HIV+ Sex

HIV+ Sex

The Psychological and
Interpersonal Dynamics
of HIV-Seropositive
Gay and Bisexual
Men's Relationships

Edited by Perry N. Halkitis,

Cynthia A. Gómez,

and Richard J. Wolitski

American Psychological Association • Washington, DC

Published by
American Psychological Association
750 First Street, NE
Washington, DC 20002
www.apa.org

To order
APA Order Department
P.O. Box 92984
Washington, DC 20090-2984
Tel: (800) 374-2721
Direct: (202) 336-5510
Fax: (202) 336-5502
TDD/TTY: (202) 336-6123
Online: www.apa.org/books/
Email: order@apa.org

In the U.K., Europe, Africa, and the Middle
East, copies may be ordered from
American Psychological Association
3 Henrietta Street
Covent Garden, London
WC2E 8LU England

Typeset in Goudy by World Composition Services, Inc., Sterling, VA

Printer: Edwards Brothers, Inc., Ann Arbor, MI
Cover Designer: Anne Masters, Washington, DC
Project Manager: Debbie Hardin, Carlsbad, CA

The opinions and statements published are the responsibility of the authors, and such
opinions and statements do not necessarily represent the policies of the American
Psychological Association. Any views expressed in chapters 1, 4, 8, 10, 11, and 15 do not
necessarily represent the views of the United States government, and the authors'
participation in the work is not meant to serve as an official endorsement.

Library of Congress Cataloging-in-Publication Data

HIV+ sex : the psychological and interpersonal dynamics of HIV-seropositive gay and
bisexual men's relationships / edited by Perry N. Halkitis, Cynthia A. Gómez, and
Richard J. Wolitski.
    p. cm.
    Includes bibliographical references and index.
    ISBN 1-59147-245-8
    1. HIV-positive men—Sexual behavior. 2. Gay men—Sexual behavior.
  I. Halkitis, Perry N.   II. Gomez, Cynthia A.   III. Wolitski, Richard J.
    RC606.6.H575 2005
    362.196'9792'0081—dc22   2004026530

British Library Cataloguing-in-Publication Data
A CIP record is available from the British Library.

Printed in the United States of America
First Edition

To the memory of our colleague and friend Robert B. Hays, PhD. Bob was an important contributor to the work described in this volume and the field of HIV prevention as a whole. His scientific acumen, kind-hearted nature, and wit are deeply missed by all of us.

CONTENTS

CONTRIBUTORS

Nicholas J. Alvarado, MPH, Center for AIDS Prevention Studies, University of California, San Francisco

Caroline J. Bailey, MA, MPH, Macro International Inc., Atlanta, GA

David S. Bimbi, MA, City University of New York, New York; Center for HIV/AIDS Educational Studies and Training, New York

Thomas M. Borkowski, MA, New York State Psychiatric Institute, Research Foundation for Mental Hygiene, New York

Cynthia A. Gómez, PhD, Center for AIDS Prevention Studies, University of California, San Francisco

Perry N. Halkitis, PhD, New York University, New York; Center for HIV/AIDS Educational Studies and Training, New York

Trevor A. Hart, PhD, York University, Toronto, Ontario, Canada

Colleen C. Hoff, PhD, Center for AIDS Prevention Studies, University of California, San Francisco

Gladys E. Ibañez, PhD, National Center for HIV, STD, and TB Prevention, Centers for Disease Control and Prevention, Atlanta, GA

Kelly R. Knight, MEd, Center for AIDS Prevention Studies, University of California, San Francisco

Anupama Manchikanti, MSc, Mailman School of Public Health, Columbia University, New York

Byron Mason, Center for AIDS Prevention Studies, University of California, San Francisco

Ann O'Leary, PhD, National Center for HIV, STD, and TB Prevention, Centers for Disease Control and Prevention, Atlanta, GA

Jeffrey T. Parsons, PhD, Hunter College, New York; City University of New York, New York; Center for HIV/AIDS Educational Studies and Training, New York

David W. Purcell, JD, PhD, National Center for HIV, STD, and TB Prevention, Centers for Disease Control and Prevention, Atlanta, GA

Robert H. Remien, PhD, New York State Psychiatric Institute, New York; Columbia University, New York

Deborah J. Schwartz, MA, National Center for HIV, STD, and TB Prevention, Centers for Disease Control and Prevention, Atlanta, GA

Michael J. Stirratt, PhD, HIV Center for Clinical and Behavioral Studies, Columbia University, New York; New York State Psychiatric Institute, New York

Kalil Vicioso, MA, City University of New York, New York; Center for HIV/AIDS Educational Studies and Training, New York

Leo Wilton, PhD, Binghamton University, State University of New York, Binghamton

Richard J. Wolitski, PhD, National Center for HIV, STD, and TB Prevention, Centers for Disease Control and Prevention, Atlanta, GA

FOREWORD

Gay and bisexual men carry the majority of the burden of HIV in the United States. Volume 14 of the Centers for Disease Control and Prevention's (CDC) *HIV/AIDS Surveillance Report, Cases of HIV/AIDS in the United States, 2002,*[1] tells us that 73% of the individuals living with HIV/AIDS are men and that 61% of that group are men who have sex with men (MSM). Another 8% are MSM who are also injection-drug users. A total of 76% of the HIV/AIDS cases among White men are MSM. For Black, Latino, Asian or Pacific Islander, and Native Americans the figures are 47%, 57%, 66%, and 60%, respectively. MSM who also inject drugs add to the totals an additional 9% to Whites, 7% to Blacks, 6% to Latinos, 4% to Asian or Pacific Islanders, and 15% to Native Americans.

Highly active antiretroviral therapy (HAART) has extended life and quality of life for individuals infected with HIV in recent years. The relatively rapid development and deployment of these drugs has meant that HIV is no longer the deadly disease it once was. Although these drugs do bring other complications to one's life, and although it is also true that people with HIV may die sooner than those who do not have HIV, the drugs make it possible for people with HIV to live relatively normal lives. Sex is a natural part of a normal life, and people with HIV want to experience and enjoy sexual relations like most other human beings. The question of the decade is how to do this, and at the same time, keep one's virus to oneself.

HIV is here to stay in the gay and bisexual communities, at least in our lifetime. This wily retrovirus has planted itself firmly and demonstrated its resilience. And, according to the CDC, HIV is endemic and the incidence

[1]Centers for Disease Control and Prevention. (2002). *HIV/AIDS surveillance report. Cases of HIV/AIDS in the United States, 2002* (Vol. 14). Atlanta, GA: Author.

of new infections has increased in the past several years. This means that HIV is a participant in every male-to-male sexual relationship. The individual who knows that he has HIV is well aware of this fact. That individual's regular sexual partners, whether positive or negative, must take that fact into account and accommodate it when engaging in sexual relations with the HIV-infected person. But HIV is also present in the sexual relationships of those who believe or declare themselves to be uninfected. Is it possible that they were infected but have not yet been diagnosed with antibodies? Is it possible that they are failing to disclose such information to their sexual partners for fear of rejection? HIV hangs over every sexual encounter among MSM.

One fact is certain: HIV has taken transmission-prevention programs to new realms. Public health rarely likes to venture into such out-of-the-mainstream areas. It is much easier, and much more sanitary, to focus on health and attempt to motivate people to keep themselves and others healthy. Messages about nonuse of tobacco, moderate exercise, and healthy diets are relatively clean and easy.

HIV is relatively hard to transmit and can only move from mother to child, or from one person to another through sharing injection equipment or through intimate sexual contact. Therefore, one would also think that it would be relatively easy to prevent transmission.

People have sexual relations for a variety of reasons: for love and intimacy, for recreation, for fun, for friendship, for money, to avoid loneliness, to be touched. The essence of sexual encounters is bonding, blending, mutual pleasure, and loss of inhibition. HIV, lurking in the background, places strict boundaries on all of those aspects of sexuality. Is it any wonder, then, that the development of effective prevention programs focused on HIV-infected people has come late in the game? Is it any wonder that such programs are difficult to develop and implement because they must take into consideration all of these factors in addition to motivating individuals to protect others from HIV infection?

This volume brings these issues into focus by presenting all of the dimensions of the sexual lives and behaviors of HIV-infected gay and bisexual men. It explores the hopes and aspirations, the dreams and desires, and the trials and difficulties associated with satisfying and safe sexual relationships. It explains what is at stake as gay and bisexual men attempt to come to terms with the meaning of HIV in their sexual lives and the risks and gambles associated with disclosure and sharing information that may say something about one's past but certainly speaks volumes about how that person is going to live and relate in the future. Most important, this book uses that information to construct an approach to HIV prevention that goes beyond a health education or cognitive–behavioral approach and attempts to place HIV prevention within a sexual context.

Positive prevention, assisting HIV-infected individuals to avoid spreading HIV to others, is a relative late-comer to the HIV prevention field. It has been difficult to find language to discuss the issue of positive prevention without victimizing or blaming the HIV-infected person. This volume begins to provide language that allows us to see HIV-infected individuals *as* individuals, striving to live the extended lives they have been given by HAART in ways that are satisfying and at the same time safe. This is the beginning of such ventures. It will be useful if others are inspired by this work to apply it. But more important is the quest to extend this work, to understand further and more deeply how HIV-infected individuals integrate their disease into their intimate lives and how that information can be used to assist people in living lives that do not spread HIV.

Thomas J. Coates
Division of Infectious Diseases
David Geffen School of Medicine
University of California, Los Angeles

PREFACE

Sex is an important aspect of the lives of HIV-positive gay and bisexual men. Like most human beings, these men navigate their way through the complexities of courtship and sexual relationships guided by the drive for physical and emotional connection with another person. Even under the best circumstances, dating rituals, sexual experiences, and relationships are demanding and challenging. Yet for HIV-positive individuals, this reality is further complicated by their serostatus.

Many HIV prevention efforts over the past 20 years have neglected the very essence of sex, treating it as a cognitive and rational construction, controlled solely by one's mind and not one's heart. Yet the essence of sex and sexuality transcend the cognitive. And these complex phenomena must be understood in relation to emotional and sociological contexts in addition to cognitive states. For HIV-positive gay and bisexual men who face daily challenges to both their physical and mental health as well as discrimination and intolerance for being both gay and HIV-positive, this idea could not be more obvious. Yet as researchers and practitioners, we have often missed the mark.

It is our hope that this volume helps to fill this gap in the literature and promote a deeper understanding of these complex realities. Thus, at the core of our work is recognition that one's sexual self is intimately connected to the cognitive, emotional, and social factors that affect and make up the totality of a person's existence.

The voices and stories of 250 individuals provide the basis of this volume. Through their words, we explore how these men live with HIV and make decisions about sex, express their sexuality, choose their sexual partners, and balance their physical and emotional health while attempting to maintain viable and responsible sex lives. To this end, these chapters seek to depict the issues gay and bisexual men face in their sex lives and how they work to resolve the internal and interpersonal conflicts that these issues sometimes present.

In the pages that follow, we highlight the struggles faced by HIV-positive gay and bisexual men as sexual beings and also describe the myriad ways in which many of these men are able to celebrate their sexuality and have satisfying sex lives that support their own and their partners' physical and mental health. It is our goal to provide insight into these men's lives by letting their words guide the reader toward a deeper understanding of the challenges and joys that they experience in their sexual relationships. We hope that the insights gained from the experiences of these men can inform the development of programs that are designed to ease the burdens that HIV-positive gay and bisexual men face on a daily basis and lead to the creation of HIV-prevention strategies that benefit gay and bisexual men, as well as help guide future researchers.

We are grateful to the 250 men from New York and San Francisco who so openly shared their stories with us as part of the Seropositive Urban Men's Study. We celebrate them and their lives.

ACKNOWLEDGMENTS

A project of this magnitude would not be possible without the contributions of many dedicated and gifted people. The Seropositive Urban Men's Study (SUMS) was a 2-year formative study funded in 1996 by the Centers for Disease Control and Prevention (CDC) to provide a scientific foundation for developing interventions that protect the health of HIV-seropositive gay and bisexual men and prevent HIV transmission to their sex partners. The funded sites were the New Jersey City University (Jeffrey Parsons, principal investigator), Rutgers University (Ann O'Leary, principal investigator), and the University of California, San Francisco (Cynthia Gómez, principal investigator). The team of researchers across the three sites worked collaboratively on the study, which was overseen by Richard Wolitski of the CDC, who drafted the original funding announcement.

Developing and implementing the qualitative research protocol was a team process that depended on the expertise and important contributions of the following individuals who constituted the collaborative teams in New York, San Francisco, and at the CDC: Timothy Ambrose, James Carey, Cynthia Gómez, Perry Halkitis, Robert Hays, Colleen Hoff, Ann O'Leary, Jeffrey Parsons, David Purcell, Robert Remien, Michael Stirratt, and Richard Wolitski. We would like to acknowledge Susan Kegeles and Robert Hays, who shared instruments developed for the Behavioral Consortium Pilot Study (funded by the National Institutes of Health) that shaped the development of the SUMS study. In addition, we would like to acknowledge the invaluable insights provided by HIV-positive men in San Francisco and New York City who served on local community advisory boards that reviewed study materials and gave feedback to the investigators.

The quality of the SUMS data reflect the skill and commitment of the many talented interviewers who worked on the study. Their ability to develop rapport and make a personal connection with the participants was instrumental to the success of this study. In particular we would like to thank Timothy Ambrose, David Bimbi, Thomas Borkowski, Michael-Anthony Brooks, Cesar Cadabes, Josiah Evans, Gene Kim, Chris Johnson, Robb MacGregor-Crowe, J. E. Miles, Tokes Obsubu, Cristobal M. Olivares, Andrew Nelson Peterson, John Sanchez, and Michael Stirratt.

Dealing with a dataset of this magnitude required that an extraordinary amount of effort be dedicated to data management and coding. In particular we would like to acknowledge James Carey, Colleen Hoff, David Purcell, and Michael Stirratt for their contributions to data management, data segmentation, and data-coding procedures. The analysis of these data would have been impossible if it were not for the months of effort that Deborah Schwartz, Caroline Bailey, and Stephanie Macari spent coding the combined dataset.

Lynne Stockton greatly improved the quality and readability of the volume. Marie Morgan provided early input on guidelines for the structure and format of chapters, which facilitated the writing and editing of the individual chapters.

Finally, we would like to acknowledge Gregory Herek and Lansing Hays, as well as the American Psychological Association for their support of this volume.

HIV+ Sex

1

UNDERSTANDING THE SEXUAL LIVES OF HIV-POSITIVE GAY AND BISEXUAL MEN: AN OVERVIEW OF THE SEROPOSITIVE URBAN MEN'S STUDY

PERRY N. HALKITIS, RICHARD J. WOLITSKI, AND
CYNTHIA A. GÓMEZ

At the onset of the HIV epidemic during the 1980s, little attention was given to the sexuality of HIV-infected individuals, aside from protective behaviors aimed at certain sex practices taken out of the context of their sexuality as whole human beings (e.g., condom use; Kok, 1999). This was true particularly for men engaging in sex with other men (MSM), most often gay and bisexual men.

Like all human beings, gay and bisexual men engage in sexual behavior on many different levels and for a variety of reasons. And, as with all human beings, "sexuality" is far deeper and more complex than the specific act of engaging in sex, incorporating issues of identity and nested within emotional,

This chapter was coauthored by an employee of the United States government as part of official duty and is considered to be in the public domain. Any views expressed herein do not necessarily represent the views of the United States government, and the author's participation in the work is not meant to serve as an official endorsement.

social, and biopsychosocial contexts, and thus needs to be viewed in a holistic perspective.

This book explores the sexuality of gay and bisexual men in terms of both men's sexuality in a holistic sense and in terms of how this translates into meaningful action in terms of prevention of HIV. This is important for several reasons, one of which is the finding that a 14% increase in new HIV infections in this population was noted between 1999 and 2001, indicating that this segment of the populations continues to account for the majority of new HIV diagnoses in the United States (Validisseri, 2003).

Exploring the sexuality of MSM is also important because little attention has been paid to HIV-positive gay and bisexual men in terms of their sexuality as human beings, despite the obvious fact that HIV-positive individuals are one source of infection for HIV-negative individuals (engaging in sex in the context of their own sexuality; Crepaz & Marks, 2002). It was not until the 12th World AIDS Conference in 1998 in Geneva, Switzerland, that the matter of sexuality among HIV-positive individuals became a recognizable focus in the presentation of research findings (Schiltz & Sandfort, 2000). Although as early as 1994, the need for prevention of HIV was clearly suggested (Wenger, Kusseling, Beck, & Shapiro, 1994), many prevention efforts did not address the role of sexuality in HIV-positive individuals until recently, through a perspective known as positive prevention.

TREATMENT ADVANCES AND HIGHLY ACTIVE ANTIRETROVIRAL THERAPY: A DOUBLE-SIDED COIN

As highly active antiretroviral therapy (HAART) has enabled HIV-positive individuals to regain hope for their lives, both in terms of length of life and quality of life, it has also affected their sexuality. On a positive note, HAART has enabled many individuals to embrace their sexuality as human beings once again. It has also lent an optimistic note to staunching the HIV epidemic (Kalichman, Nachmison, Cherry, & Williams, 1998; Kelly, Otto-Salaj, Sikkema, Pinkerton, & Bloom, 1998; Van de Ven, Prestage, Crawford, Grulich, & Kippax, 1999; Vanable, Ostrow, McKirnan, Taywaditep, & Hope, 2000). Unintended negative consequences of HAART include a false impression among some that the HIV epidemic is over (Stall, Hays, Waldo, Ekstrand, & McFarland, 2000). For some men, this optimism has led to greater complacency with regard to safer sex practices, perhaps someday leading to a second coming of the HIV epidemic in the United States (Wolitski, Valdiserri, Denning, & Levine, 2001).

Coupled with the implementation of HAART and a population of HIV-positive gay and bisexual men living longer, healthier lives and experiencing more active sex lives is a necessity to undertake more sophisticated and interdisciplinary examinations of sex and sexuality. If these same men are engaging in more unprotected sex because of a false sense of security regarding HIV, then there is significant reason to be concerned about HIV-positive gay and bisexual men spreading the infection. Recent work has documented an alarming increase in unprotected sexual behaviors among gay and bisexual men beginning in the late 1990s (Kellog, McFarland, & Katz, 1999; Van de Ven et al., 2000), especially among young men of color (Koblin et al., 2000; Valleroy et al., 2000). So too, dramatic increases in the incidence of other sexually transmitted diseases, such as gonorrhea (Centers for Disease Control and Prevention [CDC], 1999) and syphilis (Bellis, Cook, Clark, Syed, & Hoskins, 2002; de Luise, Brown, Rubin, & Blank, 2000; Kahn, Heffelfinger, & Berman, 2002) underscore the increase in sexual risk taking in the gay and bisexual male community. This population, as a result, continue to be the largest subgroup of individuals living with HIV/AIDS in the United States, with 14% to 25% of men in this population living with the disease, a prevalence rate equivalent to that in sub-Saharan African countries (Catania et al., 2001).

CONSIDERING THE WHOLE PERSON

Treatment advances, in and of themselves, seem insufficient to explain the continued sexual risk demonstrated by HIV-positive gay and bisexual men. Rather, disentangling the complex interactions of developmental, behavioral, psychological, sociological–contextual elements, in light of treatment advances, is more likely to clarify the sexual lives and sexual risk taking of these men. For example, it is likely that sexual risk taking on the part of HIV-positive gay and bisexual men is influenced by developmental elements such as childhood sexual abuse (O'Leary, Purcell, Remien, & Gómez, 2003), exacerbated by behavioral factors such as alcohol and drug use (Halkitis, Parsons, & Stirratt, 2001; Purcell, Parsons, Halkitis, Mizuno, & Woods, 2001), shaped by sexually charged environments such as bars, circuit parties, and sex clubs (Halkitis & Parsons, 2002; Parsons & Halkitis, 2002), and perhaps driven by overall mental health including levels of depression (Beck, McNally, & Petrak, 2003).

Recently, the emergence of barebacking, which some have described as intentional unprotected anal intercourse (Halkitis & Parsons, 2003, Halkitis, Parsons, & Wilton, 2003; Mansergh et al., 2002), seems to have transgressed both the behaviors and sexual identities of HIV-positive gay and bisexual men, creating a reality for HIV prevention that is much more complex than those behaviors addressed by the "use a condom every time" campaigns of the 1980s.

Finally, behavioral research indicates that after initial diagnosis, most HIV-positive gay and bisexual men engage in sex practices that pose little or no risk for HIV transmission (Higgins et al., 1991; Marks, Burris, & Peterman, 1999; Wolitski, MacGowan, Higgins, & Jorgensen, 1997). However, most do continue to partake in active sex. In fact, previous reviews of the literature (Marks et al., 1999) report that many (10%–60%) HIV-positive individuals engage in oral sex, anal sex, or both after they become aware that they are infected (Crepaz & Marks, 2002). The fact remains that as we enter the third decade of AIDS in the United States, gay and bisexual men continue to engage in unsafe sex acts (Kellog et al., 1999; Van de Ven et al., 2000; Williams, Elwood, & Bowen, 2000; Wolitiski et al., 2001). Recent trends in HIV seroconversion (Valdiserri, 2003) also support an increase in these sexual risk-taking behaviors.

PUBLIC HEALTH CONSIDERATIONS

HIV prevention is only one reason to explore sexuality of HIV-positive gay and bisexual men as we have done in this book. Another is that for many researchers and practitioners in this area, especially those who are not gay or bisexual themselves, the commonalities and differences between straight and gay men with regards to their sexuality may remain shrouded in secrecy. While these researchers and practitioners may know enough about sexual behavior to be competent in their fields of study or practice (e.g., counseling, developmental, and health psychology; public health; sociology), they may not know enough about gay sexuality, and how it is similar to and different from the sexuality of heterosexuals, to be excellent in their chosen fields. Because this book is grounded in research (see next section) both about sex and sexuality of HIV-positive gay and bisexual men, we believe that this book can contribute to such excellence.

THE SEROPOSITIVE URBAN MEN'S STUDY

Unprotected sexual behaviors place both HIV-negative and HIV-positive gay and bisexual men at a substantial risk for long-term adverse health complications. With regard to HIV-negative men, initial infection with HIV is the most immediate consequence of unsafe behavior. Seroconversion for these men carries the potential for initial infection with HIV mutant variants that are resistant to medication or are untreatable (Boden et al., 1999; Hecht et al., 1998). For HIV-positive men, unsafe sex acts may place them at risk for superinfection (i.e., reinfection with a different strain of the HIV virus; Blackard, Cohen, & Mayer, 2002), rapid loss of CD4 cells (Wiley et al., 2000), risk for contracting other STDs that may lead to immune system deterioration (Gibson, Pendo, & Wohlfeiler, 1999), and opportunistic infections (O'Brien et al., 1999; Renwick et al., 1998; Rezza et al., 1999). Because sexual intercourse is the primary route of HIV transmission for MSM in general and gay and bisexual men in particular (CDC, 2003b), the issues of sex and sexuality in the population of HIV-positive men require greater understanding in the campaign against the virus.

As suggested by Wenger and colleagues in 1994 and by the realities noted earlier, the need for HIV prevention efforts focusing on HIV-positive individuals are inevitable and essential. Community agencies recognized this reality as early as 1997 when, for example, the Gay Men's Health Crisis launched its Positive Testimonials campaign (Halkitis, 1997). To date, a small set of funded research studies have sought to effect change in the HIV epidemic by developing and field testing programs aimed at the seropositive population. The CDC has deemed such prevention efforts essential to advancing HIV prevention (CDC, 2003a).

The Seropositive Urban Men's Study (SUMS) was among the first such efforts and was rooted in the belief that by understanding HIV-positive gay and bisexual men and their sexuality, effective and meaningful programs could be developed to protect their seronegative partners from the virus. SUMS was conducted to provide information for the development of a behavioral intervention for HIV-positive gay and bisexual men that would reduce the risk for HIV transmission and promote serostatus disclosure. The objectives of SUMS were (a) to compare the feasibility of recruiting self-identified HIV-positive MSM from three community settings; (b) to describe serostatus disclosure and sex practices of HIV-positive MSM; (c) to identify factors that help or hinder serostatus disclosure and the maintenance of safer sex practices; and (d) to elicit ideas regarding risk-reduction interventions for HIV-positive MSM.

SUMS was a collaborative effort between university-based researchers and behavioral scientists at CDC. Researchers from the participating institutions jointly developed the research protocol. Protocol development was guided by reviews of published research, health behavior theory, and the insights of HIV-positive members of the research team. All study activities were approved by community advisory groups, program review panels, and the appropriate institutional review boards. Feedback from the community advisory boards was especially useful in planning the study. Each community advisory board was made up of HIV-positive gay and bisexual men and their advocates who provided their own perspectives on the research, suggested participant recruitment locations, and helped to refine the content and the structure of the qualitative and quantitative interviews.

RECRUITMENT

Potential participants were recruited from June through November 1997 in New York City and San Francisco. The sampling strategy was targeted (Watters & Biernacki, 1989), and there were quotas to ensure the representation of HIV-positive men of color from three distinct types of community venues: (a) AIDS service organizations; (b) gay community venues (e.g., bars, gay pride event sites, gay neighborhoods); and (c) public sex environments (e.g., bathhouses, sex clubs, outdoor cruising areas). The quotas were established with regard to race and ethnicity for each type of venue to ensure adequate representation of men of color from each setting. Participants were actively recruited by field staff and passively recruited through flyers placed at venues and advertisements placed in gay-oriented publications. Staff and recruitment materials asked HIV-positive men who were interested in the study to call a toll-free telephone number for additional information. To eliminate the need for men to disclose their HIV status, potential participants were told, "If this does not apply to you, please give it to someone you know." As a result, some potential participants were reached through referrals by friends. Men who called the toll-free number received information about the purpose of the study and the activities that were involved. Those who expressed interest in being a part of the study were then screened for eligibility. Eligibility criteria for the study were (a) self-identifying as HIV-seropositive; (b) having engaged in sex with a man during the past year, (c) being age 18 years or older; and (d) being of appropriate race and ethnicity and from an appropriate venue to fill recruitment quotas. Of the potential participants, 250 men met the eligibility criteria and completed a qualitative interview and a paper-and-pencil survey.

QUALITATIVE INTERVIEW

Participants who wished to remain anonymous were given the option of completing the interview over the telephone, but only a few men did so. The qualitative interviews took approximately 90 minutes to complete and were conducted by a team of racially diverse male interviewers, which made it possible to offer participants the option of being matched with an interviewer of the same race/ethnicity. Interviewers received standardized cross-site training (Carey, Parsons, & Purcell, 1997) and conducted each interview by using a standardized interview guide made up of 58 open-ended questions. As shown in Exhibit 1.1, the questions in the SUMS interview addressed a broad range of issues related to HIV and sex practices. A key component of the interview was eliciting detailed narratives about specific sexual encounters. Participants were first asked to describe their most recent

EXHIBIT 1.1
Summary of SUMS Qualitative Interview Content

- Living with HIV
- Meeting and selecting sex partners
- Dating and relationships
- Roles and meanings of sex
- Effects of HIV on sexual practices
- Detailed narrative of most recent sexual encounter
- Self-assessment of whether most recent encounter was safe
- Detailed narratives of sexual encounters—most recent safe and most recent risky
- Strategies for maintaining safer sex practices
- Reasons for unprotected sex
- Temptation to have unprotected sex
- Disclosure of HIV status to sex partners
- Condom negotiation and safer sex communication
- Accessibility of HAART and effects on sexual practices
- Suggestions for prevention with HIV-positive individuals
- Earlier participation in HIV prevention programs

sexual encounter and then asked for as much detail as possible regarding the specific sexual behaviors that occurred and the psychological, interpersonal, and environmental influences that may have affected their behavior. If the narrative included unprotected anal sex with an HIV-negative or unknown status partner, the participant was asked to describe his most recent sexual encounter that did not include this behavior (i.e., an encounter with a lower risk for HIV transmission). If the narrative did not include unprotected anal sex with an HIV-negative or unknown status partner, the participant was asked to describe his most recent encounter that included this behavior (i.e., an encounter that had a higher risk for HIV transmission). This procedure yielded two narratives for each participant: one that described a high-risk encounter with an uninfected partner and another that described an encounter with little or no risk for HIV transmission to an uninfected partner. Participants who had had sex with one or more women in the past 6 months ($n = 17$) were also asked to describe their most recent sexual encounter with a female partner. In addition to the standardized questions, interviewers were instructed to ask spontaneous follow-up questions to clarify participants' responses and provide additional information about participants' experiences. An incentive of $30 was provided to men who participated in the interview.

Paper-and-Pencil Survey

Participants were given the option of completing the paper-and-pencil survey immediately following the qualitative interview or taking it home and returning it later. The survey required about an hour to complete; it addressed issues related to sex practices, substance use, access to health care, adherence to treatment, and mental health. Participants who completed the survey were given an additional $30. Those who returned the survey within 2 weeks were entered into a lottery drawing for a cash prize at the end of the study. The survey is not a focus of this book; interested readers can learn about the survey and the quantitative findings in other SUMS publications (Courtney-Quirk, Wolitski, Hoff, Parsons, & Seropositive Urban Men's Study Group, 2003; Halkitis, Parsons, Wolitski, & Remien, 2003; Halkitis, Wilton, Parsons, & Hoff, 2004; Hart et al., 2003; Margolis, Wolitski, Parsons, & Gómez, 2001; O'Leary et al., 2003; Parsons & Halkitis, 2002; Parsons, Halkitis, Wolitski, Gomez, & the SUM Team, 2003; Purcell et al., 2001; Wolitski, Halkitis, Parsons, & Gómez, 2001).

Qualitative Data Coding and Analysis

All interviews were tape-recorded and transcribed. Completed transcripts were reviewed for accuracy (with few exceptions, this was done by the person who conducted the interview); errors made during the transcription process were corrected before data analysis.

Transcribed text from the interviews was organized into smaller segments that were defined by groups of similar questions in the interview guide. The segments were entered into a cross-site database using CDC EZ-Text Qualitative Analysis Software for data coding and analysis (Carey, Wenzel, Reilly, Sheridan, & Steinberg, 1998). The data were centrally coded by a team of three people trained in qualitative research methods; they used a code book that was developed a priori by a cross-site team of researchers using procedures for multisite studies (MacQueen, McLellann, Kay, & Milstein, 1998). The code book was refined during data coding to reflect emergent themes and to improve the reliability of the coding. The final code book had a total of 195 codes. Intercoder reliability was evaluated by comparing their coding of sets of one to five complete interviews from each site (Carey, Morgan, & Oxtoby, 1996). The final intercoder reliability was high; 85% of the segments were identically coded by two coders. An intercoder reliability of $\kappa \geq .70$ was achieved for 95% of the individual codes that were applied to each segment.

Authors of the individual chapters began their analysis with the precoded dataset. In most instances, the authors organized their analyses around a limited number of the standardized interview questions or used the presence of global codes to identify relevant responses regardless of where they appeared in the interview. Limiting the analysis to one section of the interview or selecting cases on the basis of having specific codes resulted in a more manageable dataset that contained only responses that were relevant to a given chapter. The analyses that were conducted for all the chapters involved at least some additional coding. In some instances, the authors developed additional a priori codes that were applied to the data subset. In others, themes emerged from reading the data, and codes were applied that reflected these themes. With one exception, the starting point for analysis was the full set of 250 interview transcripts. The exception was the analysis used in chapter 7 (this volume), for which a smaller subset of interviews was selected for analysis to permit the secondary coding of relevant information wherever it appeared in the complete interview transcript.

Characteristics of Participants

Men who participated in SUMS were diverse in many ways; the diversity of this sample is one of the major strengths of the study. The men came from varying socioeconomic backgrounds (see Table 1.1). They were recruited from a range of venues, although compared with men from San Francisco, a greater percentage of men from New York were recruited in public sex environments and fewer came from AIDS service organizations. By design, most participants were men of color and accounted for 70% of the sample. However, in New York a larger percentage of participants were Black or Latino, compared with San Francisco, where more Asian or Pacific Islanders were sampled. Although participants described themselves as gay, queer, or homosexual (84%) and bisexual (10%), a minority (6%) did not use one of these labels to describe their sexual orientation. The participants' ages ranged from 20 to 67 years (M = 37.6, SD = 9.2). Most had at least some college education, and 40% were college graduates. More than half of the SUMS participants were unemployed at the time, and 45% reported that their annual income was less than $10,000.

The amount of time that participants had been living with HIV and the effects that the virus had had on their health also varied (see Table 1.1). Although some participants had only recently learned that they were infected, most had known that they were HIV-positive for many years, with an average time since HIV diagnosis of 6 years. Almost half had received a diagnosis of AIDS. Most had access to medical care, including tests used to assess the progression of HIV disease. Almost all knew their CD4, or T-cell, count. One third reported that their CD4 count was below 200, which is a sign of severe immunosuppression. The difference in the percentage of men who had a diagnosis of AIDS and those with a recent CD4 count below 200 (which would classify them as having AIDS) may reflect the rapid advances in HIV treatment and the emergence of active antiretroviral therapy in the mid-1990s. In addition, nearly half of the men (103 out of 209) knew their viral load (a measure of the amount of HIV present in blood) and reported that it was undetectable. Although HAART regimens that included protease inhibitors were relatively new at the time the study was conducted, 58% of participants reported that they were taking a

TABLE 1.1
Selected Characteristics of SUMS Participants

	Total (N = 250)[a]	New York (n = 159)	San Francisco (n = 91)	p[b]
Source of recruitment				<.005
AIDS service organization	75 (30%)	39 (25%)	36 (40%)	
Gay community venues	56 (22%)	37 (23%)	19 (21%)	
Public sex environments	74 (30%)	59 (37%)	15 (17%)	
Referral	45 (18%)	24 (15%)	21 (23%)	
Race/ethnicity				<.001
Black	72 (29%)	50 (31%)	22 (24%)	
Asian or Pacific Islander	16 (6%)	2 (1%)	14 (15%)	
Latino	59 (24%)	43 (27%)	16 (18%)	
White	75 (30%)	49 (31%)	26 (29%)	
Native American	5 (2%)	1 (1%)	4 (4%)	
Mixed race/ethnicity, other	23 (9%)	14 (9%)	9 (10%)	
Education				ns
Less than high school	15 (6%)	9 (6%)	6 (7%)	
High school graduate	42 (17%)	32 (21%)	10 (11%)	
Some college	90 (37%)	54 (35%)	36 (40%)	
Bachelor's degree	68 (28%)	37 (24%)	31 (34%)	
Advanced degree	31 (13%)	23 (15%)	8 (9%)	
Current employment				ns
Full-time	47 (19%)	35 (23%)	12 (13%)	
Part-time	29 (12%)	16 (10%)	13 (14%)	
Unemployed—student	15 (6%)	8 (5%)	7 (8%)	
Unemployed—disabled	85 (35%)	52 (34%)	33 (37%)	
Unemployed—other	69 (28%)	44 (28%)	25 (28%)	
Current annual income				ns
Less than $10,000	108 (45%)	70 (46%)	38 (43%)	
$10,000 to $29,999	91 (38%)	53 (35%)	38 (43%)	
$30,000 to $49,999	30 (12%)	20 (13%)	10 (11%)	
$50,000 or more	12 (5%)	9 (6%)	3 (3%)	

(continued)

treatment regimen that included one or more protease inhibitors. This finding and others (see Halkitis et al., 2003) are important indicators of the access that most men in the study had to basic HIV-related medical care.

Strengths and Weaknesses of the Seropositive Urban Men's Study

SUMS, like all studies, has particular strengths and weaknesses that affect the conclusions that can be drawn from it. A particular strength of SUMS is that the sampling strategy included a significant number of non-White men from a diverse range of community settings. Other significant strengths include the involvement of HIV-positive gay and bisexual men in the design and implementation of the study, the use of standardized

TABLE 1.1 *(Continued)*

	Total (N = 250)[a]	New York (n = 159)	San Francisco (n = 91)	p[b]
Sexual orientation				ns
Gay, queer, homosexual	205 (84%)	130 (86%)	75 (82%)	
Bisexual	23 (10%)	16 (11%)	7 (8%)	
Straight, heterosexual	2 (1%)	1 (1%)	1 (1%)	
None of the above, not sure	13 (5%)	5 (3%)	8 (9%)	
Ever diagnosed with AIDS	119 (48%)	69 (44%)	50 (55%)	ns
Most recent CD4 count (cells/µl)				ns
Below 200	78 (32%)	54 (34%)	24 (26%)	
200–499	104 (42%)	59 (38%)	45 (50%)	
500 or above	57 (23%)	38 (24%)	19 (21%)	
Not tested, do not know	9 (4%)	6 (4%)	3 (3%)	
Most recent viral load count				ns
Undetectable	103 (42%)	57 (37%)	46 (51%)	
Detectable	106 (43%)	72 (46%)	34 (38%)	
Not tested, do not know	27 (15%)	27 (17%)	10 (11%)	
Current HIV treatment				ns
Not taking HIV medications	62 (25%)	40 (25%)	22 (24%)	
Taking HIV medications—without protease inhibitor	42 (17%)	25 (16%)	17 (19%)	
Taking HIV medications—with protease inhibitor	145 (58%)	93 (59%)	52 (57%)	

[a]*Number of respondents does not always add up to 250 because of missing data for some variables. Percentages are rounded to the nearest whole number.*
[b]*Chi-square tests were performed to test for city differences. A significance level of p <.05 was chosen for all comparisons. ns = not significant.*

training and research protocols in two HIV-epicenters, the unprecedented size of the study sample, the preparation of verbatim transcripts, and the high level of reliability achieved in the coding of these data. Some characteristics of the study limited the interpretation of study findings. Although the sampling procedures ensured the representation of key population segments, study participants cannot be considered to be representative of all gay and bisexual men living with HIV in New York or San Francisco. Like all cross-sectional studies, care must be taken when inferring causality from these data. In some instances, participants talked about their own perceptions of the factors that influenced their sexual relationships and practices. In other instances, the investigators inferred causality from the data. It is possible that participants' beliefs about the factors that affect their behavior are inaccurate or represent after-the-fact justifications for past sex practices. Similarly, the research team may have made some incorrect conclusions about causality because of the cross-sectional nature of the data. Firm conclusions about causality can only be drawn from longitudinal research in which participants are followed up over time. Despite the potential uncertainty of inferences about cause-and-effect relationships, the information provided by SUMS makes a significant contribution to our understanding of how HIV-positive gay and bisexual men view their sexuality and the factors *they* believe affect their sexual relationships and practices.

ORGANIZATION OF THIS VOLUME

This volume contains 15 chapters that are based on the qualitative interviews conducted with 250 SUMS participants. Chapters 2 through 6 focus on the sexuality for HIV-positive gay and bisexual men in the context of their relationships in general. Chapter 2 elucidates the meanings that these men attach to their sexual behavior and the psychological motivations behind these meanings that drive their sexuality. Chapters 3 and 4 describe the range of sexual relationships and practices of the HIV-positive gay and bisexual men in the study. Chapter 5 examines sexual negotiation and communication strategies used by HIV-positive men with their sexual partners. Chapter 6 examines the role of race and ethnicity on sex behavior among HIV-positive gay and bisexual men.

In terms of sex, sexuality, and relationship dynamics, chapter 7 focuses on issues of serostatus disclosure by HIV-positive gay and bisexual men with their sexual partners, and chapter 8 examines the assumptions that some men make when serostatus is not disclosed.

Chapters 9 through 13 focus on general and specific intrapsychic and contextual factors that influence sexuality and also have important implications for preventing the spread of HIV. Chapter 9 describes how HIV-positive men's beliefs about how they became infected affects their sexual behavior. Chapter 10 examines SUMS participants' beliefs about their responsibility to protect others from HIV and how beliefs about personal responsibility affect the risk of HIV transmission to uninfected partners. Patterns of alcohol and drug use (including the use of club drugs, which have become increasingly present in the gay community) and the effects of substance on risk behavior are considered in chapter 11. The effect of physical and social environments on sexual behavior has been inadequately studied, and thus chapter 12 makes important contributions by describing the motivations of HIV-positive men who meet sex partners in bathhouses, sex clubs, and other public sex environments and the challenges of disclosing HIV status and maintaining safer sex practices in these settings. The availability of HAART has been life-changing for many individuals living with HIV; the positive and negative effects of HAART on the sex behavior of SUMS participants is the focus of chapter 13.

We conclude this volume with chapter 14, which describes the role of support systems in the lives of HIV-positive gay and bisexual men, and chapter 15, which summarizes the findings of our work in terms of psychological and public health perspectives.

This book tells the whole story of HIV-positive gay and bisexual men as viable and sexual beings. To this end, the stories provided by each of the 250 men living with HIV or AIDS form the basis of the ideas that are presented in this volume. It is through their words that we have come to better understand their lives and the manifestation of sexuality in the lives of HIV-positive gay and bisexual men.

REFERENCES

Beck, A., McNally, I., & Petrak, J. (2003). Psychosocial predictors of HIV/STI risk behaviours in a sample of homosexual men. *Sexually Transmitted Infections*, 79, 142–146.

Bellis, M. A., Cook, P., Clark, P., Syed, Q., & Hoskins, A. (2002). Re-emerging syphilis in gay men: A case-control study of behavioural risk factors and HIV status. *Journal of Epidemiology and Community Health*, 56, 235–236.

Blackard, J. T., Cohen, D. E., & Mayer, K. H. (2002). Human immunodeficiency virus superinfection and recombination: Current state of knowledge and potential clinical consequences. *Clinical Infectious Diseases*, 34, 1108–1114.

Boden, D., Hurley, A., Zhang, L., Cao, Y., Jones, E., Tsay, J., et al. (1999). HIV-1 drug resistance in newly infected individuals. *Journal of the American Medical Association*, 282, 135–141.

Carey, J. W., Morgan, M., & Oxtoby, M. (1996). Intercoder agreement in analysis of responses to open-ended interview questions: Examples from tuberculosis research. *Cultural Anthropology Methods*, 9, 1–5.

Carey, J. W., Parsons, J. T., & Purcell, D. (1997). *Formative behavioral intervention research on the prevention of sexual transmission by HIV-seropositive men: Qualitative interviewing skills training workshop manual*. Atlanta, GA: Centers for Disease Control and Prevention.

Carey, J. W., Wenzel, P. H., Reilly, C., Sheridan, J., & Steinberg, J. M. (1998). CDC EZ-Text: Software for management and analysis of semistructured qualitative data sets. *Cultural Anthropology Methods*, 10, 14–20.

Catania, J. A., Osmond, D., Stall, R. D., Pollack, L., Paul, J. P., Blower, S., et al. (2001). The continuing HIV epidemic among men who have sex with men. *American Journal of Public Health*, 91, 907–914.

Centers for Disease Control and Prevention. (1999). Increases in unsafe sex and rectal gonorrhea among men who have sex with men—San Francisco, California, 1994–1997. *Morbidity and Mortality Weekly Report*, 48, 45–58.

Centers for Disease Control and Prevention. (2003a) Advancing HIV prevention: New strategies of a changing HIV epidemic—United States, 2003. *Morbidity and Mortality Weekly Report*, 52, 329–332.

Centers for Disease Control and Prevention. (2003b). *HIV/AIDS surveillance report, Volume 15.* Washington, DC: U.S. Department of Health and Human Services.

Courtenay-Quirk, C., Wolitski, R. J., Hoff, C., Parsons, J. T., & Seropositive Urban Men's Study Group. (2003). Interest of HIV-seropositive men who have sex with men in prevention and support services. *AIDS Education and Prevention, 15,* 401–412.

Crepaz, N., & Marks, G. (2002). Towards an understanding of sexual risk behavior in people living with HIV: A review of social, psychological, and medical findings. *AIDS, 16,* 135–149.

de Luise, C., Brown, J., Rubin, S., & Blank, S. (2000). *Emerging patterns in primary and secondary syphilis among men: NYC: January–September 2000.* New York: Author.

Gibson, P., Pendo, M., & Wohlfeiler, D. (1999). Risk, HIV, and STD prevention. *Focus: A Guide to AIDS Research and Counseling, 14*(7), 1–5.

Halkitis, P. N. (1997, August). *Positive testimonials: The role of HIV positive gay men in HIV prevention.* Paper presented at the meeting of the American Psychological Association, Chicago.

Halkitis, P. N., & Parsons, J. T. (2002). Recreational drug use and HIV risk sexual behavior among men frequenting urban gay venues. *Journal of Gay and Lesbian Social Services, 14,* 19–38.

Halkitis, P. N., & Parsons, J. T. (2003). Intentional unsafe sex (barebacking) among men who meet sexual partners on the Internet. *AIDS Care, 15,* 367–378.

Halkitis, P. N., Parsons, J. T., & Stirratt, M. (2001). A double epidemic: Crystal methamphetamine use and its relation to HIV prevention among gay men. *Journal of Homosexuality, 41,* 17–35.

Halkitis, P. N., Parsons, J. T., & Wilton, L. (2003). Barebacking among gay and bisexual men in New York City. *Archives of Sexual Behavior, 32,* 351–358.

Halkitis, P. N., Parsons, J. T., Wolitski, R. J., & Remien, R. H. (2003). Characteristics of HIV antiretroviral treatments and adherence in an ethnically diverse sample of men who have sex with men. *AIDS Care, 15,* 89–102.

Halkitis, P. N., Wilton, L., Parsons, J. T., & Hoff, C. (2004). Sexual risk taking among HIV-positive gay men in seroconcordant primary partner relationships. *Psychology, Health, and Medicine, 9,* 99–113.

Hart, T. A., Wolitski, R. J., Purcell, D. W., Gómez, C. A., Halkitis, P., & the Seropositive Urban Men's Study Group. (2003). Sexual behavior among HIV-seropositive men who have sex with men: What's in a label? *Journal of Sex Research, 40,* 179–188.

Hecht, F. M., Grant, R. M., Petropoulos, C. J., Dillon, B., Chesney, M. A., Tian, H., et al. (1998). Sexual transmission of HIV-1 variant resistant to multiple reverse-transcriptase and protease inhibitors. *New England Journal of Medicine, 339,* 307–311.

Higgins, D. L., Galavotti, C., O'Reilly, K. R., Schnell, D. J., Moore, M., Rugg, D., et al. (1991). Evidence for the effects of HIV antibody testing on risk behaviors. *Journal of the American Medical Association, 266,* 2419–2429.

Kahn, R. H., Heffelfinger, J. D., & Berman, S. M. (2002). Syphilis outbreaks among men who have sex with men: A public health trend of concern. *Sexually Transmitted Diseases, 29*, 285–287.

Kalichman, S. C., Nachimson, D., Cherry, C., & Williams, E. (1998). AIDS treatment advances and behavioral prevention setbacks: Preliminary assessment of reduced threat to HIV-AIDS. *Health Psychology, 17*, 546–550.

Kellogg, T., McFarland, W., & Katz, M. (1999). Recent increase in HIV seroconversions among repeat anonymous testers in San Francisco. *AIDS, 13*, 2303–2304.

Kelly, J. A., Otto-Salaj, L. L., Sikkema, K. J., Pinkerton, S. D., & Bloom, F. R. (1998). Implications of HIV treatment advances for behavioral research on AIDS: Protease inhibitors and new challenges for HIV secondary infection. *Health Psychology, 17*, 310–319.

Koblin, B. A., Torian, L. V., Gulin, V., Ren, L., MacKellar, D. A., & Valleroy, L. A. (2000). High prevalence of HIV infection among young men who have sex with men in New York City. *AIDS, 14*, 1793–1800.

Kok, G. (1999). Targeted prevention for people with HIV/AIDS: Feasible and desirable? *Patient Education and Counseling, 36*, 239–246.

MacQueen, K. M., McLellan, E., Kay, K., & Milstein, B. (1998). Codebook development for team-based qualitative analysis. *Cultural Anthropology Methods, 10*, 31–36.

Mansergh, G., Marks, G., Colfax, G., Guzman, R., Rader, M., & Buchbinder, S. (2002). Barebacking in a diverse sample of men who have sex with men. *AIDS, 16*, 653–659.

Margolis, A. D., Wolitski, R. J., Parsons, J. T., & Gómez, C. A. (2001). Are healthcare providers talking to HIV-seropositive patients about safer sex? *AIDS, 15*, 2335–2337.

Marks, G., Burris, S., & Peterman, T. A. (1999). Reducing sexual transmission of HIV from those who know they are infected: The need for personal and collective responsibility. *AIDS, 13*, 297–306.

O'Brien, T. R., Kedes, D., Ganem, D., Macrae, D., Rosenberg, P., Molden, J., et al. (1999). Evidence of concurrent epidemics of human herpesvirus 8 and human immunodeficiency virus type 1 in US homosexual men: Rates, risk factors, and relationship to Kaposi's sarcoma. *Journal of Infectious Diseases, 180*, 1010–1017.

O'Leary, A., Purcell, D., Remien, R. H., & Gómez, C. A. (2003). Childhood sexual abuse and sexual transmission risk behaviour among HIV-positive men who have sex with men. *AIDS Care, 15*, 17–26.

Parsons, J. T., & Halkitis, P. N. (2002). Sexual and drug using practices of HIV+ men who frequent public and commercial sex environments. *AIDS Care, 14*, 816–826.

Parsons, J. T., Halkitis, P. N., Wolitski, R. J., Gómez, C. A., & the Seropositive Urban Men's Study (SUMS) Team. (2003). Correlates of sexual risk behavior among HIV+ men who have sex with men. *AIDS Education and Prevention, 15*, 383–400.

Purcell, D. W., Parsons, J. T., Halkitis, P. N., Mizuno, Y., & Woods, W. J. (2001). Substance use and sexual transmission risk behavior of HIV-seropositive men who have sex with men. *Journal of Substance Abuse, 13,* 1–16.

Renwick, N., Halby, T., Weverling, G., Dukers, N., Simpson, G. R., Coutinho, R. A., et al. (1998). Seroconversion for human herpersvirus 8 during HIV infection is highly predictive of Kaposi's sarcoma. *AIDS, 12,* 2481–2488.

Rezza, G., Andreoni, M., Dorrucci, M., Pezzotti, P., Monini, P., Zerboni, R., et al. (1999). Human herpesvirus 8 seropositivity and risk of Kaposi's sarcoma and other acquired immunodeficiency syndrome related diseases. *Journal of the National Cancer Institute, 91,* 1468–1474.

Schiltz, M. A., & Sandfort, T. G. (2000). HIV-positive people, risk, and sexual behaviours. *Social Science and Medicine, 50,* 1571–1588.

Stall, R., Hays, R. B., Waldo, C. R., Ekstrand, M., & McFarland, W. (2000). The gay '90s: A review of research in the 1990s on sexual behavior and HIV risk among men who have sex with men. *AIDS, 14*(Suppl. 3), S1–S14.

Valdiserri, R. O. (2003, February). *Preventing new HIV infections in the US: What can we hope to achieve?* Paper presented at the 10th Conference on Retroviruses and Opportunistic Infections, Boston.

Valleroy, L., MacKellar, D. A., Karon, J. M., Rosen, D. H., MacFarland, W., Shehan, D. A., et al. (2000). HIV prevalance and associated risks in young men who have sex with men. *Journal of the American Medical Association, 282,* 198–204.

Van de Ven, P., Prestage, G., Crawford, J., Grulich, A., & Kippax, S. (2000). Sexual risk behavior increases and is associated with HIV optimism among HIV-negative and HIV-positive gay men in Sydney over the 4 year period to February 2000. *AIDS, 18,* 2951–2953.

Vanable, P. A., Ostrow, D. G., McKirnan, D. J., Taywaditep, K. J., & Hope, B. A. (2000). Impact of combination therapies on HIV risk perceptions and sexual risk taking among HIV-positive and HIV-negative gay and bisexual men. *Health Psychology, 19,* 134–145.

Watters, J. K., & Biernacki, P. (1989). Targeted sampling: Options for the study of hidden populations. *Social Problems, 36,* 416–430.

Wenger, N., Kusseling, F., Beck, K., & Shapiro, M. (1994). Sexual behavior of individuals infected with the human immunodeficiency virus: The need for intervention. *Archives of Internal Medicine, 153,* 1849–1854.

Wiley, D. J., Visscher, B. R., Grosser, S., Hoover, D. R., Day, R., Gange, S., et al. (2000). Evidence that anoreceptive intercourse with ejaculate exposure is associated with rapid CD4 loss. *AIDS, 14,* 707–715.

Williams, M. L., Elwood, W. N., & Bowen, A. M. (2000). Escape from risk: A qualitative exploration of relapse to unprotected anal sex among men who have sex with men. *Journal of Psychology and Human Sexuality, 11,* 25–49.

Wolitski, R. J., Halkitis, P. N., Parsons, J. T., & Gómez, C. A. (2001). Awareness and use of untested barrier methods by HIV-seropositive gay and bisexual men. *AIDS Education and Prevention, 13,* 291–301.

Wolitski, R. J., MacGowan, R. J., Higgins, D. L., & Jorgensen, C. M. (1997). The effects of HIV counseling and testing on risk-related practices and help-seeking behavior. *AIDS Education and Prevention, 9*(Suppl. B), 52–67.

Wolitski, R., Valdiserri, R. O., Denning, P. H., & Levine, W. C. (2001). Are we headed for a resurgence in the HIV epidemic among men who have sex with men? *American Journal of Public Health, 91,* 883–888.

2

THE MEANINGS OF SEX FOR HIV-POSITIVE GAY AND BISEXUAL MEN: EMOTIONS, PHYSICALITY, AND AFFIRMATIONS OF SELF

PERRY N. HALKITIS AND LEO WILTON

Sex is a source of pleasure that encompasses biological, psychological, and sociological realities (Reiss, 1989). To this end, sexual behavior and the meanings that individuals assign to sex are directly linked to the social, cultural, and interpersonal contexts of their lives (Heyl, 1989), and sexual identities transgress the act of sex.

For gay and bisexual men, however, the same-sex act is often the foundation on which they construct their sexual and social identities. Thus, the meanings that they assign to sex may be closely linked to the act of sex itself. It may be, in fact, a source of life or of "the self" (Sadownick, 1996). In the era of AIDS, as HIV-positive gay and bisexual men attempt to maintain their roles as active and viable sexual beings and in turn maintain their sexual identities, the formation and maintenance of these identities

The authors acknowledge the invaluable assistance of David Zade, Michael Shrem, and Allison Duffy in the analyses of these interviews.

21

have been complicated by the physical and psychological effects of the disease (Halkitis, 1999).

For most HIV-positive gay and bisexual men in the United States, sexual intercourse with another man represents the primary route of transmission for HIV (Centers for Disease Control and Prevention, 2001). Despite the fact that one sex act in their lives had caused irreparable damage, not surprisingly, most continue to actively engage in sex (Parsons, Halkitis, Wolitski, Gómez, & the Seropositive Urban Men's Study Team, 2003). Yet their identities as sexual beings often are intertwined with their identities as HIV-seropositive individuals, creating a reality that permeates their physical, emotional, and social lives (Halkitis, 2001). These men, like all HIV-positive individuals, must somehow make meaning of their sexual identities in lives already burdened by the physical effects of the disease (Schaefer, Coleman, & Moore, 1995), the social and emotional burden of disclosing an HIV status to sex partners (see chap. 7, this volume), and the need to protect their sex partners from seroconversion and themselves from acquiring other sexually transmitted infections or the possibility of superinfection with a different strain of the HIV virus (Schiltz & Sandfort, 2000).

If the act of sex itself is crucial to understanding the sexual identities of HIV-positive gay and bisexual men, then sexual behaviors must be viewed holistically and in terms of all of the meanings that men ascribe to sex, as well as the social, emotional, and cognitive factors that influence their sexual decision making and practices. However, in our attempts to prevent the further spread of HIV, our efforts traditionally have been based on the assumption that sex is a cognitive phenomenon (Ajzen, 1991; Bandura, 1990; Fisher & Fisher, 2000), and thus the sexual decision making of HIV-positive men have been viewed from this perspective (Schonnesson & Clement, 1995). Research, however, has consistently shown that although such perspectives have been successful to some extent in understanding sexual behavior, they have failed to encompass the notion that sex is more than a cognitive act and that strong social and emotional components influence sexual behavior (Halkitis, 2001; Poppen & Reisen, 1997). For HIV-positive individuals, in particular, the need to feel wanted or desirable (Halkitis, 1999, 2001), the need to escape the realities of HIV (McKirnan, Ostrow, & Hope, 1996), and the need to avoid feelings of stasis, rejection, or death (Klitzman, 1997) may strongly influence the type of sex in which these men engage, the meanings that they assign to sex in their lives, and their maintenance of sexual identities.

More recently, with the advent of successful HIV antiretroviral treatments and the possibility of HIV being transformed into a manageable and chronic disease (Gallo, 1996; Vittinghoff et al., 1999), a new consciousness has emerged with regard to the sexuality and sexual behaviors of HIV-positive individuals, which has created an additional complexity in attempts to prevent further spread of the disease. These treatments seem to have created a sense of optimism (see chap. 13, this volume) that may give HIV-positive individuals "permission" to engage more freely in risky sexual behaviors that are more physically and emotionally satisfying. The emergence of intentionally unsafe sex acts between HIV-positive men and their partners, known colloquially as barebacking (Halkitis & Parsons, 2003; Halkitis, Parsons, & Wilton, 2003; Mansergh et al., 2002; Suarez & Miller, 2001), may be one such outcome of these treatment advances and appears to be a mechanism by which HIV-positive men can realize the physical, emotional, and social needs provided by sex.

HIV-positive gay and bisexual men are sexual beings. To understand how this group of men negotiate safety and make decisions with regard to their sexual behaviors and, in turn, affect the further spread of HIV, it is crucial to consider the role that sex plays in their lives. More pointedly, it is important to examine the meanings that they give to their sexual behaviors through lenses that incorporate the physical, emotional, and social aspects of these behaviors. Only then can we fully understand how HIV-positive men make sense of sex in their lives and in effect develop HIV prevention strategies that are true to the sexual realities of HIV-positive gay or bisexual men. With this idea in mind, we considered the stories of 250 HIV-seropositive gay or bisexual men who participated in the Seropositive Urban Men's Study (SUMS; see chap. 1, this volume) in terms of the meanings they ascribed to the role of sex in their lives.

THE ROLES OF SEX

All 250 of the men with whom we spoke discussed the role and meaning of sex in their lives with reference to temporal and interpersonal paradigms. Many indicated that the role of sex had changed as a result of HIV seroconversion, and some discussed sex as it related to the sex partners that they chose and the manner in which they interacted with these sex partners. These matters are addressed in other aspects of this volume (in this volume, see chap. 3, for a description of the types of relationships in which HIV-positive men engage; chap. 9, for a discussion of attributions of seroconversion and their effects; and chap. 10 for an examination of the role of responsibility in sexual relationships). Our purpose was to disentangle the intrapersonal aspects of sex for HIV-positive gay and bisexual men and specifically to consider how these men make meaning of sex in their lives. We found that most of the men discussed the roles of sex in their lives along three main lines: the emotional role of sex as a mood stabilizer, stress reducer, and facilitator of intimacy; the physical role of sex as a biological release, a tactile connection, or an indication of physical ability; and the affirmation of identity, existence, and life through the vehicle of the sex act.

Emotional Roles

For many of the men in our study (approximately 74%), sex was highly related to their emotional state in that the act of sex both helped to deal with difficult and upsetting emotions and provided an escape, a reduction in stress, or a new emotional high. For others, the meaning and role of sex were related to a feeling of connectedness to another person. For this latter group, sex was the vehicle by which they were able to achieve intimacy in their lives.

The emotional burdens of being gay, being HIV-positive, and for some being single were, at times, overwhelming for many of the men. These burdens led to feelings of loneliness, depression, and guilt. And although many of the men acknowledged the presence of social structural systems, such as therapists, community-based agencies, families, and friends, to help deal with these emotional states, many indicated that sex was a means to eradicate these negative feelings, albeit only temporarily: "It's a fix. It's a drug. It's something to make me feel better. It makes me feel less lonely" (White male, age 46, New York). Sex is used a means of coping with emotions, "If I have a very, very bad day with someone, tension, depression, stuff like that" (Black male, age 35, San Francisco). Frequently, loneliness was the negative affect that many of the men sought to escape through sexual encounters:

> And being gay—it's really hard; it's just really hard. And it can be a pretty lonely life, you know, and having sex with even people I don't know, somehow relieves the loneliness. (Asian or Pacific Islander male, age 31, San Francisco)

> The loneliness, you know. Just the feeling of being screwed. Just being penetrated, period. That's a good feeling for me and I enjoy it, so that's what satisfies me. That's what I like. (Black male, age 28, New York)

In this regard, the use of sex as an emotional stabilizer and as a means to escape negative feelings was directly linked to the search for anonymous sex partners by some of the men. For instance, one of the men described his need to overcome his feelings of loneliness by seeking an anonymous sexual encounter as follows:

> I guess it's the tension like you get, you build inside, of being alone, so you seek a stranger—And I don't know. It's just . . . it's a release. It's

a release for me to—instead of being home, watching TV, doing nothing, I go and I seek a stranger. (Latino male, age 26, New York)

In addition, feelings of guilt or sorrow also were viewed as emotional states that could be alleviated through sex. The need for anonymous and often multiple partners was exacerbated by these emotional states for many of the men. Thus, sex could help ease those feelings:

> Oh, definitely it fulfills guilt, or if I am sad about anything, or like if I went to the race track and I lost like a couple of hundred dollars or something, and I like I did the other night and I just got so disgusted with myself, that my immediate, like some people would reach for a beer or a line of cocaine. I reach for a hard cock, you know, and I love it; and it is like after I am done with that one, I want a different one. And it is like the excitement of that person you have never met before, and just having that person touch you and just really do you really good and it is a great feeling, after you done. (White male, age 28, New York)

The loneliness, shame, and guilt that men experienced also resulted in stress in their lives. Thus, very often the men expressed the role of sex in their lives as a means of stress relief or "stress reduction. You know, relaxation" (Black male, age 28, New York). These feelings of stress that the men experienced were linked to the emotional states described earlier as well as the physical demands of their lives. Sex was seen as a means of deflating the feelings of stress that they were experiencing. One participant said about sex: "It relieves me. I feel—after I finish having sex I feel relaxed and, you know, I just feel good." (Black male, age 32, New York). Another commented, "At times too, I guess, it's a tool to release anger. Frustrations" (Black male, age 40, New York); and yet another noted that sex was helpful "to get off frustration, to get off tension" (Black male, age 36, New York). Elaborating on this notion of stress reduction, men described the role of sex as follows:

> That's a good stress relief, that's for sure. I think just the need to, just kind of be with somebody and have some kind of connection there. There were times where it was just a bad week and I hated everyone at work and everyone I had to deal with you. That would be a time for me to just say, "Okay, I'm going to go out and get laid." I need it, it's a clarifier, it's a relaxer, it's wonderful stuff. (White male, age 27, New York)

> It is just a great release of stress; it feels good and it just makes me forget certain problems. And it is a great like substitute for cocaine or drugs or liquor or crime or beating someone up or anything, stealing. I would rather go and get my ass reamed and then just take a shower

and go home. So, to release stress definitely. (White male, age 28, New York)

As some men described the role of anonymous sexual encounters to modulate negative emotional states, some described these experiences in terms of stress reduction:

To let off steam. Coming from a tense day, tense workday or a visit with my parents. I find no, you know, I can, you know, go on to a sex party or a bar or whatever I could meet someone and then let off steam. Translate the job frustration and tension into something positive, to a sexual situation. (White male, age 46, New York)

Despite the fact that many of the men believed that sex relieved stress in their lives and modulated difficult emotions, there was a general consensus among those who described the emotional role of sex that sex was only a temporary solution to the problems that they were facing: "If you're tied up in knots because of anxiety, tension, or stress, it tends to relieve a lot of that. So physically speaking, I think it relieves a lot of stress. Emotionally, I think the same problems are there before and after" (White male, age 55, San Francisco). Nonetheless, many of the men frequently used sex as a means of maintaining their emotional states and, at least temporarily, achieving an emotional high. Despite the shortcoming of this behavioral strategy, it was the only behavior that some men trusted or knew how to use, "It provides me with an emotional catharsis at times, a catharsis that I need, and that I don't feel that I can express in other ways" (mixed race/ethnicity male, age 39, San Francisco).

In addition to describing sex as a means for confronting difficult emotions, men described the feelings of emotional connectedness that they were able to achieve through their sexual behaviors. For example, some of the men expressed the belief that "intimacy is sex" (mixed race/ethnicity male, age 32, San Francisco) and sex was described as a way "to create or enhance intimacy" (White male, age 46, New York). Specifically, some participants spoke of sex as a facilitator for intimacy and oftentimes as the primary manner in which they were able to achieve intimacy in their lives. Sex is for some men "a major route to intimacy; you know, it allows you to get close to a person" (White male, age 42, New York). One participant described what sex provided him as follows:

I guess a sense of closeness, a sense of fulfillment and attachment and closeness and intimacy. Other than that, that's a need that I have. And sex temporarily fills that. (White male, age 46, New York)

For some men, sexual encounters are the only avenue that they have to reach intimacy, even if a sexual exchange is not what they are seeking:

> Sometimes sex is a way of—what I really need is intimacy, but what I end up getting is sex in exchange for the intimacy, although I really don't want to have sex. (White male, age 34, San Francisco)

Similarly, another man described sex as the means of achieving intimacy as follows:

> It's like a gesture, like a ritual, part of the intimacy process I guess, to show closeness . . . and an expression of my feelings toward the other person and vice versa. (Asian or Pacific Islander male, age 32, San Francisco)

In addition, some believed that the role of sex was not only to enhance intimacy between just those who were engaging in the sex act but the whole gay community: "I believe sex is the glue that sticks gay men together. And that's a philosophical point of view, and that there is a bond among gay men" (White male, age 67, New York).

> When I'm having sex, it just symbolizes to me a bond between you know, me and my lover or me and another person you know, even if it is with a stranger for a couple of minutes. (White male, age 46, New York)

For some the search for intimacy through sex partners was related to the need to love and be loved and ultimately, perhaps, to fall in love, a need of every individual:

> It feels good; it feels like it makes up—it is nice to be loved; everyone likes to be loved and held and cuddled and touched, something that every human being craves for, you know. (White male, age 28, New York)

> I think it's—like I said, I think it's beautiful. I think—that if two hearts could just have the same mind, the same purpose, I think it could be— it could take you to another level, mentally. (Latino male, age 33, New York)

Ultimately, the need for love, the desire for intimacy, the desire to feel good and escape emotional burdens and reduce stress represent various interconnected emotional roles that sex provides for many HIV-positive gay and bisexual men. The multifaceted emotional meaning of sex in the lives of the men is best summarized by the words of one participant as follows:

> It plays many different roles. Sometimes I use it for instant gratification. Sometimes I use it to relieve stress. Sometimes I use it to validate my self-esteem. Sometimes I use it for just pleasure. And the most important one to me is that I use it to share with another person basically, you know, share feelings, love, caring, you know affection for someone. But I use it for many different reasons, and I'm aware of that. (Black male, age 32, New York)

Physical Roles

Sex as a fulfillment of a physical state emerged as another theme in the narratives of the HIV-positive men, with 66% of the men describing sex in this manner. In that regard, the men described sex as a medium through which they were able to satisfy a biological function. Further, many of the men discussed the physical connectedness that sex provided them. This latter notion was often but not always related to the emotional intimacy that was described earlier. Related to this matter of connectedness and among a smaller subset of the men, sex was a manifestation of physical power and control.

Frequently, men described sex as vehicle to satisfy a biological need. In this regard, one participant said, "It is normally just a physical desire" (mixed race/ethnicity male, age 28, New York). Similarly, some of the men related the physical role of sex to other biological realities: "It's like eating a meal. It's just something that your body needs" (Latino male, age 30, New York), and, "Well, I guess sex is an act. . . . It's a desire. I guess it's like eating, sleeping, exercising (Black male, age 29, New York). Another elaborated as follows:

> Mostly, it's just a physical need. It's a need for release, it's like eating or breathing or having an alcoholic beverage or something. It's a need, it's a pleasure, it's something that I just need to do periodically. (White male, age 42, New York)

This view of sex as a physical need and as a necessary biological function allowed some of the men to be able to separate the sex act from any form of emotion within themselves or in relation to their partners and simply to consider it in terms of their own physical satisfaction. To this end, sex as a physical construction was not related solely to an exchange with another man but also to the act of masturbation as a means of fulfilling a desire. As stated by one participant, "You know sex is sex. Anyway sex is like an ejaculation. It's just—just something you do just to do it" (Black male, age 40, New York). Others described this notion as follows:

> What I get out of it is an orgasm. Sex to me, how I define it is a roll on the sheets. It's just two people getting together to get physical, you know. Sex, it's just it. It's no—really, for me it's no feelings, it's no emotion, it's just, other than a good orgasm. (Black male, age 37, San Francisco)

> Only physical, yeah, I don't think about, you know, I just try to satisfy myself, physical, you know, not spiritual or nothing, just physical. Satisfy my sexual appetite besides doing it with a person I like. (Latino male, age 29, New York)

It's a sexual need that—it's just satisfying or gratifying, knowing that you can still have sex with somebody but not have to be emotionally involved. And I can turn that emotion off very easily. I can turn off the idea that knowing that a relationship has ended, I can turn off my emotions that way too. (Latino male, age 39, San Francisco)

In addition, when sex was viewed as separate from emotions, partners were viewed as simply a tool for self-gratification: "Sex is, you know, a . . . you know, you're horny and you want to get off" (White male, age 40, San Francisco). In relation to their ability to separate the physical meaning from any emotional connection of sex, others expressed the following:

Well I mean—cuz I'm a man, and we have these sexual urges. So, even if I'm not in a bathhouse, even if I'm just in my room, I get these urges, so—but sometimes I just gotta find someone to perform my sexual urges with. (Asian or Pacific Islander male, age 31, San Francisco)

In addition, a small set of the men described a clear distinction of sex acts for physical fulfillment from those acts in which sex was immersed in the emotional elements described earlier. This often varied by the partner or the man's particular needs at a fixed point in time:

Mmm, sex to me is just sex. It's just pleasing yourselves, because I feel I have two different things. I have sex and I have making love, there's a difference to me. So, when I have sex with someone, it means I'm having sex with them; he's not something—I have no feelings for them, and after we're done, I say goodbye and never care if I ever see them again. But, when you're involved with someone, and you have feelings for them, then the whole act of sex becomes very special, and the feelings play into that, and everything gets really emotional and gets, furthermore, deeper. So, for me there's like two different—there's two levels of sex. There's just pure ecstasy, pleasing yourself, and then there's another side of being involved and actually yearning for somebody special, not just anybody. (Black male, age 25, San Francisco)

Just having sex, just like getting your rocks off. It's just a, there's a physical thing there as a, you know. It's good while you're doing it there, but having sex with a partner is more than that. You take your time. (Latino male, age 28, New York)

Apart from the physical, I would say not much, not much. Because as I say, when I have sex with my boyfriend, the person I'm going out with, still sex is sex with him. What makes it special is what you make after sex, what you create and what you are able to see in the other person after sex. It's very important. (Latino male, age 35, New York)

The gratification of the tactile sense was key for some of the men who described the physical connectedness that sex provided. This expression was occasionally but not always related to the emotional connectedness described earlier. This role of sex was described as a source of enormous pleasure to many of the men as well as to their partners. Specifically, the act of physical touch through caressing, kissing, massaging, as well as other forms of touch affirmed the sensuality of physical closeness or relatedness: "I like pleasure, I like giving pleasure, I like the touching and the feeling and all that shit man" (mixed race/ethnicity male, age 37, New York). Others described it as follows:

> Well, I guess probably the biggest need is just to be touched. . . . Maybe that's probably why I go still with this married guy because with him you can just hold him, or whatever, and that's enough. (Black male, age 43, New York)

> Certainly I, I prefer a lot of hugging and caressing and kissing and just physical closeness as well as emotional closeness and intimacy on any physical and emotional level. (Black male, age 45, New York)

> I like the caressing part, the kissing part, the oral part, the closeness, and, you know, the touching, the holding. You feel loved, and you feel important. (Black male, age 29, San Francisco)

For some of the men, the need for a physical connection and the ensuring acts superseded the need for any particular act other than demonstrations of affection through human touch:

> Sometimes I have hard-core sex, but other times it's just holding, kissing, and mutual masturbation, which is just as satisfying and gratifying as the actual hard-core stuff. So, it depends on what you want. Sometimes I'll be in that like I need that hard-core sex, and other times I'll be like I just want to be comforted. So, it depends on what you need. (Black male, age 32, San Francisco)

> And I need that warmth and affection from a very masculine body, next to 'em and stuff like that. And I get off on his body, you know, the crushing, the holding during—the rough holding and touching. (Black male, age 35, San Francisco)

> Sometimes just being touched by another human being, sometimes everything and sometimes nothing like the most recent one. I just did it because I wanted somebody to kiss me and I wanted to be kissed in a relaxed manner not in a rushed way. (Latino male, age 43, New York)

Less often, the men described the physical power and physical dominance that sex offered them. This notion was related to a potential need to take control of a sex partner and, in turn, experience a sense of sexual competency and empowerment offered by the act of power and control: "It's very empowering, very fulfilling, dominating" (White male, age 32, San Francisco). This physical aspect of sex as power was constructed within the paradigms of being the active or "top" person in the sex act. The few men that discussed this physical aspect of sex in their lives described it as follows:

> And also test my ability against theirs, how good are you, can you fuck real well, or can't you, you just, do I have to teach you some things, you know, or can we kind of have a friendly competition that's like real nice and we kind of get our groove on and it's like wow, it's like we're seeing fireworks and I stimulate you, and you stimulate me and it kind of feeds off itself sort of incestuously in terms of roles. (Black male, age 39, New York)

> What really turned me on was when he was like saying, "Well, your dick is so big. You gonna put that all up me? You can't put that all up me." (mixed race/ethnicity male, age 36, San Francisco)

AFFIRMATION OF SELF

Affirmation of self served as the third primary theme to emerge from the narratives in relation to the sexual experiences of the men. In particular, approximately 19% of the participants described sex as a condition that provided affirmations of their physical attractiveness and sexual desirability as well as a manifesto for their sexual identity as gay men.

Many of the men discussed the importance of body image and, as a result, physical attractiveness in their lives and how the act of sex validated their feelings of sexual desirability. According to one participant, "It [sex] makes me feel like attractive and, you know, that somebody wants me" (Latino male, age 30, New York). Another expressed the role of sex as follows: "Maybe some validation things, maybe some reminders that I'm attractive, attractive to other people" (Black male, age 37, New York). For many men, sex means: "I feel wanted, attractive" (Black male, age 30, New York) and "I feel very attractive when somebody is making love to me or fucking me or something or sexually attracted to me" (Latino male, age 31, New York). Others elaborated on this concept of sex as an affirmation of physical desirability and attractiveness:

> It helps validate me as a person, makes me feel I'm attractive at least. I've been looking for, I've been ready for a relationship for nine years, eight years, seven years, something like that, and I have not found anybody who's really interested in me to develop a relationship with me. So going to the baths or going out and meeting somebody validates that, at least, they might not like me as a person, but they at least find me attractive enough as a body to have sex with. (White male, age 44, New York)

> Mentally, I think the fact of being with someone who's enjoying being with me, that's self-satisfying for my persona I guess. It makes me feel

good knowing that someone was attracted to me and . . . got from it the same thing that I got out of it. (Latino male, age 33, New York)

To the same extent, a few of the men described how their sex partners or potential sex partners simply function to fulfill their need to feel attractive, and how sex, in turn, provides them with this affirmation regardless of the sex partner:

I guess there's a certain kind of attention. I mean, I guess for a long time, early on, I would judge myself, my sexual identity. I would use it as a gauge like oh there's a great looking guy in the bar over there. If I can get him, then I'm somebody. You know? And, there's an ugly guy over there, you know, and I can get him. And, if I can't wow then I'm really a loser. So, sometimes you go to these bars where like there's really ugly people just so you can make yourself feel better about yourself knowing that you can have anybody that you want. (White male, age 34, New York)

They could sit there and promise you the world and tell you how good looking you are and how sexy and beautiful you are, and you go like, "Oh, thank you, thank you, thank you," and you go through it and when it's over you don't talk to that person ever again. But, you have that need fulfilled. (White male, age 27, New York)

For a smaller subset of men, the need for acceptance and the ensuing affirmation of self was provided by sex and was used as a means of compensating for other rejections in their life. One man best described it as follows:

So, uhm, I don't know if that [sex] makes me an addict, but, you know, it's something that I use as a crutch, you know. I mean it's just—and I think it has to do with, uhm, in the industry that I'm in there's a lot of rejection, you know. You deal with a lot of, you know, oh, you didn't get this part, or you didn't get this gig, or whatever. So, you deal with a lot of that. And, going and having anonymous sex with someone, it's like, you know, acceptance. (White male, age 42, New York)

Since the onset of the HIV epidemic, gay men have endured unrelenting forms of heterosexism along with individual, institutional, and cultural forms of homophobia and AIDS-phobia. In essence, the sexual behavior of gay men has been negatively constructed as "deviant" or "pathological" within these hegemonic structures. These sociopolitical and sociohistorical realities for gay men have been accentuated by the physical demands of HIV on the body. As a result, the physical effects of the virus have become a core issue connected to body image for gay men. Connected to these themes, some of the narratives of the men demonstrated that issues of physical attractiveness and sexual desire were connected to the physical effects of living with the HIV virus:

Sex has been a security blanket. It's like, well, I'm having sex. Somebody cares about me for a little while. It's also been a distraction from being HIV-positive, just running out and, well, I'm alive, I'm free, I can have some sex as I want to. (Black male, age 30, New York)

It's reassuring that someone still finds me attractive, that I'm still wanted, that they can still love me, so it's really—that is the necessary reassurance. This has been very difficult because I've had KS [Kaposi sarcoma] everywhere. Everywhere. So, sex has helped me, you know, if someone finds me attractive and it makes me feel like maybe I'm not a leper. And, I'm still desirable and that I can still have that kind of intimacy. And, you know, because you still need to be touched and held and wanted. So, it has served a purpose. Apart from orgasms, and, you know, pleasure, that kind of sexual pleasure. It's gratifying. For my self-esteem. That I'm still, you know, whatever. (White male, age 40, New York)

The issues of physical attraction and the need for sexual desirability become even more complex for older gay men in terms of aging. Thus, affirmations of desirability were connected to both the physical realities of HIV as well as the developmental process of aging.

It's [sex] a meaning that there is a [sighs] energy that's in me at 50 years old that when I'm sexually stimulated, when someone is caressing my body or admiring my body, it permits me to—somehow like feel very proud, very, very, very strong. Strong not in the way of battle strong, but it's nice to be admired. (White male, age 51, New York)

It [sex] proves to me that I'm attractive. It shows to me that I'm still in the race. I don't mean culture. I mean in the running. I mean, like, I can still pull someone who's like, then, 15 years younger than me, and that kind of turns me on because of the fact that I am not in that age group anymore. It turns me on that I can seduce a man, and I have, you know, literally seduced men. I guess it's a power trip. (Black male, age 35, New York)

In many cases, the men discussed the centrality of the sex act in affirming HIV-positive gay men's sexuality, including their sexual identity. In this sense, the act of sexual intercourse served a critical role in the synergistic negotiation of multiple identities or concepts of self with the merging of a gay "self" and the HIV-positive "self." With regard to affirmations of gay identity, one man said, "I think that's basically where, you know, sometimes sex plays a part of my life as being a gay male" (mixed race/ethnicity male, age 41, New York). The role of sex also was described as a route to feeling whole: "It helps me feel—I feel sexy. I think that is part of being a whole person" (Latino male, age 40, New York). Another elaborated on the role of sex as an affirmation of identity:

Well, it [sex] is a way to sort of express my sexual freedom. . . . Yes, what I want to say was, you know, I grew up in a family and it was very homophobic. And maybe with growing up with very homophobics it's kind of, you know, a way to sort of express myself. Sexual freedom now. And now I'm just like starting to come out. Actually, I'm starting to come out of the closet recently. But, it's a way to sort of kind of liberate myself. (White male, age 37, New York)

This affirmation of identity also was connected to the sense of being alive even in light of HIV infection. One man described it as follows: "Well, I guess it makes me feel like I'm alive. Part of the world, I guess" (White male, age 47, New York). Another stated, "I associate sex with health, being healthy (Asian or Pacific Islander male, age 35, San Francisco). Others expressed the affirmation of life through sex as follows:

> Ah, it makes me feel healthy. It makes me feel I have a very positive attitude, about masturbation and stuff like that. I feel, ah—it makes me feel like I'm healthy because when I'm not healthy, I, I don't, ah, feel sexual. (White male, age 39, New York)

> It means that I'm alive. It means that I'm living fully. It means that— it means that I'm worthwhile. It means that I can get what I want. It means that I'm an effective person. I'm gay. And I'm actively gay. I'm very interested in sex, and sex is very important to myself and in some way my self-image and my self-esteem, in ways that I partly understand and in ways that I'm probably just beginning to look at and better understand what this means. (White male, age 46, New York)

DISCUSSION

Based on these narratives, sex appears to have multifaceted meanings for HIV-positive gay and bisexual men. Sex functions on many levels and incorporates intrapersonal, interpersonal, and temporal paradigms. In this chapter, we assessed the intrapersonal aspects of sex. Within the person, sex appears to synergistically fulfill the emotional and physical needs of an HIV-positive man while simultaneously affirming one's existence as a gay man, an HIV-positive man, and an attractive man. These ideas appear consistently across the narratives, regardless of themes, ages, races, and ethnicities. This suggests a consciousness with regard to sex for HIV-positive gay and bisexual men that may parallel the realities for gay men as a whole, as well as some heterosexuals, while also incorporating the realities faced by those who are infected with HIV.

Sex provides personal fulfillment for HIV-positive gay and bisexual men. This fulfillment takes the form of alleviating negative emotions or feelings, relieving many types of stress, and providing a biological release. All of these aspects of sexual meanings represent forms of coping. Thus, for many of the men with whom we spoke, sex appeared to function as a mechanism for coping with the realities of their lives, including the stressors of their emotional and personal lives, the physical realities of HIV disease, and the isolation and loneliness experienced by being gay and HIV-positive. These ideas were corroborated by the fact that many of the men also spoke of sex as a tool for affirming that one is still alive, vibrant, and desirable. Although it appears that sex helps HIV-positive gay and bisexual men adapt to the emotionally and physically burdensome aspects of their lives, it also helps, at least temporarily, emotionally lift their spirits or affirm their places in the world.

In addition, many HIV-positive gay and bisexual men view sex as the primary way to experience intimacy with another individual. Men discussed the role of sex as a means of realizing both emotional and physical connectedness, and some described sex as the only tool with which they were able to achieve this goal. Clearly, this need for connectedness is important to HIV-positive gay and bisexual men. But what is essential, as articulated by many of the men, is that sex is viewed as the primary means for obtaining this desired outcome.

To this end, understanding the meanings that HIV-positive gay and bisexual men ascribe to their sexual behaviors and sexual identities helps us understand their motivation for engaging in HIV risk-related behaviors. As HIV-related prevention efforts have recently begun to address the role of HIV-positive individuals in the transmission of this disease, the findings presented in this chapter are timely and sensitive to the complexities faced by those who are living as both HIV-positive and sexual beings. Such information can be used to tailor programs that are true to the lives of HIV-positive gay and bisexual men without ostracizing or asking them to curtail their sex lives. The information can be used to develop messages and interventions that incorporate the meanings that these men ascribe to sex and seek means to ensure safety without compromising the important role that sex plays in their lives.

REFERENCES

Ajzen, I. (1991). The theory of planned behavior. *Organizational Behavior and Human Decisions Processes, 50,* 179–211.

Bandura, A. (1990). Perceived self-efficacy in the exercise of control over AIDS infection. *Evaluation and Program Planning, 13,* 9–17.

Centers for Disease Control and Prevention. (2001). *HIV/AIDS Surveillance Report, 13*(1), 1–40.

Fisher, J. D., & Fisher, W. A. (2000). Theoretical approaches to individual-level change in HIV risk behavior. In J. L. Peterson & R. J. DiClemente (Eds.), *Handbook of HIV prevention* (pp. 1–55). New York: Kluwer Academic.

Gallo, R. C. (1996). AIDS as a clinically curable disease: The growing optimism. *AIDS Patient Care and STDs, 10,* 7–9.

Halkitis, P. N. (1999). Redefining masculinity in the age of AIDS: Seropositive gay men and the buff agenda. In P. Nardi (Ed.), *Gay masculinities* (pp. 130–151). Newbury Park, CA: Sage.

Halkitis, P. N. (2001). An exploration of perceptions of masculinity among gay men living with HIV. *Journal of Men's Studies, 9,* 413–429.

Halkitis, P. N., & Parsons, J. T. (2003). Intentional unsafe sex (barebacking) among men who meet sexual partners on the Internet. *AIDS Care, 15,* 367–378.

Halkitis, P. N., Parsons, J. T., & Wilton, L. (2003). Intentional unsafe sex, or barebacking, among gay/bisexual men in New York City. *Archives of Sexual Behavior, 32,* 351–358.

Heyl, B. S. (1989). Homosexuality: A social phenomenon. In K. McKinney & S. Sprecher (Eds.), *Human sexuality: The societal and interpersonal context* (pp. 321–349). Norwood, NJ: Ablex.

Klitzman, R. (1997). *Being positive: The lives of men and women with HIV.* Chicago: Ivan R. Dee.

Mansergh, G., Marks, G., Colfax, G., Guzman, R., Rader, M., & Buchbinder, S. (2002). Barebacking in a diverse sample of men who have sex with men. *AIDS, 16,* 653–659.

McKirnan, D., Ostrow, D. G., & Hope, B. (1996). Sex, drugs, and escape: A psychological model of HIV-risk sexual behaviors. *AIDS Care, 8,* 655–669.

Parsons, J. T., Halkitis, P. N., Wolitski, R. J., Gómez, C. A., & the Seropositive Urban Men's Study Team. (2003). Correlates of sexual risk behaviors among HIV+ men who have sex with men. *AIDS Education and Prevention, 15,* 383–400.

Poppen, P., & Reisen, C. (1997). Perception of risk and sexual self-protective behavior: A methodological critique. *AIDS Education and Prevention, 9,* 373–390.

Reiss, I. L. (1989). Society and sexuality: A sociological explanation. In K. McKinney & S. Sprecher (Eds.), *Human sexuality: The societal and interpersonal context* (pp. 3–29). Norwood, NJ: Ablex.

Sadownick, D. (1996). *Sex between men.* New York: HarperCollins.

Schaefer, S., Coleman, E., & Moore, A. M. (1995). Sexual aspects of adaptation to HIV/AIDS. *Journal of Psychology and Human Sexuality, 7,* 59–71.

Schiltz, M. A., & Sandfort, T. G. M. (2000). HIV-positive people, risk, and sexual behaviours. *Social Science and Medicine, 50,* 1571–1588.

Schonnesson, L. N., & Clement, U. (1995). Sexual attitudinal conflicts and sexual behavior changes among homosexual HIV-positive men. *Journal of Psychology and Human Sexuality, 7,* 41–58.

Suarez, T., & Miller, J. (2001). Negotiating risks in context: A perspective on unprotected anal intercourse and barebacking among men who have sex with men—Where do we go from here? *Archives of Sexual Behavior, 30,* 287–300.

Vittinghoff, E., Scheer, S., O'Malley, P., Colfax, G., Holmberg, S. D., & Buchbinder, S. P. (1999). Combination antiretroviral therapy and recent declines in AIDS incidence and mortality. *Journal of Infectious Diseases, 179,* 717–720.

3

HIV-POSITIVE GAY AND BISEXUAL MEN'S PERSPECTIVES ON ESTABLISHING AND MAINTAINING RELATIONSHIPS

CAROLINE J. BAILEY AND TREVOR A. HART

Since the advent of the AIDS epidemic, sexuality has typically been studied in terms of the health risks associated with specific sexual practices. This has been especially true of research on HIV-positive gay and bisexual men, for whom most studies have focused on individual risks for transmission of HIV. This narrow view of human sexuality often ignores the psychological meaning of sexual interactions, the motivations of HIV-positive gay and bisexual men to initiate and maintain intimate relationships, and the benefits and challenges in these relationships.

Like other populations, HIV-positive gay and bisexual men have sexual relationships to fulfill basic needs for emotional intimacy and physical contact (Remien, Wagner, Dolezal, & Carballo-Dieguez, 2001). These relationships can take various forms, including long-term relationships, dating relationships, and one-time sexual encounters. However, few researchers have examined psychological issues in the short- and long-term sexual relationships of HIV-positive gay and bisexual men. As a result, relatively little is known about the needs that sexual relationships fulfill and the barriers to the initiation and maintenance of these relationships that are faced by HIV-positive gay and bisexual men. A more complete understanding of these relationships is essential to better address mental health needs of HIV-positive gay and bisexual men and to develop feasible and sustainable HIV prevention programs that support these men in adopting and maintaining safer sex practices that protect them and their partners.

Similarities are likely to be found between the relationships of HIV-positive gay and bisexual men and the relationships of other populations. For example, research has found that social support received in long-term sexual relationships serves as a support for both physically ill heterosexual individuals with cancer and for HIV-positive gay and bisexual men; for both of these populations, such social support in the context of these partnerships helps to increase relationship satisfaction (Haas, 2002; Hagedoorn et al., 2000). Also likely are similarities between these populations in terms of barriers to establishing and maintaining sexual relationships. Common challenges may include finding potential partners, experiencing frustration while searching for a relationship, attending to the health and psychological needs of one's partner, and defining the emotional and sexual boundaries of relationships.

Despite the potential similarities, some differences have been noted. Sexual relationships among gay and bisexual men take place in a broader culture that is often not supportive of same-sex relationships (Wagner, Brondolo, & Rabkin, 1996) and that provides far less social and legal support for the maintenance of relationships. Sexual relationships of gay and bisexual men are likely to be affected not only by societal antigay attitudes but also by internalized homophobia (Derlega, Sherburne, & Lewis, 1998; Herek, 2002; Herek, Gillis, Cogan, & Glunt, 1997; Herek & Glunt, 1993), which may lower the individual's perception of his ability to initiate and maintain long-term relationships. Another difference between gay and bisexual men and heterosexual couples is the level of distress caused by sexual activity outside the relationship. In one sample of 75 serodiscordant gay and bisexual couples (in which one partner is HIV-positive and one is HIV-negative), 72% of relationships were not monogamous (Wagner, Remien, & Carballo-Dieguez, 1998). Of the couples that were not monogamous, a quarter reported having an agreement permitting sexual activity outside the relationship, often called an open relationship. Yet another fifth reported they had at least some knowledge that sexual acts occurred outside the relationship. The study suggested that extrarelationship sexual activity may not automatically cause distress, especially if both partners agree to an open relationship.

Living with HIV also appears to add to the difficulty of initiating or maintaining sexual relationships (Cusick & Rhodes, 2000; Rolland, 1994). In fact, HIV-positive gay and bisexual men are less likely to have a main partner than are their HIV-negative peers (Hoff, Coates, Barrett, & Collette, 1996). The difficulties associated with having HIV may often be compounded when one's partner is HIV-negative or of unknown serostatus. To avoid transmitting the virus to their partner, HIV-positive gay and bisexual men must consider which risk reduction measures they want to take regarding sexual intercourse. Although some data indicate that many serodiscordant partners discuss safer-sex behaviors, or negotiate safety (Crawford, Rodden, Kippax, & Van de Ven, 2000; Davidovich, de Wit, & Stroebe, 2000; Kippax, 2002), other studies have found that the need for consistent condom use is often perceived as interfering with emotional intimacy (Carballo-Dieguez, Remien, Dolezal, & Wagner, 1997; Remien, Carballo-Dieguez, & Wagner, 1995). Other challenges specific to HIV-positive gay and bisexual men include fear of being rejected for being HIV-positive, feeling hopelessness about finding a long-term partner, fear of infecting a partner, and for some fear of losing another partner to HIV.

This chapter illustrates many of the added challenges that HIV-positive men face in initiating and establishing sexual relationships and maintaining dating and long-term relationships. We will use data from 250 interviews of men who participated in the Seropositive Urban Men's Study (SUMS) to explore sexuality among men with main partners, men in or wanting dating relationships, and men not in relationships who do not want to date or have a long-term relationship but do want to engage in sexual behavior from time to time. A complete narrative of the research methods used in SUMS is presented in chapter 1 (this volume). We describe how relationships and sexual behavior are initiated and identify issues that may affect relationships or the lack thereof among these men.

SEXUALITY AND RELATIONSHIPS: FINDINGS FROM THE SEROPOSITIVE URBAN MEN'S STUDY

Three major types of sexual relationships were discussed by respondents in the narratives. The men either had a main partner, were dating or wanting to date, or were not seeking a romantic relationship. The following sections go into detail about each of these main categories.

Men With Main Partners

Almost a quarter (22%) of the men in the sample reported having a main partner, referred to as a lover, partner, or boyfriend. Three major themes emerged from the interviews of men with main partners: the emotional and sexual boundaries of relationships, the benefits and drawbacks of having an

HIV-positive partner, and fears of infecting a partner of unknown or negative HIV status.

Emotional and Sexual Boundaries of Relationships

Men in this study varied considerably in their approach to sexual fidelity. Most of the respondents with main partners did not discuss the benefit of having a monogamous relationship. However, among the few men who did discuss benefits, one main advantage was security, decreased concern about their partner leaving them for someone else. Another advantage of monogamy was avoiding infecting new partners with HIV: "I don't want to infect anybody else no matter what. And . . . I think maybe that's one large reason why for 10 years I was so monogamous" (Black male, 42, New York).

Some men reported being in open relationships. Respondents in such relationships tended to discriminate between sexual fidelity and emotional commitment. As one respondent reported:

> Sexually, it's open. . . . But as far as the commitment, I think it's there. We've done a lot of stuff together, invested a lot of stuff for the future, and, you know, it's pretty stable I feel. It's working and . . . I get support from it. (White male, age 48, San Francisco)

Others engaged in sexual activity outside their relationship without the consent of their main partner. One respondent reported ambivalence about his behavior:

> I'm trying to—it's like 51% of me is saying, "Yes, I do want a steady partner, I want somebody to be with for the remainder of my life." 49% is saying, "Well, I do, but maybe I want to finagle a little bit, at least for a little while, until I'm . . . really dead sure that this is going to be the one and only for the rest of my life. (Black male, age 39, New York)

Along with ambivalence about committing to their main partner sexually, some reported that engaging in casual intercourse with a new partner was exciting because of the novelty of a new partner. One respondent described anonymous sex as being more "intense" than sex with his main partner:

> Much more intense . . . with the one-night stand because you know after so many years in a relationship, you just get like humdrum about it, and you miss that spontaneity of just like cruising the bushes and things like that. . . . The intensity of it because you know that you probably won't see that person again and just not know how they are going to perform, how they will react to your body. (White male, age 36, New York)

Benefits and Drawbacks of Having an HIV-Positive Partner

Half of the men with main partners reported being in a relationship with an HIV-positive man. Many of these men reported benefits of having a committed relationship with someone of the same serostatus, such as not having to be concerned about one's partner contracting HIV and being able to share their common experiences living with HIV. However, having an HIV-positive partner also appeared to have its own set of difficulties. Some respondents reported concern that their partner would get sick or die:

> My partner is HIV-positive, and I really love him. I worry about him. . . . I get real upset about it when he's sick. I'm scared that something will happen. Very scared something—he'll get sick, because I don't want to go through losing somebody. . . . We love each other. We couldn't be without each other. (Latino male, age 44, New York)

Although most respondents appeared to be interested in caring for their partners, a few reported that it was difficult when both partners in the relationship had health problems. One respondent reported resenting spending much of his time taking care of his HIV-positive partner:

> He's physically ill. . . . I don't want to be a caregiver and a lover too, because I have needs too. And I know that sounds very selfish. . . . I've got to tell you that health care plays a big role, bigger than I ever thought it would. (Black male, age 50, San Francisco)

Fears of Infecting a Partner

A common theme that emerged among men with main partners of HIV-negative or unknown HIV status was the fear of infecting their sexual partner. Many reported that they would experience extreme guilt if they infected their partner:

> I'm scared to even touch him or kiss him. . . . I feel like I'm gonna hurt him, and I can't handle it. I won't allow myself to feel like that, that's it gonna be my fault if anything happens to him. I mean, I'm thinking like if a condom breaks. (Latino male, age 20, San Francisco)

This fear was typically more intense among men with main partners than those with other types of partners possibly because of the greater emotional intimacy in these relationships:

> I'm even more protective with him [respondent's boyfriend] than I would be with a stranger. . . . With my lover, as much as there's the love, and that has its own connection, it's very charged. It's constantly charged because we're very aware of our situation. . . . When I'm with anonymous partners, I don't have that. I feel more free. I feel more— I don't have to talk about things so much. I don't have all the baggage. (White male, age 37, New York)

Many men reported that fear of infecting a partner caused not only personal distress but also caused conflict in their relationship. For example, one man reported that his HIV-negative boyfriend was frustrated by always having to use condoms:

> You know, there were areas where he kind of like expressed, you know, at some point there was frustration that I was—that I was positive, and there were things that he wanted to do we couldn't do because we had to have safe sex. So you know, I think there were some tensions there. (White male, age 37, San Francisco)

Despite concerns about infecting their partners, some HIV-positive men decided that unsafe sex was at least somewhat acceptable when their partners knew about their serostatus and therefore were able to make an informed decision. One man reported reduced concern because his partner knew that the respondent was living with HIV and the partner had not seroconverted thus far:

> Well, I talk to him about safe sex. I tried hard to get him to use a condom. But like I say, we've been together 4 years and he hasn't been infected yet. (Black male, age 31, New York)

Men Who Were Dating or Wanting to Date

Most (78%) respondents stated that they currently did not have a main partner. However, approximately two thirds of this group acknowledged that they would like to pursue a romantic relationship. This included 111 men who stated that they were currently single. Men who were dating (27% of the total sample) relayed some of the same sentiments as men who were in relationships, such as fear of infecting a partner as well as concerns about their partner's serostatus. Dating men also discussed difficulties in meeting partners because of one's HIV status, hopelessness about prospects of meeting a partner, and the effects of recent HIV treatments on dating interest and behavior.

Effects of HIV Seropositivity on Dating

Men who wanted to date and develop relationships would sometimes express that the "dating pool" was much more limited for HIV-positive men. Respondents also discussed having been rejected by HIV-negative men or at least expressed a belief that HIV-negative men would not want to date someone who was HIV-positive. Others just felt more comfortable with someone else who was HIV-positive and would exclusively seek other HIV-positive men for dating. One respondent who wanted to date expressed how HIV had affected his dating, including fear of rejection:

It affects it a lot. I think I've not been able to find a boyfriend. That there is a much smaller market for what it is that I want. That when people who are not positive find out that [I am], they probably don't want me, I think. (White male, age 46, New York)

This fear of being rejected for being HIV-positive played a major role in many men's decisions toward remaining single or dating.

Actually and coincidentally, probably I usually date a lot of people who don't have that virus. And it has its advantages and disadvantages, and I have a lot of rejection within dating people who don't have the virus. (White male, age 30, New York)

Similar to men in relationships, men who were dating reported that the fear of infecting an HIV-negative partner was a prominent concern. For men who were dating, this concern sometimes led to added distress:

I have three people I'm dealing with, not sexually, but to see which one is the right one for me. And it scares me because two of them are not HIV-positive. (Latino male, age 28, New York)

Although some men expressed a concern that HIV-negative gay and bisexual men would not want to date them, others reported that they preferred dating someone of like serostatus. This preference was often discussed as a means to avoid potential fears or conflicts associated with having a relationship with a partner who was not infected: "Well it complicates it, and this is why I say I wouldn't date anybody who is not HIV-positive" (White male, age 40, San Francisco). Some men felt more comfortable with other HIV-positive gay and bisexual men because of a sense of commonality around shared experiences regarding living with the virus: "I feel more comfortable [dating someone who is HIV-positive]. I think we have more, a lot more in common" (White male, age 51, New York). Others preferred dating an HIV-positive man to avoid concern about transmitting HIV:

I just feel more comfortable in a sexual situation with someone who is positive. I mean, you know, I've had relationships with negative guys, and that's always been in the back of my mind. That's the point where I think about my HIV the most, is—you know, I always have safe sex now, but I also always fear the fact that "What if?" Even though I'm pretty educated on the transmission of this disease, but, you know, you never can be sure. (Asian or Pacific Islander, male, age 32, San Francisco)

Hopelessness About Prospects for Relationships

Others expressed their desire to date but believed that other gay and bisexual men in their community did not share this desire. As one respondent expressed, "It's very hard to have a relationship. Nobody wants a relationship;

everybody wants just sex" (Black male, age 36, New York). Another respondent expressed a similar sentiment:

> Everybody is on a marathon to date everybody in New York at least once, and I'm looking for somebody to date; and I don't know, I wear my heart on my sleeve, and it doesn't happen. (Latino male, age 33, New York)

Discussing HIV With Dating Partners

When asked about issues surrounding dating, respondents discussed the effect that disclosing their HIV status had on their relationships. Chances of discussing one's HIV status with dating partners were occasionally lessened by fear of the potentially deleterious consequences on the longevity of the relationship. Those who were afraid of being rejected often preferred to wait until they had a better sense of their partner's potential reactions to having an HIV-positive partner or until they were more confident that this was a relationship worth pursuing. One respondent summed up his perspective when asked to discuss how HIV affected how he felt about dating or having a boyfriend:

> I have to meet somebody that I think I would have to date them for a while so I could know how they are going to deal with it. I just can't blurt it out, "I have AIDS." It is a hard thing to do. You just don't know what the reaction will be. I am kind of sensitive; I hate rejection. I try not to set myself up for rejection; I would rather be without than to just be rejected for some reason. I never handle rejection well. (White male, age 34, New York)

Another respondent also avoided disclosing until he knew that a relationship was going to be serious:

> So I don't usually discuss my HIV status with no one, unless I find myself getting serious about them and they're getting serious with me; then I may tell them. But if I feel that it's just going to be something that's going to be a sexual thing and they're sleeping around with other people too, I don't feel a need to discuss it with anybody. So I don't tell no one. (Latino male, age 34, New York)

Dating Again Because of Improved HIV Treatments

Improved treatment for HIV had become widely available 1 or 2 years before these men were interviewed. Many men reported that before these treatment advances, having HIV dramatically decreased their interest in dating. After highly active antiretroviral therapy (HAART) became available, many attitudes changed, and men reported a renewed interest in dating. This renewed interest in dating appears to stem from the introduction of

HAART, allowing HIV-positive men to have hope that they might be able to live with HIV as a chronic illness instead of as a death sentence. One respondent expressed the following:

> I'm not emotionally invested in anyone. . . . And [I] just started dating
> . . . decided that because of the protease inhibitors in my life, I'm not
> dying or I'm not going to a hundred percent die . . . with the protease
> inhibitor and the information that the blood was going in a positive
> direction rather than negative one, I have come up with a new discov-
> ered energy that included starting relationships once again. (White
> male, age 51, New York)

Fear of Losing Another Partner to AIDS

Having lost a lover to AIDS greatly affected men's views of relationships and the types of relationships that they sought. This theme recurred through-out the narratives. When asked about the types of sexual relationships in which they engaged, many men spoke of having lost their former partners to AIDS. Although men in relationships also discussed this fear, men who were dating expressed this fear more frequently. The emotional effect of this loss was expressed in the following narratives:

> [My lover] passed away in '93. I don't think I ever could see anybody
> again. It wouldn't work. . . . There's this one person that I date . . . but
> it hasn't been going good because of the age difference. My age group
> is already dead. Everybody in their 40s is already dead. (Latino male,
> age 38, San Francisco)

> My lover died in December of '96. I'm not in a lover relationship. I do
> see people but primarily sexually. Most of my relationships with people
> are around recovery and around certain friendships. But for sexual—
> and I really look at it as sexual acting out more than, you know, I'm
> not in any kind of committed, fulfilling, intimate relationship. (Black
> male, age 50, New York)

Some men mentioned that these losses to HIV/AIDS negatively af-fected their current relationship. One man discussed his current situation with a man he was seeing:

> We're not sure where it want to go, and my friend buried his other half
> about—almost 2 years ago, and—because of AIDS—and doesn't know
> if he really want to go through with it again. (White male, age 32,
> New York)

Fear of Infecting a Dating Partner

Similar to the men with main partners, men who were dating reported anxiety about the possibility of infecting an HIV-negative dating partner.

Occasionally, concerns about transmitting HIV led some respondents to leave their HIV-negative partner altogether:

> I was in a relationship for 3 years. . . . I made him believe that I was cheating on him so he would leave me . . . but if he doesn't know how much I loved him to send him away, because he was negative . . . but I just didn't want him to go through all that, and he was a young man. (Latino male, age 26, New York)

> We're a lot alike. He's younger than I am, of course. There are not many people my age left. We have a good relationship, but at this point we basically don't have sex anymore. My guilt. He's HIV-negative. He has a long and bright future ahead of him, and I don't want to be responsible for anything like that. (Latino male, age 41, San Francisco)

Men Not Seeking a Relationship

Although most men without main partners reported having an interest in meeting people to date, some chose to not become emotionally involved with their sexual partners. Explanations for wanting to remain single varied. Similar to the men who had main partners but were not monogamous, some men who were not seeking relationships reported that they enjoyed the novelty of new partners. However, most of the explanations for choosing to remain single related to feeling lack of interest because of past negative experiences, avoiding being rejected for being HIV-positive, and preferring anonymous sex to avoid emotional intimacy.

Feeling Lack of Interest Because of Past Negative Experiences

Some men had recently broken up with a partner and had negative feelings toward relationships. Often these negative experiences had little or nothing to do with HIV serostatus and involved instead recollections of intense relationship conflict and ensuing emotional distress. For one respondent, his memories had to do with both conflict and how he contracted HIV:

> [I'm] Single and plan to stay that way. . . . I don't even need it, 'cause I went through 4 and a half years with a guy that I believe that I contracted this [HIV] with, a very violent, very vicious relationship with him, and I don't even—I don't want to ever go through that no more. (Black male, age 37, San Francisco)

Avoiding Being Rejected for Being HIV-Positive

For some men, fear of being rejected because of their HIV status resulted in lack of interest in establishing relationships. As opposed to the men who were seeking or were in relationships, some men decided that the benefits of a relationship were outweighed by the potential negative consequences of being rejected by someone with whom they were emotionally intimate:

> I'm single right now . . . you meet people but nothing like for a lasting relationship because maybe the HIV situation. . . . So if you go out to—let's say a club or whatever—you go and you see a person that you really like. And the conversation about the HIV situation doesn't happen; it's hard, you know. So you're better off to let that person go and forget about the situation. (Latino male, age 41, New York)

Many of the respondents who were not interested in pursuing a relationship recalled past experiences with rejection when they had disclosed their HIV status. When asked if having HIV was an issue in dating, one respondent stated:

> I am very, very cautious, and frankly afraid—in fact, it affected me for years. I didn't do anything because I didn't want to knowingly contact or communicate this to anybody. Because in my mind, it requires me talking to the partner about it, not about sex, but about HIV. (White male, age 64, San Francisco)

> It makes me not want to or not consider looking for—it steers me away from looking for a serious relationship, you know; it makes me feel like I just want to go and have sex real quick, get it over with and not deal with all that trauma that goes along with like, you know, revealing your status and talking about it and then the rejection that comes along with it and all that kind of crap. (Latino male, age 33, New York)

Preferring Anonymous Sex to Avoid Emotional Intimacy

A related theme was men frequenting anonymous sex venues such as sex clubs and adult bookstores as an alternative to the emotional intimacy of dating or having a long-term relationship. Many of the single respondents reported that they attended these settings to replace relationships, to avoid discussing their HIV status with a dating partner, or to remain anonymous. The following excerpts describe how fears of being rejected led to a desire to have anonymous sex:

> It has stopped me from getting a boyfriend; that's why I go to the East Side Club. I'm afraid that if I find someone . . . and I tell them I'm HIV-positive, it's gonna make a difference. I'm afraid of getting rejected, so for there I want someone who's not gonna reject me. So I want to pick someone who's anonymous, or a stranger, so that I don't have any stigmatism [sic] later on. (Latino male, age 26, New York)

> I hardly ever go anywhere now where I put myself in a position where I'm going to meet someone and develop a serious relationship. . . . I've kind of fallen into—I feel secure with not having to deal with those

issues by going to sex clubs. It's just anonymous sex. (mixed race/ethnicity male, age 46, New York)

I think a lot of my fascination with sex clubs, it's emotionally safer and it's a lot easier and I don't have to deal with a lot of the shit that I have to deal with when I'm more emotionally involved with someone. (White male, age 37, New York)

DISCUSSION

These data demonstrate some of the challenges faced by HIV-positive gay and bisexual men in their sexual relationships, which vary, ranging from one-time sexual liaisons to long-term committed relationships. They may be nontraditional, such as long-term relationships in which partners are permitted to engage in sexual activities with outside partners. And because a large percentage of men in primary relationships reported engaging in sexual activities outside their main relationship, it may be incorrect to assume monogamy within long-term relationships in this population.

The availability of HAART had a noticeable effect on the willingness of HIV-positive men to establish sexual relationships. Some men who were single mentioned that before these treatment advances, they had little interest or motivation to date or seek a long-term relationship. These men's concerns varied from fear of infecting an HIV-negative partner to fear of being rejected for being HIV-positive. One concern that was not mentioned was the fear or experience of any of the appearance-altering side effects of protease inhibitors. This is likely a result of the sampling time frame of the study, in which HAART had recently been introduced. Although the men in our sample did not report this concern, concerns about the effects of HAART on appearance may also affect the attitudes and behavior of HIV-positive gay and bisexual men in sexual relationships.

The data provide important insights about why HIV-positive men are less likely than other gay and bisexual men to be involved in long-term relationships (Hoff, McKusick, Hilliard, & Coates, 1994). Men not in relationships reported that it was more difficult to meet romantic partners because of HIV-related stigma. Many men reported reluctance to disclose their HIV-positive status because of fears or because of having previously been rejected on disclosure. Additional discussion of the effect of disclosure on the lives of HIV-positive gay and bisexual men can be found in a later chapter (see chap. 7, this volume). Even among men who established a romantic relationship with a serodiscordant partner, fears of infecting the partner and frustration about having to consistently use condoms for the entire duration of the relationship served as additional stressors that were perceived as decreasing intimacy and increasing relationship conflicts. For these reasons, some had given up on ever meeting someone to share emotional intimacy, instead resorting to casual or anonymous sexual encounters in which they did not feel the need to discuss their serostatus and could at least experience temporary human contact and affection.

Some of the themes presented in this chapter add new insights to data already discussed in the literature. For example, many studies describe sexual behavior in sex clubs and other anonymous sex venues, and others describe the sexual behavior of HIV-positive men with and without main partners (e.g., Binson et al., 2001), but little research has explored why HIV-positive men might frequent anonymous sex venues in the first place. Our data provide preliminary evidence that men frequent anonymous sex venues to avoid emotional intimacy or to experience the excitement of having sex with a new partner. Although many single men in the study desired a long-term relationship, these men were highly aware of the challenges in establishing and maintaining such a relationship. Specifically, they reported that they were concerned about being rejected for being HIV-positive, losing another partner to HIV, or infecting an HIV-negative main partner. Our results show that men are especially concerned about infecting a main partner because of the greater guilt associated with infecting someone with whom they are emotionally involved.

The themes discussed in this chapter are not likely to represent the totality of attitudes, emotions, and contextual details regarding sexual relationships. For example, these themes do not discuss many of the benefits of being single, such as making independent decisions and having greater personal space. They also do not discuss the benefits of being in a relationship, such as being able to share financial responsibilities or having increased social support (Haas, 2002). The data are also limited in that questions were not designed to elicit specific responses to details such as whether men were married, the lengths of their relationships, and if men lived with their partners.

The data suggest significant differences in the level of emotional intimacy between the three different types of relationships discussed in this chapter: main partner, dating, and casual sex. The data suggest that despite differences among men in this group, men with main partners remain in relationships longer; communicate better about difficult issues such as HIV, safer sex, and monogamy; and experience greater emotional intimacy. Men who were dating or looking to date were not able to rely on this level of emotional intimacy; they reported concern about their ability, both as gay or bisexual men and as men living with HIV, to establish emotional intimacy. In contrast, casual sex encounters were often used as alternatives to emotional intimacy and, occasionally, to avoid the consequences of being rejected or otherwise losing one's partner. These findings regarding attitudes and behavior associated with sexual relationships are likely to be common to a variety of populations; however, more qualitative and quantitative research among different populations is warranted.

This chapter illustrated many of the added challenges that HIV-positive men face in establishing and maintaining short- and long-term sexual relationships. These findings present a psychological context for previous research focusing on the sexual behaviors of this population and demonstrate a potential interaction between the psychological issues faced by HIV-positive men and their sexual behavior. Addressing these concerns is likely not only to decrease distress and improve relationship functioning but may also reduce the spread of HIV and other sexually transmitted diseases.

REFERENCES

Binson, D., Woods, W. J., Pollack, L., Paul, J., Stall, R., & Catania, J. A. (2001). Differential HIV risk in bathhouses and public cruising areas. *American Journal of Public Health, 91,* 1482–1486.

Carballo-Dieguez, A., Remien, R. H., Dolezal, C., & Wagner, G. (1997). Unsafe sex in the main relationships of Puerto Rican men who have sex with men. *AIDS and Behavior, 1,* 9–17.

Crawford, J. M., Rodden, P., Kippax, S., & Van de Ven, P. (2000). Negotiated safety and other agreements between men in relationships: Risk practice redefined. *International Journal of STD and AIDS, 12,* 164–170.

Cusick, L., & Rhodes, T. (2000). Sustaining sexual safety in relationships: HIV positive people and their sexual partners. *Culture, Health and Sexuality, 2,* 473–487.

Davidovich, U., de Wit, J. B. F., & Stroebe, W. (2000). Assessing sexual risk behaviour of young gay men in primary relationships: The incorporation of negotiated safety and negotiated safety compliance. *AIDS, 14,* 701–706.

Derlega, V. J., Sherburne, S., & Lewis, R. J. (1998). Reactions to an HIV-positive man: Impact of his sexual orientation, cause of infection, and research participant's gender. *AIDS and Behavior, 2,* 339–348.

Haas, S. M. (2002). Social support as relationship maintenance in gay male couples coping with HIV or AIDS. *Journal of Social and Personal Relationships, 19,* 87–112.

Hagedoorn, M., Kuijer, R. G., Buunk, B. P., DeJong, G. M., Wobbes, T., & Sanderman, R. (2000). Marital satisfaction in patients with cancer: Does support from intimate partners benefit those who need it most? *Health Psychology, 19,* 274–282.

Herek, G. M. (2002). Heterosexuals' attitudes toward bisexual men and women in the United States. *Journal of Sex Research, 39,* 264–274.

Herek, G. M., Gillis, J. R., Cogan, J. C., & Glunt, E. K. (1997). Hate crime victimization among lesbian, gay, and bisexual adults. *Journal of Interpersonal Violence, 12,* 195–215.

Herek, G. M., & Glunt, E. K. (1993). Interpersonal contact and heterosexuals' attitudes toward gay men: Results from a national survey. *Journal of Sex Research, 30*, 239–244.

Hoff, C. C., Coates, T. J., Barrett, D. C., & Collette, L. (1996). Differences between gay men in primary relationships and single men: Implications for prevention. *AIDS Education and Prevention, 8*, 546–559.

Hoff, C. C., McKusick, L., Hilliard, B., & Coates, T. J. (1994). The impact of HIV antibody status on gay men's partner preferences: A community perspective. *AIDS Education and Prevention, 4*, 197–204.

Kippax, S. (2002). Negotiated safety agreements among gay men. In A. O'Leary (Ed.), *Beyond condoms: Alternative approaches to HIV prevention* (pp. 1–15). New York: Kluwer Academic.

Remien, R. H., Carballo-Dieguez, A., & Wagner, G. (1995). Intimacy and sexual risk behavior in serodiscordant male couples. *AIDS Care, 7*, 429–438.

Remien, R. H., Wagner, G., Dolezal, C., & Carballo-Dieguez, A. (2001). Factors associated with HIV sexual risk behavior in male couples of mixed HIV status. *Journal of Psychology and Human Sexuality, 13*, 31–48.

Rolland, J. S. (1984). Toward a psychosocial typology of chronic and life-threatening illness. *Family Systems Medicine, 2*, 245–262.

Wagner, G., Brondolo, E., & Rabkin, J. (1996). Internalized homophobia in a sample of HIV+ gay men, and its relationship to psychological distress, coping, and illness progression. *Journal of Homosexuality, 32*, 91–106.

Wagner, G., Remien, R. H., & Carballo-Dieguez, A. (1998). "Extramarital" sex: Is there an increased risk for HIV transmission? A study of male couples of mixed HIV status. *AIDS Education and Prevention, 102*, 245–256.

4

BETWEEN THE SHEETS AND BETWEEN THE EARS: SEXUAL PRACTICES AND RISK BELIEFS OF HIV-POSITIVE GAY AND BISEXUAL MEN

DEBORAH J. SCHWARTZ AND CAROLINE J. BAILEY

Many variables influence whether the sexual behaviors of gay and bisexual men protect them from HIV, sexually transmitted diseases (STDs), and other diseases or place them at greater risk for contracting these infections. The issues are complex and include dynamics of relationships with partners, condom use and other issues with condoms, pleasure-seeking, beliefs about HIV risk with regard to new advances in HIV/AIDS treatments, substance use, communication and negotiation skills, mood and affect, and knowledge and beliefs about how HIV and other STDs are transmitted (Gold, 2002; Gold & Skinner, 1992, 2001; Gold, Skinner, Grant, &

This chapter was coauthored by an employee of the United States government as part of official duty and is considered to be in the public domain. Any views expressed herein do not necessarily represent the views of the United States government, and the author's participation in the work is not meant to serve as an official endorsement.

Plummer, 1991; Kalichman, Rompa, Austin, Luke, & DiFonzo, 2001; Suarez & Miller, 2001; Suarez et al., 2001; Vanable, Ostrow, McKirnan, Taywaditep, & Hope, 2000; see also Stall, Hays, Waldo, Ekstrand, & McFarland, 2000, for a review of the research). For gay and bisexual men, addressing these issues within the context of sexual decision making requires that they assimilate and understand the variables that affect their risk for HIV and STDs and balance this understanding with the demands of sexual desire.

Little research has been done to specifically understand how HIV-positive gay and bisexual men navigate these complex issues or how these issues affect HIV transmission (Kok, 1999; Schiltz & Sandfort, 2000). Exploring how HIV-positive gay and bisexual men perceive safety and risk in their sexual decision making and how these perceptions guide the behaviors they choose to engage in is an important step in understanding how to decrease sexual risk for HIV-positive men and their sex partners. This chapter presents findings from the Seropositive Urban Men's Study (SUMS) on the sexual practices and risk beliefs of 250 HIV-positive gay and bisexual men in New York City and San Francisco (see chap. 1, this volume, for more information about SUMS). Beliefs about the perceived risks of specific sex acts (anal sex, oral sex, and other sex acts) will be discussed, and these discussions include knowledge and beliefs about HIV transmission, condom use, substance use, sex partners, and other factors perceived as influencing risk in sexual situations.

BRIEF REVIEW OF RELEVANT LITERATURE

The influence of multiple variables on the decision to be sexually safe or risky is well documented in the literature. Advances in HIV treatments, such as highly active antiretroviral treatment (HAART), often result in reduced viral load and improved immune functioning and overall health. This has resulted in the perception of HIV as a chronic, manageable disease. Research conducted by Vanable, Ostrow, McKirnan, Taywaditap, and Hope (2000) involving a convenience sample of well-educated gay men indicated that unprotected sex with HIV-positive partners taking antiretroviral drug therapies was seen as less risky than unprotected sex prior to the availability of antiretroviral therapies, especially if their partners had an undetectable viral load. Kalichman, Rompa, Austin, Luke, and DiFonzo (2001) also showed that HIV-positive gay and bisexual men perceived themselves as being less infectious because of reduced viral load and that, as a result, they participated in increased unprotected anal sex. In another study, gay and bisexual men perceived having sex with partners who had a low viral load as a result of taking HAART as less risky than having sex with an HIV-positive partner not taking HAART (Suarez et al., 2001).

Types of partners involved in a sexual encounter (anonymous or steady partner) influence the decision to engage in unprotected anal intercourse (Stall et al., 2000). Common reasons (especially among young gay and bisexual men) for unsafe encounters with anonymous partners of unknown HIV status include believing that (a) partners who exhibit healthy characteristics (e.g., physical health, personal wealth, high educational achievement, and nice personalities) are unlikely to be infected; (b) not thinking about HIV to avoid ruining the sexually positive mood, and (c) withdrawing early when having anal sex to avoid exchanging fluids avoids some risk for infection (Gold & Skinner, 1992). In contrast, unprotected anal sex between steady partners or boyfriends may not be perceived as risky (Bosga et al., 1995; Gold et al., 1991; Hays, Kegeles, & Coates, 1997). If unprotected anal sex has already occurred between partners, the necessity to stop is considered small (Gold & Skinner, 2001). Barebacking, or the conscious and consensual decision to have unprotected anal sex, occurs between primary partners as an expression of intimacy and trust (Boulton, McLean, Fitzpatrick, & Hart, 1995; Suarez & Miller, 2001). When asked why they barebacked, men most often state that their main reason is to experience the physical stimulation and pleasure of unprotected sex (Mansergh et al., 2002). For gay and bisexual men, the motivation for engaging in unsafe sexual behavior is sometimes a result of succumbing to powerful emotional and sexual needs and desires (such as intimacy and trust; Boulton et al., 1995). Furthermore, the motivation for engaging in safer sexual behavior may involve a number of reasons, including concern for their sex partner, an ethical commitment to safety, concerns about infecting others, or concerns about the future and well-being of the gay community (Nimmons, 1998; Nimmons & Folkman, 1999; see also chap. 10, this volume).

Pinkerton and Abramson (1992) suggested that risky sex can be the result of gay and bisexual men weighing options of perceived threat or safety against perceived pleasure and intimacy. Men calculate the risk factors influencing a sexual situation, and their actions directly reflect that calculation of risk (Boulton et al., 1995). The result is a variety of measures used to balance threat or safety with pleasure and intimacy, including withdrawing early, inconsistent condom use during a sexual encounter, taking care to not exchange body fluids, having unprotected but not rough sex, and agreeing to not use condoms for anal sex with seroconcordant partners.

The knowledge and beliefs of gay and bisexual men about HIV transmission in specific sexual behaviors has been shown to affect sexual decision making (Gold & Skinner, 2001). Assumptions about HIV transmission, stemming partly from advances in antiretroviral treatments, have been found to be related to the strategies men used to ensure safety in their sexual encounters (such as early withdrawal) and the sexual roles men chose (men perceived encounters as less risky for HIV transmission if the infected partner was the receptive partner; Gold & Skinner, 2001). These researchers also found that HIV-positive men were more likely than other gay and bisexual men to underestimate transmissibility (especially for isolated experiences of unprotected anal insertive sex with no exchange of semen or preejaculative sex and even of isolated unprotected anal sex encounters with ejaculation; Gold & Skinner, 2001). This research suggests that beliefs and knowledge about HIV transmission, especially perceived safety of early withdrawal, affect gay and bisexual men's decisions to engage in unprotected anal sex.

As this brief review of the literature demonstrates, many variables influence the decisions gay and bisexual men make during sex to determine to what degree their encounter will be safe or risky. The literature supports the concept of calculating risk and strategizing sex behaviors. Assumptions about the health and HIV status of a partner and the risks involved in unprotected sex with that partner are probably common approaches to sexual decision making for gay and bisexual men. HIV-positive men also weigh all of these options and, in addition, negotiate a second layer of complexity around their own HIV status and their responsibility to protect the health of their partners and themselves. The SUMS sexual narratives reflect many of the issues raised in this brief literature review. In addition, our analyses reinforce that these issues are not isolated factors, but rather are complex and muddled issues that affect nearly all aspects of the sexual lives of HIV-positive gay and bisexual men and require an equally complex approach on the part of HIV prevention efforts.

SPECIFIC SEX ACTS

The narratives indicate that HIV-positive gay and bisexual men participate in a multitude of sexual practices, including insertive and receptive anal sex, oral sex, and mutual masturbation. To a lesser degree, men also reported participating in one or more other sexual activities such as using dildos, rimming (oral to anal contact), and fisting (inserting a fist into the partner's rectum).

More men in this sample were the receptive partner for anal sex (almost half) than were the insertive partner (less than a third). Less than 10% of the sample reported barebacking with another HIV-positive man or a man of negative or unknown HIV status. About half of the respondents reported having participated in oral sex with their partners. Sexual encounters were not limited to specific sexual acts; most men in this sample also engaged in a range of sexual activities during their sexual encounters.

SEX ACTS AND PERCEIVED RISK FOR HIV

Men interpreted the risk involved in their sex acts in many different ways. Few (less than 15%) perceived sexual role (being the anal insertive top or the anal receptive bottom) as important to their safety. Of those who did, one respondent stated, "I was the bottom, so I was taking more risk anyway" (white male, age 34, New York). Another, describing sex with an HIV-negative partner, stated, "I feel like the top has a less risk factor than the bottom" (Latino male, age 33, New York).

Oral sex was believed by almost a quarter of respondents to carry low or no risk. As one man stated:

> To me, oral sex—all right, there is a slight possibility, but it is very small about contracting HIV. I personally don't know anybody that I have met in the circles of having HIV who have ever said that they got it from oral sex. (White male, age 34, New York)

Some men believed that their sexual encounter was safe because they actually participated in noninsertive sexual acts, such as rimming or rubbing or mutual masturbation (33%). In addition, a few men believed that they were safer in their sexual encounters if they avoided rough sex or even kissing (5%). As one respondent stated, "I think it was safe because I don't kiss guys" (Black male, age 34, New York). Another stated:

> Go slow, you know, I think I didn't want—you know, you have hard, rough, ready sex, it's gonna, you know, you can break condoms, lot of bleeding, and, you know. (Native American male, age 29, San Francisco)

ANAL SEX

Knowledge and Beliefs About Condom Use and Risk for HIV

Almost half of the HIV-positive gay and bisexual men in this sample believed that anal sex contributed to risk for HIV transmission (46%). In addition, almost half believed that they were at risk for transmitting HIV or STDs during receptive anal sex when no condom was used. For example, when asked about what he thought made his sexual interaction with a partner of HIV-negative or unknown status unsafe, one respondent replied:

> I guess in a way it's . . . we're not talking about HIV alone . . . when you have unprotected sex, it could be . . . we can expose each other to VDs . . . hepatitis . . . things like that. Especially . . . anal sex and

and rimming and things like that. (Asian or Pacific Islander male, age 32, San Francisco)

Respondents who did not use a condom for anal sex and who believed that this put their partner at risk for HIV stated that they did so at their partner's request or because their relationship involved some degree of emotional intimacy or trust (20%). One respondent said this about his partner's (of HIV-negative or unknown status) request to not use a condom:

> Now, if he wanted me to put on a condom, I would have because I had them there. I always carry them. If he had insisted on that, I would have done that. But he didn't. So, I didn't. (Black male, age 48, New York)

In contrast to perceiving the encounter as risky because condoms were not used, 56% of the men felt that their sexual encounter was safe because they did use a condom (for anal and oral sex). As one respondent stated, "I had the condom on and there was no exchange of fluid in the mouth or ass. So that is safe" (Latino male, age 41, New York).

Some men indicated beliefs and knowledge about condoms and HIV transmission that suggested they could justify not using a condom and still feel safe (26%). These strategies for safe but unprotected sex offer important insight into the creative ways that HIV-positive men find to balance the affirming aspects of unburdened sexuality with conscious awareness of HIV transmission.

Some men (8%) perceived their sexual encounters without using a condom as safe because their partner was of the same HIV status. As one respondent stated about not using condoms for anal sex with his HIV-positive partner:

> Well, I know that his . . . health is good and my health is excellent and . . . we both know we don't have any other STDs. So, yes, I think it was pretty safe. As far as reinfecting each other with HIV, I don't believe it happens. Vancouver [the AIDS conference] last year taught me that you can't reinfect someone with HIV. That used to be what they thought was true. . . . So, sexually, in terms of HIV transmission, since we both have HIV, I guess it was safe, well, since you can't transmit it again, so yes, it was safe. (mixed race/ethnicity male, age 37, New York)

A few believed that they were safe when not using a condom because they did not participate in rough sex (5%), as described by one respondent with a partner of HIV-negative or unknown status:

> I believe that usually when HIV is transmitted to the receiver, there has to be a tear in the intestine, which to me would be either violent sex or—just that, violent sex. I don't think—it's just my belief, and

I've never heard any different, that if it's comfortable sex, that there shouldn't be any rip in the intestine, and you have some protection there naturally. So, if there was any semen, I wouldn't think that [inaudible], but that doesn't really count there, unless we were both infected. So no, there was no condom. (Black male, age 32, San Francisco)

In general, not using a condom to protect against HIV and other STDs was perceived as the most prevalent risk behavior. Other beliefs relating to condom use (perceived by 12% of the men) included the opinions that condoms hurt or felt bad, that respondents disliked using condoms, that condoms were only used on occasion (only for anal sex when the respondent or his partner believed that they were going to ejaculate), that condoms were not available during the sexual encounter, or that sex was better or more natural without a condom. One respondent vividly described the difficulty of using condoms and the resultant anxiety:

I do not want to mess with this little packet. Look, my hands are full of lube, right, because I just reset either my butt or my dick, and then I've got to tear this thing and—and then take the thing that has— who knows what's been on my finger . . . you've got to bite it, bite this thing open, take the condom out right, now figure out which end is up . . . and try to figure out which way to try to scroll this on my dick. Meanwhile, my dick is getting soft and I have to try to figure out how to put this thing on. I put it on; it doesn't fit. It's like the wrong size suit; it's not meant for me. . . . All this stuff makes it really complicated . . . it makes me all anxious, and I'm losing my hard-on already, and by then its, like, all over. (White male, age 46, New York)

Knowledge and Beliefs About Exchanging Body Fluids and Risk for HIV

Reinfection with another strain of HIV was a concern expressed by 34% of men. Reinfection was a concern if there had been an exchange of fluids during the sexual encounter or if the respondent had come into contact with a partner's sores or cuts. Men were specifically concerned about the risk for transmission from ejaculating inside the partner and thereby exchanging fluids.

Avoiding exchange of fluids during sex did not necessarily include a strategy of using condoms for anal sex (more than two thirds of these men had alternative strategies for avoiding fluid exchange that did not involve condom use, such as not penetrating partners, pulling out before ejaculation, implementing pre- and postsex cleanliness rituals). For example, one respondent explained his belief about risk after an encounter in a sex club with multiple partners of unknown HIV status:

I was able to have what I considered natural sex without much thought. HIV by and large . . . is simply not an issue . . . I just had good sexual encounters. And like I said, it was unprotected. . . . I also felt really good because even though it was unprotected, it wasn't what I really consider risky or dangerous because no one orgasmed [sic] inside of the other. At least, for myself, when I was inside of the one guy, I'm pretty confident I didn't have pre-semen. So I felt good about that. (White male, age 37, New York)

For a few men, not penetrating their partners or not being penetrated by partners was the only way to completely avoid fluid exchange and have a sexual encounter they perceived as safe. For example, one respondent stated:

There was no exchange of body fluids. There was no bodily punctures, no blood, no rough sex, no penetration. It's hard to imagine it could have been much safer. (White male, age 42, New York)

Men were also concerned about contracting other health-damaging STDs and infections through exchange of and contact with body fluids during the sexual encounter. As part of their concern about exchanging body fluids, some men discussed beliefs about hygiene, specifically practicing good hygiene as a way to ensure safety in their sexual encounters. Some men devised specific routines and rituals around cleanliness. One respondent described the routine that made him feel safe:

It's just that afterwards, I just soak my—I know that sounds stupid, but I just soak myself in a hot . . . tub or hot water. And I double-check that I have no cuts or nothing in my—in my head [of the penis], and—and I just think that, that helps get rid of any—most of the stuff there. (Asian or Pacific Islander male, age 38, San Francisco)

Another respondent said this about sex with a partner of HIV-negative or unknown status:

I know I was clean; I didn't have anybody on me, and I'd cleaned with bacterial soap even before I slept with him, so I know that that was pretty unrisky. (mixed race/ethnicity male, age 30, San Francisco)

Few men discussed pulling out, or withdrawing before ejaculating, as a strategy for safer sex. As one respondent stated about his HIV-positive partner:

I was safe, because he didn't come inside of me. He pulled out, and I think it was . . . he pulled out because maybe he was trying to protect me, or maybe he was trying to protect himself. I mean, I know that the virus can be communicated without coming, but I would say it was safe. We didn't use condoms, but I feel okay with that, with the encounter we had. (Latino male, age 38, San Francisco)

Knowledge and Beliefs About Sex Partners

The principle aspect of this series of knowledge and beliefs involves the nature of the relationship to the sex partner; the dynamics of the sexual relationship with the partner (casual, anonymous, or romantic) were believed to contribute to sexual risk by 45% of the men. One respondent said this about anal sex with an HIV-negative main partner: "I [had unprotected anal sex] because I loved the man" (Asian or Pacific Islander male, age 41, San Francisco). Another respondent suggested his intimate relationship with his HIV-negative partner affected his ability to use a condom during anal sex:

> Well, I've been trying to get him to use a condom. He doesn't want to use them; he says it stops him from coming. It slows his metabolism down or something, you know. So he refuses to wear them, you know. (Black male, age 31, New York)

HIV status of partners (whether seroconcordant or serodiscordant) was a persuasive factor in determining risky or safe sexual encounters. One respondent did not perceive his encounter with an HIV-negative partner as risky because of the level of intimacy he shared with his partner:

> I guess we figured that he's only having sex with me, I'm only having sex with him. We have come to the conclusion that we are just going to have sex with each other, and we're not going to have sex with anybody else, and we not every time have to use protection . . . he is the only person I'm sleeping with, so this whole concept of safe and unsafe doesn't even come into play. (mixed race/ethnicity male, age 28, New York)

Risk perception differed when sex was with an anonymous partner. One respondent discussed his risk with an anonymous partner of unknown HIV status whom he had met at a sex club:

> At the time when I was doing the unsafe thing (anal insertive without a condom), the HIV issue hadn't been brought up so—so at that time, I didn't think about it because I assume everyone is positive when I have sex with them on that level in a sexual club . . . see, now I have a hard issue about this because who was in control, you know? Is it the guy who's getting it up the butt who's in the more vulnerable position than the top? Who is the one that has the responsible part? . . . Because, as far as I was concerned, someone who sits back on a dick without a condom (laughter) is probably positive. (Latino male, age 33, New York)

Perceived risk is also affected when sex partners are known to have other partners. One HIV-positive respondent said this about sexual risk with his partner: "Because I don't know where he is . . . I may not be his only partner . . . and all I know is what is in front of me: a dick that's not covered" (White male, age 51, New York).

Intimacy and trust with a main partner was a predominant theme. Almost a third of respondents believed that anal sex was safer because they trusted their partner or the relationship was mutually respectful. One respondent said this about not having anal sex with his HIV-positive partner:

> As a person who has had to deal with the problems and symptoms, and the life-threatening things that AIDS can bring on a person, I wouldn't want to pass that on to somebody else that I care about. (Latino male, age 31, San Francisco)

For some respondents, the encounter was perceived as safe because safer sex was discussed in the relationship before the sexual encounter took place (16%). One respondent, when asked what made the interaction with his long-term partner safe, replied, "Our behavior, I think our understanding of each other, of what we talked about when we first met, which I think is very important" (Latino male, age 41, New York).

For some men, the sexual encounter was perceived as safe if both partners were known to be HIV-positive. As one respondent summed it up, "We're both already infected, so you aren't going to catch anything you already have" (White male, age 42, San Francisco).

Knowledge and Beliefs About Substance Use and Risk for HIV

Only 18% of the gay and bisexual men in this sample perceived alcohol or drug use as contributing to unprotected anal sex. For these men, using alcohol or drugs was believed to impair the respondent's ability to avoid exposing himself to HIV. As one respondent described using alcohol with his partner of HIV-negative or unknown status:

> With alcohol you're driving, that beer, it like do something to your brain, your mind, it be saying, "Well, you don't need no rubbers," you know. You don't think about using them. You don't want to use them. (Black male, age 37, New York)

Another respondent described using drugs with a partner of unknown or HIV-negative status:

> You just get high. You don't care. You just think about yourself. You don't think about anyone else. You could give two shits about anybody else. And all that's going through your mind is just what's happening. Nothing. Just making sure you're having a good time. (Latino male, age 31, New York)

Another man stated that drug use affected his decision to have safer sex with his HIV-positive partner:

> I guess it was the first time since I was HIV-positive that I had unprotected anal sex with a partner. And it was enjoyable, but at the same time it was like, you know, I had been bombarded with all this safe-sex information and messages, so—but I did it anyway, because I think the drug had kind of gave me the feeling that we were both positive anyway, so there wasn't going to be a risk of infecting him, so I just continued anyway. (White male, age 48, San Francisco)

When asked about his unsafe anal sex encounter and drug use with a partner of HIV-negative or unknown status, one respondent stated:

> It was a direct derivative of being totally incapacitated and being unaware of my surroundings in summary . . . it was a reflection on being able to lose my control of the situation. (White male, age 26, New York)

(For more information about substance use and sexual risk, see chap. 11, this volume.)

Knowledge and Beliefs About Pleasure Seeking and Risk for HIV

Some of the HIV-positive gay and bisexual men associated their risk for unprotected anal sex during a sexual encounter with pleasure seeking and the desire for gratification (11%). One respondent, after having had unprotected anal sex with a partner of HIV-negative or unknown status, stated:

> I think that there is a part of me that wants to . . . escape the reality that I have this virus and that I have to use protection, and I have to protect me and somebody else. (Latino male, age 25, New York)

When asked to explain why they perceived one sexual encounter as safe and another as risky, 40% of respondents perceived the main reasons to be physical. Reasons included differences in physical desire and in sexual behaviors and activities (anal sex being perceived as more risky than oral sex), degree of arousal, quality of sex, heat of the moment, intensity, condom use, and access to condoms. When describing an unsafe sexual encounter in a park (as opposed to a safe encounter with his boyfriend), a participant stated the anonymous encounter was different because it was physically intense:

> The not knowing. The spontaneity. What they like or what they don't like. The intensity of it because you know that you probably won't see that person again and just that not knowing how they are going to perform, how they will react to your body. Not knowing when you put

your hands in somebody's pants what you're going to get; it's like Cracker Jacks, you get a surprise inside. So, you know, and if it's a surprise you like—you know, and you hopefully would like to run into them again. (White male, age 36, New York)

Men also stated the difference between a perceived risky encounter and a perceived safe encounter was a result of characteristics associated with their sex partners (40%). These included attraction, attachment, familiarity with partner, type of partner (main or casual), partner preference, and partner HIV status. For example, one respondent described the differences between sex with an HIV-negative long-term partner and sex with an anonymous partner of unknown status:

With T, it was much more safer. We were using condoms. I don't love this guy, so I guess its sort of like saying, "Fuck you, I don't give a fuck. You want to kill yourself, it's up to you." With him, it's like I said, an emotional attachment, so I'm going to shield him, I'm going to protect him. (Latino male, age 33, New York)

Describing the difference between a safe encounter with a hustler (a male prostitute) and an unsafe encounter with a boyfriend, one respondent stated:

Where my emotions—my emotions are there and I want to please somebody, I'm more willing to have unsafe sex. When it's a matter of pleasing myself, I'm willing to; you know, I normally will have safe sex. (White male, age 48, New York)

Some men suggested that the differences between their safer and riskier sexual encounters were the result of their emotional state at the time of the encounter (10%). These included feeling lonely, feeling depressed, feeling physically attractive or unattractive, or needing someone to pay them some attention. Describing why he has risky sexual encounters with HIV-positive partners, one respondent stated:

More attractive sexually, more horny for the person I am, I want him to fuck me. And that strong feeling. The stronger it is, the more difficult for me—it is for me to control the safeness of the relationship. The more attracted I am, it is more difficult to control that aspect. (Latino male, age 44, New York)

In general, pleasure and sensation seeking as a means to escape reality or fulfill a sexual fantasy affected risk in several ways: by overpowering decision making related to preventing risk (because men choose to not think about risk or HIV because it affects their sexual experience) or by simply not caring about risk because of the strong desire to gratify their physical and emotional needs.

ORAL SEX

Knowledge and Beliefs About Condom Use and Risk for HIV

Men in this sample of HIV-positive gay and bisexual men expressed confusion and ambiguity about the need for condoms when practicing oral sex. Not using a condom for oral sex (receptive or insertive) was perceived as less risky than unprotected anal sex. However, HIV-positive gay and bisexual men concerned about transmission through oral sex developed strategies for determining levels of risk. For example, one respondent described how he perceived his level of risk during a sexual encounter at a peep show with a partner of HIV-negative or unknown status. When asked what he felt made the interaction unsafe, he replied:

> My sucking his dick. The fact that, you know, I check it. It's weird. I check it, I smell it, I lick it. First, I smell it. Then I look at it. I looked at it; I inspected his penis; I jerked it a few times to see if there was anything coming out of it. Everything looked good. . . . You know, the guy must have knew I was doing this because I was like I'm now going into a medical field. I inspected it thoroughly, and, you know, it looked good; the light was on it, so it's like, okay. I don't think it's very safe, though, still, because—well, they say you can't get it; he can't get it from saliva, but I could get it from maybe his penis itself. (Black male, age 35, New York)

In general, not using a condom during oral sex to protect against HIV and other STDs was perceived as the most prevalent risk factor, especially by Latino men (52% compared to 19% White and Black men; see chap. 6, this volume, for more discussion on differences in the men by race/ethnicity and culture). One respondent, a Latino man with a first-time partner of HIV-negative or unknown status, described his belief about why his oral sex was risky:

> I normally use a condom, even to give a blow job. And that particular day, I didn't. Because I do worry about, you know, venereal warts and other stuff like that . . . and there's just other STDs and other stuff that we should worry about. You know? A lot of people don't, you know? When you're giving someone a blow job, HIV is the least of your worries [laughter], you know. (Latino male, age 31, New York)

Men often determined the safety of a particular sex act visually, by the healthy appearance of the partner (32%). For example, one respondent discussed having safe unprotected oral sex with a partner of HIV-negative or unknown status by stating, "As long as you don't have open cuts or sores in your mouth, or open cuts or anything on your dick, I think it is relatively safe" (Latino male, age 40, New York). Another respondent spoke of his encounters in bathhouses with multiple partners of unknown HIV status:

> Um, before sucking dicks or do something, I make a little exam. I look for warts or openings or blood, bad smell or something like that, and I—I stop. (Latino male, age 39, New York)

OTHER SEX ACTS

Although there are no known cases of HIV transmission associated with oral–anal contact, some men expressed concern over the risk involved with rimming. As one respondent stated:

> You could have—he could have an open cut on his tongue, and I could have an open cut in my behind, and that's very unsafe, because, once— you don't even have to have a cut on your tongue. Once somebody's blood hits his tongue, 'cause, his tongue, remember, that's open flesh; that's always open. That's not—you know, that don't have no skin on; that's always open. (Black male, age 20, New York)

Of the respondents 64% believed that preventing the exchange of fluids during the sexual encounter made the event safe. Avoiding the exchange of fluids (semen, pre-semen, or blood) by, for example, rimming and kissing was believed to be safe by 49% of men. For example, one respondent believed that his encounter with a partner of HIV-negative or unknown status was almost completely safe because, "There was no exchange of body fluids" (White male, age 34, New York).

In terms of practicing good hygiene as a way to ensure safety in a sexual encounter, one respondent discussed the safety of rimming with a partner of HIV-negative or unknown status, "Unless there's a sore, I consider it safe" (White male, age 38, New York).

Others believed that using lubricant with condoms or checking condoms regularly for tears increased their feeling of safety in their sexual interaction. As one respondent described:

> The oral sex was with condoms. The anal sex was with condoms and then later with gloves [for fisting] . . . and as I changed activities, I am very careful to clear up old stuff and put down new stuff every time there is a break. (White male, age 52, New York)

DISCUSSION

Many variables affect the practice of safer sex for HIV-positive gay and bisexual men. Men in this sample experienced many of the issues discussed in the introduction to this chapter, such as relationships with partners, condom use, and transmission risk related to specific sex acts. In addition, men were concerned about body fluid exchange and hygiene and had highly individualized strategies for reducing risk during sexual encounters. HIV risk was perceived as a combination of these interdependent variables (some more dominant than others) rather than as the result of any one specific variable. In addition, men often used different strategies for different combinations of perceived risk factors (for example, for a long-term partner or anonymous partner, for an HIV-negative partner or HIV-positive partner). Often HIV risk-reduction strategies corresponded to accepted HIV prevention messages (such as using a condom for anal sex). In some instances, however, men devised unique risk-reduction strategies that were personally acceptable and tailored to specific sexual situations but were not necessarily effective for reducing risk for HIV or other STDs. Many of these strategies provided little or no HIV and STD prevention but were based on misinformation, anecdotes, confusion, or myths. As these findings suggest, men who have tested HIV-positive and who may be receiving HIV treatment do not necessarily have accurate information about HIV risk and transmission. It is therefore important to understand the factors that influence individual HIV prevention strategies for future HIV prevention efforts within this population.

Relationships with sex partners, condom use, beliefs about HIV transmission and risk, and the perceived safety of specific sexual acts form a core set of beliefs and perceptions guiding how men negotiate HIV risk and which strategies they use to reduce this risk. Men often felt that they put themselves at greater risk as the result of wanting to please a partner (for intimacy and trust in long-term relationships or, perhaps, to maintain the sexual interest of an anonymous or one-time partner). In many instances, men made heat-of-the-moment sexual health decisions with first-time partners that often incurred unplanned risk. The type of sex partner and individual attitudes toward condoms affected risk-reduction strategies adopted during sex. The HIV-positive gay and bisexual men in this sample often decided to not use traditional protective measures (condoms) in long-term relationships with their main partner but rather they used individualized strategies for risk reduction (for example, deliberately avoiding exchanging fluids or pre-semen and early withdrawal). In addition, risk could be one-sided, in which one partner assumed much of the risk in the encounter in contrast to the other (for example, as a direct result of the expressed desires of the partner or because of emotional feelings for the partner or beliefs about responsibility for protecting the partner from HIV). Barebacking was not directly discussed by men in this sample (the study was conducted before the widespread discussion about barebacking); however, some men described consensual anal sex without condoms with partners of the same, HIV-negative, or unknown status. Reasons for consensual unprotected sex included intimacy and trust with the partner or having the same HIV serostatus as the partner.

The knowledge and beliefs about HIV transmission evident in this sample illustrate the wide range of information available to HIV-positive gay and bisexual men. Most men were aware of standard information about HIV prevention (for example, using condoms for anal sex) as well as anecdotal information and misinformation, such as avoiding rough sex as a safer sex strategy, or avoiding kissing. Information about HIV and STD risk was often used to create individual strategies and rituals for risk reduction. For example, some men in the sample visually inspected themselves and their partners. Being unclean, having poor personal hygiene, or having visible cuts and sores were considered risk factors. Of course, although the personal health and hygiene of sex partners is important, these are not prevention strategies and should not be relied upon to guide sexual decision making. Prevention agencies need to address these perceptions of risk reduction with HIV-positive individuals.

Avoiding body fluids (such as preejaculate, semen, saliva, or blood) was also a common theme. Men considered their sexual experiences safer if they used strategies to avoid the exchange of body fluids, such as withdrawing early; avoiding rough sex; and, in some instances, avoiding kissing. Again, HIV prevention efforts for HIV-positive gay and bisexual men need to address these issues. The findings from this sample of men suggest that HIV-positive gay and bisexual men have absorbed and assimilated much HIV prevention information but that in an effort to devise safer sex strategies for themselves (beyond condom-only strategies), the men are perhaps unaware of the risk inherent in their chosen alternatives. This is especially true for men in long-term and committed relationships, who require new and innovative ways to safely express their desire for sexual intimacy and trust.

This sample of HIV-positive gay and bisexual men clearly demonstrates the complexity involved in weighing risk factors in the context of sexual encounters. In addition to the challenges that the literature illustrates are common to most gay and bisexual men negotiating sexual relationships, HIV-positive gay and bisexual men have unique challenges relating to their HIV status. HIV-positive men, like other gay and bisexual men, weigh options and calculate risk in their sexual situations, resulting in the adoption of specific tactics for reducing risk. In addition, HIV-positive gay and bisexual men must somehow negotiate the fact that they bring to all sexual situations the potential transmission of a deadly virus. This creates a series of tensions that include responsibility for the partner's safety, responsibility for their own health, and responsibility for disclosure. These narratives illustrate certain realities for HIV-positive gay and bisexual men: confusion about who should be the responsible partner, hypersensitivity to the risk inherent in every sexual act, confusion about oral sex, and frustration with condom use in general. Conspicuously absent in this sample of men is the lack of prominence attached to variables widely discussed in the literature, such as substance use or new HIV treatments as perceived factors influencing risk. Beliefs and perceptions about HIV risk discussed by these men highlight the importance of developing HIV prevention messages and programs specifically for HIV-positive gay and bisexual men that take into consideration the many influences on their sexual decision making. Efforts should be made especially to engage HIV-positive gay and bisexual men in effective HIV and STD prevention strategies that include, but also go beyond, condom use.

REFERENCES

Bosga, M. B., de Wit, J. B., de Vroome, E. M., Houweling, H., Schop, W., & Sandfort, T. G. (1995). Differences in perception of risk for HIV infection with steady and non-steady partners among homosexual men. *AIDS Education and Prevention, 7*, 103–115.

Boulton, M., McLean, J., Fitzpatrick, R., & Hart, G. (1995). Gay men's accounts of unsafe sex. *AIDS Care, 7*, 619–630.

Gold, R. S. (2002). The effects of mood states on the AIDS related judgments of gay men. *International Journal of STDs and AIDS, 13*, 475–481.

Gold, R. S., & Skinner, M. J. (1992). Situational factors and thought processes associated with unprotected intercourse among young gay men. *AIDS, 6*, 1021–1030.

Gold, R. S., & Skinner, M. J. (2001). Gay men's estimates of the likelihood of HIV transmission in sexual behaviours. *International Journal of STD and AIDS, 12*, 245–255.

Gold, R. S., Skinner, M. J., Grant, P. J., & Plummer, D. C. (1991). Situational factors and thought processes associated with unprotected intercourse in gay men. *Psychology and Health, 5*, 259–278.

Hays, R. B., Kegeles, S. M., & Coates, T. J. (1997). Unprotected sex and HIV risk taking among young gay men within boyfriend relationships. *AIDS Education and Prevention, 9*, 314–329.

Kalichman, S. C., Rompa, D., Austin, J., Luke, W., & DiFonzo, K. (2001). Viral load, perceived infectivity, and unprotected intercourse. *Journal of Acquired Immune Deficiency Syndromes, 28*, 303–305.

Kok, G. (1999). Targeted prevention for people with HIV/AIDS: Feasible and desirable? *Patient Education and Counseling, 36*, 239–246.

Mansergh, G., Marks, G., Colfax, G. N., Guzman, R., Rader, M., & Buchbinder, S. (2002). "Barebacking" in a diverse sample of men who have sex with men. *AIDS, 16*, 653–659.

Nimmons, D. (1998). In this together: The limits of prevention based on self-interest and the role of altruism in HIV safety. *Journal of Psychology and Human Sexuality, 10*, 75–87.

Nimmons, D., & Folkman, S. (1999). Other-sensitive motivation for safer sex among gay men: Expanding paradigms for HIV prevention. *AIDS and Behavior, 3*, 313–324.

Pinkerton, S. D., & Abramson, P. R. (1992). Is risky sex rational? *Journal of Sex Research, 29*, 561–568.

Schiltz, M. A., & Sandfort, T. G. M. (2000). HIV-positive people, risk and sexual behaviour. *Social Science and Medicine, 50*, 1571–1588.

Stall, R. D., Hays, R. B., Waldo, C. R., Ekstrand, M., & McFarland, W. (2000). The gay '90s: A review of research in the 1990s on sexual behavior and HIV risk among men who have sex with men. *AIDS, 14*(Suppl. 3), S101–S114.

Suarez, T. P., Kelly, J. A., Pinkerton, S. D., Stevenson, Y. L., Hayat, M., Smith, M. D., et al. (2001). Influence of a partner's HIV serostatus, use of highly active antiretroviral therapy, and viral load on perceptions of sexual risk behavior in a community sample of men who have sex with men. *Journal of Acquired Immune Deficiency Syndromes, 28*, 471–477.

Suarez, T. P., & Miller, J. (2001). Negotiating risks in context: A perspective on unprotected anal intercourse and barebacking among men who have sex with men—Where do we go from here? *Archives of Sexual Behavior, 30*, 287–300.

Vanable, P., Ostrow, D. G., McKirnan, D. J., Taywaditep, K. J., & Hope, B. A. (2000). Impact of combination therapies on HIV risk perceptions and sexual risk among HIV-positive and HIV-negative gay and bisexual men. *Health Psychology, 19*, 134–145.

5

SPOKEN AND UNSPOKEN DESIRES: SEXUAL NEGOTIATION AND COMMUNICATION STRATEGIES AMONG HIV-POSITIVE GAY AND BISEXUAL MEN

COLLEEN C. HOFF AND ANUPAMA MANCHIKANTI

Sexual communication between partners lies at the heart of understanding risk for HIV transmission. The quality of sexual communication between sex partners is affected by myriad elements, including fear of conveying mistrust or being rejected by one's partner, environmental situations and substance use, and cultural issues, such as history of sexual silence in the family and ethnic community of origin, nonconfrontational styles of communication, and a tendency to avoid intimate topics in the absence of closeness and trust (Appleby, Miller, & Rothspan, 1999; Díaz, Morales, Bein, Dilan, & Rodriguez, 1999; Manalansan, 1996; Pares-Avila & Montano-Lopez, 1994). Despite these complications, research has shown that communication about sex and HIV exposure is associated with more condom use and less unprotected sex (Catania, Coates, Golden, & Dolcini, 1994; Hays, Kegeles, & Coates, 1997; Mays & Cochran, 1993; Molitor,

Facer, & Ruiz, 1999). When a desire for safer sex is not communicated, unsafe sex is more likely to occur (Gold & Skinner, 1992).

Sexual negotiation is a communication process by which partners agree to use a protective strategy to reduce risk for HIV, sexually transmitted diseases (STDs), or pregnancy (Gold & Skinner, 1992; Kippax et al., 1997). It has become an important focus in HIV prevention. Various negotiation strategies have been identified, which, when applied in appropriate situations, are thought to be useful for HIV prevention. These include refusing unsafe sex, eroticizing safer sex, reassuring the partner of love and trust, discussing the consequences of unsafe sex, and focusing on the future of the relationship. It has also been found that indirect negotiation styles (e.g., vague and nonconfrontational) are used more frequently than direct styles (Williams, Gardos, Ortiz-Torres, Tross, & Ehrhardt, 2001). Another strategy—negotiated safety—is one in which HIV-negative primary partners agree to have protected sex with outside partners so they can engage in unprotected sex together. This strategy has been found to be predictive of safer sex with outside partners when compared with couples who have no agreement (Crawford, Rodden, Kippax, & Van de Ven, 2001).

Research in the area of sexual communication and negotiation is still in its infancy. The findings just mentioned are critical to promoting safer sex and HIV prevention but limited in that they do not address communication and negotiations that occur during a sexual encounter. In fact, there is a disparity between one's intention to have safer sex before an encounter and one's behavior during the encounter (Gold & Skinner, 1992). Competing factors, such as emotional issues, environmental stimuli, and interpersonal relations, can make sexual negotiation challenging for even the most well-intended. These challenges, particularly in the excitement of a sexual encounter, may interfere with or limit sexual negotiations and lead to unsafe sex. A better understanding of how men communicate with each other during sexual encounters is necessary, given the complexities of sexual situations and the potential for risk.

This chapter describes how HIV-positive gay and bisexual men communicate a desire for and negotiate safer sex during sexual encounters with a main partner (i.e., primary or boyfriend); repeat partners (i.e., partners who are known to each other and have sex but are not in a committed relationship, sometimes referred to as "fuck buddies"); and one-time partners (i.e., partners with whom participants engaged in one-time sexual encounters). It also describes how men communicate their sexual preferences and how these communications sometimes lead to negotiation for safer sex.

We reviewed detailed narratives from 250 HIV-positive men who participated in the Seropositive Urban Men's Study (SUMS; see chap. 1, this volume). Each participant described two sexual encounters, one safe and one unsafe, for a total of 500 narratives. To categorize the encounters as safe or unsafe, we used the participant's definition of what was considered safe or unsafe for him or his partner in each particular encounter. Narratives were spontaneous, and interviewers were not instructed to directly question participants about communication during the encounters. Thus, sexual communication and negotiations were detected in 260 encounters and compared for safe and unsafe practices. These encounters were also compared to determine whether communication and negotiations varied according to partner type (i.e., main, repeat, or one-time).

Protection of sex partners by using condoms and responsibility for disclosure of HIV-positive status are important elements of sexual negotiation. However, because these issues are addressed elsewhere (see chaps. 7 and 10, this volume), they are not a focus of this chapter.

COMMUNICATION AND NEGOTIATION

Narratives revealed that communication occurs verbally (during and before sexual encounters) and nonverbally (through directive behavior, body positioning, environmental cues, and normative cues). They also showed normative communication within couples, which indicated precedents set by previous communication with main or repeat partners.

Verbal Communication

Verbal communication was the most direct and frequent form of sexual negotiation. This strategy was used before or during sexual encounters and appeared to allow participants to most easily and clearly communicate their desires and, in many cases, have their desires fulfilled.

Verbal Communication Before Sexual Encounters

Communication before sex often set boundaries for the encounter and allowed the participants and their partners to negotiate sexual behaviors and safety. In many instances, verbal communication before sex shaped the direction of the encounter. In one bathhouse situation, the negotiation led to masturbation, which the participant described as safer sex:

> And then he had quite a healthy erection with which he was flipping— moving the towel that was draped across him. So I took hold of his penis and asked him if [he] wanted a blow job, and he said, "No, actually I wouldn't. But would you like to jack me off?" So I did. (White male, age 48, San Francisco)

Verbal communication before sexual encounters also provided a way for participants to set the tone and ensure a safe situation. For example, in an encounter in a public sex environment, one participant set the grounds for safe sex before any physical contact occurred:

> I met this cute little young blonde . . . and he came up to me and he said, "Oh, black daddy, I want you to fuck me," and I said, "Okay, sure, why not?" So, I asked him if he had any condoms, and he said "No." I said, "Well, we can't do it without condoms," and he wanted to do it without a condom. Fortunately, I had one in my wallet. (Black male, age 32, San Francisco)

As with many of the forms of communication, the attitudes of participants and their partners were reflected and played an important role in successful negotiation for safer sex: "And he was adamant about using a condom, even in my giving him a blow job. He was not going [to] allow me to do that without a condom" (Black male, age 34, San Francisco).

Verbal communication was not necessarily direct, as some couples used a verbal code to communicate sexual desires. For one couple, the partner was uninterested in sex, so the participant verbally communicated his sexual interest: "I said, 'Let me cuddle,' and that's that. He knows what it means. It just means that I rub up against him and come" (Latino male, age 51, New York).

As expected, there were fewer instances of verbal communication and sexual negotiation before unsafe sexual encounters. This indicates that verbal communication before sexual encounters may perhaps be a predictor for safer sex, although it also reflects a proactive attitude on the part of many participants and partners to create safer sex situations.

Verbal Communication During Sexual Encounters

Many spontaneous descriptions of conversation during sexual encounters involved reaffirming sexual interest and directing sexual behavior and safety. A number of exchanges involved negotiation of different types of sex as well as negotiation of safe or unsafe sex. Some participants described using strong language as a way to bypass the need for sexual negotiation. These interviews reflected an attitude of safe sex or no sex and left little room for misunderstanding:

> Whenever I have sex with someone, I tell them straight up. I won't tell them I'm positive. I won't ask them if they are, but I'll tell them, "Look, I want you to put on two condoms, one condom, whatever . . ." [If] they'll take it off . . . I'm walking out the door, and you can get yourself off. (White male, age 24, San Francisco)

> He was naked, I was naked, and then he tried to penetrate me without a condom, without a lube; and so because of those two reasons without the condom and without any lube, I say, "No," and then I reach for

the condom and lube and say, "Well, if you want to do it, use this." And so he did. (Latino male, age 35, New York)

There were also many instances in which communication led to sexual negotiation for sexual behaviors and safety. Discussions occurred to decide what would happen during the sexual act and how it would happen:

> Things became really apparent, very quickly. He said, "The bottom line is, I want to get fucked. What is the best way to go about this?" I said, "Well, I have to do what is going to be comfortable with you. Don't worry, I am going to use condoms, but what is your deal?" He said, "I just want you to fuck me, and I want us to both be comfortable about it." We actually talked about this. I said, "Why don't I put two rubbers on," and . . . as a matter of fact, we did. (Latino male, age 40, New York)

> I said, "You got a condom on?" And he goes, "No." I said, "Well, you need to put one on." And he goes, "I can't because I get soft." I said, "Well, just put it on. You won't get soft." I said—I said, "Why don't you put it on?" And massage my anus while he was putting it on, and he didn't get soft at all. It's all up here [in the mind]. (Latino male, age 26, New York)

One partner wanted the participant to perform insertive anal sex:

> So I told him my status. . . . But I was like, "Well, you know, I don't know if this is safe." And he is like, "It is all right, it is all right, we don't even have to use anything." I am like, "Well, I still don't know," you know. . . . And I wound up winning the argument. I am like, "Well, if we want to do this, I just want to be safe, I'm sorry." And he is like, "Fine, fine, fine," reluctantly. So, he scrambled to the bathroom for condom. (Latino male, age 20, New York)

At another level, verbal communication provided a way of turning potentially unsafe sex situations into safer sex encounters:

> At first I had a problem 'cause I got mad at him because we was having sex and at a point he wanted to do it raw, and I told him, "No, you shouldn't be doing it raw" . . . I said, "I hope whoever else you're having sex with, you're not telling them the same thing, 'cause I don't want you to get hurt. You're a nice person, you know. Anything can happen to you." So, yes, we used protection, some protection. (Black male, age 23, New York)

In one encounter, a partner pushed the participant's legs up during sex to enter him anally, and the participant said, "No," leading to a negotiation for safe sex:

> I remember he wanted to fuck me, and there wasn't a condom right by us, and we sort of talked there. He said, "You know, I want to. It feels

good without it." I said, "No, you know, we need to get a condom." So we got one. (Asian or Pacific Islander male, age 36, San Francisco)

Nonverbal Communication

During sexual encounters, nonverbal communication occurred at many different levels. Although many forms of nonverbal communication seemed simple to convey, they also left much room for interpretation. It also appeared somewhat difficult to negotiate entirely without words. In many instances, nonverbal communication would be countered with other nonverbal and verbal communications for negotiation. Nonverbal communication was examined in the following categories: directive behavior, body positioning, environmental cues, and normative cues.

Directive Behavior

Directive behavior consisted of one partner directing the other partner into a sexual behavior, either by literally moving his body or by signaling. Directive behavior was used to negotiate sex and safety in some instances; more often, it was used to communicate sexual preferences. Frequent examples of directive behavior were flipping a partner onto his stomach to communicate readiness for anal sex and pushing a partner onto a bed to indicate sexual interest:

> Well, this time I felt like getting fucked, so I rolled him over on top of me and put my legs up over his shoulders (mixed race/ethnicity male, age 37, New York).

> Well, I was thrown back on the bed and he gave me some head, and the next thing we know, we're in a 69 and then, oh, then we went into anal sex. (Black male, age 36, San Francisco)

> He was sort of like putting—holding my penis right near his ass. And I was saying, "Oh, you want some? You want some?" So he was like, "Sure." So I slipped on the condom, put on the lotion or lubrication, and I slipped it in. (Black male, age 28, New York)

In only a few instances was there a back-and-forth nonverbal discussion using directive action:

> I just didn't feel like sucking dick at that time. I mean, I guess I didn't feel like sucking his. So I didn't. And he kind of pushed me that way, and I pushed back a "no," and that's when he started to jerk himself off. (Latino male, age 37, San Francisco)

Directive behavior was an effective method of communication for some because it led to verbal communication and negotiation for safer sex:

I found him attractive, so I, you know, turned him over and stuck my tongue up his ass and then played with the area and came to the conclusion that he wanted me to fuck him. And he handed me a condom, you know, which is the international symbol for, "I want you to use a condom." So grudgingly, you know, in my own mind, grudgingly, I put it on, and I fucked him. (White male, age 34, New York)

In one encounter, directive behavior proved to be an effective method of negotiation because a participant (White male, age 39, New York) was able to prevent what he perceived as unsafe sex by pushing away the shoulders of a partner who was giving him oral sex. Directive behavior occurred similarly in encounters with all partner types.

Body Positioning

Body positioning, defined as a participant or his partner moving his own body to sexually communicate, mostly indicated preferences for certain sexual behaviors (e.g., bending over to position for anal sex). On its own, body positioning was not usually pertinent to sexual negotiation for safer sex, "He gave me his back; and then once the back is given to you, it's a definite sign that this person is passive" (Latino male, age 32, New York).

And then before you know it, he would take his shirt off, and he would take his pants off, his socks and his shoes, and then he would jump into my bed, and he would just like spread-eagle, and then, you know, I would just do my thing. (Asian or Pacific Islander male, age 51, San Francisco)

During many encounters, body positioning occurred along with other forms of communication. When body positioning was the sole form of communication, lack of communication and little negotiation were apparent. Partner type did not seem to be relevant to the use of body positioning.

Environmental Cues

Environmental cues were used infrequently to communicate participants' or their partners' interest in safer sex. In some situations, an environmental cue served as an initial step, leading to negotiation for safer sex or to communication that safe sex does not have to be negotiated. The most common example was leaving condoms and lubricant in a visible location to provide the option for or indicate interest in protected anal sex:

The condoms was right there. He already prepared. He was very cute in putting the condoms there and the lubricant there right next to the sofa because he knew that was where he was going to lay me; and we just—it was no words, there was not words. (Latino male, age 35, New York)

You know, basically, the condoms were there in open sight, you know, with non–oil-based lubricant in open, you know, everything there openly, so basically, I meant that set the . . . tone from the very beginning. (White male, age 44, New York)

The weakness of environmental cues is that although they may convey the option for safer sex, they do not necessarily lead to it. On its own, this form of communication sometimes fell short of creating safer sex situations because some partners chose to ignore the presence of condoms, and participants felt that by visibly providing condoms, there was no need for discussion of safer sex. There were also instances in which participants felt that by providing condoms, they placed the responsibility on their partners to communicate a desire for or initiate safer sex, "Well, the condoms were there—there was some on the bedside table, so they were there for him." In response to the interviewer asking whether the partner picked them up, the participant said, "Right, and I wasn't too pushy because I'm already positive" (White male, age 40, New York).

I even saw the condom there, and that crossed my mind like, "Why is it that I didn't ask him to use a condom? Why is it that he didn't initiate to put a condom himself? Why is that he didn't ask me about my status?" (Asian or Pacific Islander male, age 27, San Francisco)

Environmental cues seemed most relevant to participants with one-time and repeat partners.

Normative Cues

Communication between sex partners included behaviors and external cues that seemed to have universal meaning among gay and bisexual men. These cues were nonverbal yet were clearly understood by participants and tended to direct the sexual encounter:

And I grabbed his ass, and he didn't move, so I knew that it was all right, that he wanted me to fuck; so I reached for the condom, and I was putting the condom on and he was moving his asshole up. (White male, age 34, New York)

Several men reported that when a partner inserted his finger into his anus, it meant that the partner wanted anal sex; having this information gave participants the opportunity to make a decision about whether they wanted to continue, "He started playing with my butt, and I knew that he wanted to turn me over and start fucking" (Asian or Pacific Islander male, age 39, San Francisco). Said another, "He kept sticking his finger in my ass and I told him, 'No'" (Latino male, age 30, New York).

> Yes, he started touching on the behind before anything else ... my behind ... so I could tell that's what he wanted. So we did. I put the condom on him because I was getting the biggest risk—double condoms, as a matter a fact—and we just had love. (Latino male, age 41, New York)

In public sex environments, a desire for sex was indicated by many normative cues, such as walking past a person's room several times or touching one's crotch while looking at the person with whom he wants to have sex. Normative communication cues occurred before and during sexual encounters also but were somewhat unreliable:

> And he was wearing his keys on the left, and I assumed that he was a top. Okay. He started sucking mine. And then I put my hand down by his ass and his legs went up in the air immediately. I was kind of surprised, because I thought he was the dominant one. He wasn't. The guys that I like to fuck are very masculine, and who, I think, are tops, and then they end up to be bottoms. And I went to go get a condom and open it, and he said that, "No, not now," you know. I didn't want to [not use a condom], so I stopped. (White male, age 32, San Francisco)

NORMATIVE COMMUNICATION
WITHIN COUPLES

Couples had norms that had been previously communicated and were strongly adhered to within a sexual encounter, usually without additional communication. These norms were indicated by both verbal and nonverbal communications. Because norms within couples seemed to establish precedence with regard to safer sex, some couples appeared to have little need to communicate with each other during sex:

> We just basically know how each other reacts to each other's touches, and we know what each touch reaction means to the other. We know what each other like, because we've been doing this for years. So we pretty much know how to follow the pattern of a touch or what we want to do. (Black male, age 34, New York)

When asked about the communication leading up to a partner's putting on a condom, one participant replied, "Well, he always puts the condom on" (White male, age 27, New York).

ABSENCE OF COMMUNICATION

Several sexual encounters with a lack of communication resulted in unsafe sex. Had some kind of dialogue taken place, a safer sexual encounter may have occurred. Assumptions about what a partner wanted, issues of responsibility, and deference to a sexual partner all contributed to an absence of communication:

> Now, if he wanted me to put on a condom, I would have because I had them there. I always carry them. If he had insisted on that I would have done that. But he didn't. So I didn't. (Black male, age 48, New York)

> You know he didn't want me to use a condom. So I should have said that I am HIV-positive. Maybe we should use something. But I didn't, you know. I figured he knows what he's doing. (Black male, age 34, New York)

> I wanted to be more cautious than he, and when it was [clear] we were going to continue and he didn't even put a condom on, I wasn't going to push the issue because that was going to be his destiny anyway as far as he was concerned. (Latino male, age 33, New York)

Men with main partners also encountered situations where a lack of communication resulted in unsafe sex, although less frequently than men with repeat and one-time partners.

> And when we woke up, he wanted to have intercourse. So I allowed him first to do me, and then I did him afterwards, and we were both without thinking . . . and I said, "Well, you know what we did, don't you?" He said, "Yeah." I said, "Well, how do you feel about it?" And he said, "Well, I feel really guilty right now," and I says, "Yeah." (Latino male, age 39, San Francisco)

DISCUSSION

Communication and negotiation are important for safe sex. Clearly, participants who communicated a desire for safer sex were more likely to achieve it. It was also apparent that sexual position preferences were much more frequently and easily communicated than were desires for safer sex.

Verbal communication—before and during sexual encounters—seemed to be the most commonly used and effective method of ensuring safer sex and was useful in most sexual situations. Verbal communication was also the most direct method, leaving much less room for ambiguity than nonverbal communication.

Nonverbal methods of communication as a stand-alone safer sex strategy appeared largely problematic. This strategy was useful in initiating negotiation, but participants had difficulty actually negotiating safety using only nonverbal communication. These types of communication may be better used in conjunction with other more direct strategies or with partners with whom sexual boundaries are already established. Directive behavior seemed a possible way to communicate disinterest in unsafe sex; however, this method of communication, as well as body positioning, was used more often to indicate preferences for certain sexual behaviors than for safe sex. Participants who relied on normative cues may be particularly vulnerable because they were often making inferences about partners they did not know well, and the cues themselves tended to be unreliable. Similarly, environmental cues involved many assumptions about the partner's desire to have safe or unsafe sex.

In the absence of negotiation, many participants consciously decided to not communicate with their partners and often to not take an active role in creating a safer sex situation. One participant indicated that negotiation was not necessarily an act that he associated with sexual desire or even considered during a sexual encounter: "God, those words: negotiate sex. I negotiate contracts, but . . . I don't negotiate sex" (Native American male, age 64, San Francisco). Furthermore, lack of communication often led to participants getting carried away with the excitement of the sexual encounter, causing them to not consider safety until it was too late.

Analysis of these data was somewhat limited because the information about communication was provided spontaneously. Most participants were not asked explicitly about sexual communication or negotiation. The absence of descriptions of communication in many narratives does not necessarily mean communication did not occur. Furthermore, participants focused on specific sexual behaviors and preferences rather than communication of desires for safe or unsafe sex. With so little literature on communication during a sexual encounter, it is not clear whether these communication styles are unique to HIV-positive gay and bisexual men.

Clearly, HIV-positive men used sexual communication and negotiation in a variety of situations. It has been reported that men with steady partners are more likely to negotiate for condom use than men with anonymous partners (Semple, Patterson, & Grant, 2000); however, among our participants, communication and negotiation varied little with regard to partner type. Not surprisingly, certain communication approaches seemed to be more effective in achieving a safe sexual encounter (i.e., verbal communication) than others, yet a great deal can be learned from HIV-positive men who are successful in negotiating safer sex nonverbally.

HIV prevention interventions for gay and bisexual men should address communication and negotiation strategies. Our study suggests specifically that verbal communication before and during sex is the most direct method of communicating desires for safe sex. When verbal communication is not possible, men need to be aware that nonverbal methods should be used in conjunction with other safer sex strategies—for example, carrying condoms or including condoms in sex play. Assertive communication is also necessary for those situations in which a partner is passive or insists on unsafe sex. Existing literature and many prevention programs have focused on communication and negotiation before sex, and although this is important, men also need effective skills for negotiating safer sex during sexual encounters.

Future prevention efforts need to highlight the complexity of sexual encounters, particularly nonverbal encounters. Although many nonverbal cues are considered to be "universal conventions" among gay men, we found there was substantial opportunity for misinterpretation of cues. It is important to more thoroughly understand what men are intending to communicate via nonverbal sexual cues and how their partners perceive the cues. Determining whether nonverbal cues are interpreted differently in various contexts is important as well. From this, we can move toward the development of more effective nonverbal negotiation strategies and more consistent safer sex practices among gay men.

REFERENCES

Appleby, P. R., Miller, L. C., & Rothspan, S. (1999). The paradox of trust for male couples: When risking is part of loving. *Personal Relationships, 6*, 81–93.

Catania, J. A., Coates, T., Golden, E., & Dolcini, M. (1994). Correlates of condom use among Black, Hispanic, and White heterosexuals in San Francisco: The AMEN longitudinal study. *AIDS Education and Prevention, 6*, 12–26.

Crawford, J. M., Rodden, P., Kippax, S., & Van de Ven, P. (2001). Negotiated safety and other agreements between men in relationships: Risk practice redefined. *International Journal of STD and AIDS, 12*, 164–170.

Díaz, R. M., Morales, E., Bein, E., Dilan, E., & Rodriguez, R. (1999). Predictors of sexual risk in Latino gay/bisexual men: The role of demographic, developmental, social cognitive and behavioral variables. *Hispanic Journal of Behavioral Sciences, 21*, 414–420.

Gold, R. S., & Skinner, M. J. (1992). Situational factors and thought processes associated with unprotected intercourse in young gay men. *AIDS, 6*, 1012–1030.

Hays, R. B., Kegeles, S. M., & Coates, T. (1997). Unprotected sex and HIV risk taking among young gay men within boyfriend relationships. *AIDS Education and Prevention, 9*, 314–329.

Kippax, S., Noble, J., Prestage, G., Crawford, J. M., Campbell, D., Baxter, D., et al. (1997). Sexual negotiation in the AIDS era: Negotiated safety revisited. *AIDS, 11*, 191–197.

Manalansan, M. F. (1996). Double minorities: Latino, Black, and Asian men who have sex with men. In R. K. Savin-Williams & K. M. Cohen (Eds.), *The lives of lesbians, gays, and bisexuals: Children to adult* (pp. 393–415). Ft. Worth, TX: Harcourt Brace.

Mays, V. M., & Cochran, S. D. (1993). Ethnic and gender differences in beliefs about sex partner questioning to reduce HIV risk. *Journal of Adolescent Research, 8*, 77–88.

Molitor, F. M., Facer, M., & Ruiz, J. (1999). Safer sex communication and unsafe sexual behavior among young men who have sex with men in California. *Archives of Sexual Behavior, 28*, 335–343.

Pares-Avila, J. A., & Montano-Lopez, R. (1994). Issues in the psychosocial care of Latino gay men with HIV infection. In S. A. Cadwell, R. A. Burnham, Jr., & M. Forstein (Eds.), *Therapists on the front line: Psychotherapy with gay men in the age of AIDS* (pp. 339–362). Washington, DC: American Psychiatric Association.

Semple, S. J., Patterson, T., & Grant, I. (2000). The sexual negotiation behavior of HIV-positive gay and bisexual men. *Journal of Consulting and Clinical Psychology, 68*, 934–937.

Williams, S. P., Gardos, P. S., Ortiz-Torres, B., Tross, S., & Ehrhardt, A. A. (2001). Urban women's negotiation strategies for safer sex with their male partners. *Women and Health, 33*, 133–149.

6

CULTURE MATTERS: THE ROLE OF RACE AND ETHNICITY IN THE SEXUAL LIVES OF HIV-POSITIVE GAY AND BISEXUAL MEN

CYNTHIA A. GÓMEZ, BYRON MASON, AND
NICHOLAS J. ALVARADO

The contributions of race, ethnicity, and culture in forming one's life experiences—particularly sexual experiences, beliefs, and attitudes—are intertwined and difficult to disentangle. However, for most people, these variables have some core influence on their sexuality (Gregersen, 1994).

In this chapter, we recognize the influence of race and ethnicity on how men make meaning of sex in their lives. For many men, race, culture, religion, family history, and HIV serostatus affect the role that sex plays in their lives, including the partners they select.

Beyond the core or internalized influence related to race, ethnicity, and culture, sexuality is also affected by the attitudes of society as a whole. In the United States, most gay and bisexual men deal with common challenges such as homophobia and types of stigmatization (social, ethnic, and religious; Herek, 1991). Non-White gay and bisexual men face additional challenges such as racism, stereotyping, and discrimination (Díaz & Ayala, 2000).

Gay and bisexual men of color often report a sense of isolation that comes from the combination of being rejected by their families and ethnic communities because of their homosexuality and of being rejected by the mainstream White gay community because of their race or ethnicity. Some men feel that they must choose between embracing their ethnic identity and embracing their sexual identity (Choi et al., 1999; Díaz, 1997; Manalansan, 1996; Pares-Avila & Montano-Lopez, 1994; Stokes & Peterson, 1998). Previous studies among gay and bisexual men, both HIV-infected and HIV-uninfected, have suggested these stressful challenges and negative experiences can produce harmful outcomes such as depression, substance abuse, and increased high-risk sexual behaviors (Crawford, Allison, Zamboni, & Soto, 2002; Díaz, 1999; Myers, Javanbakht, Martinez, & Obediah, 2003).

Gay and bisexual men who are HIV-positive carry the additional burdens of social stigma and living with a life-threatening disease (Herek, 2002). Their level of isolation resulting from race or sexuality is now taken to even greater depths because many members of society experience antipathy for people living with HIV. These new challenges can further affect men's psychological well-being, such that they engage in behaviors that increases their risk of transmitting HIV and of acquiring other sexually transmitted diseases that can further compromise their overall health (Alonzo & Reynolds, 1995; Díaz, Ayala, & Marin, 2000).

Understanding how HIV-positive gay and bisexual men, particularly men of color, view their sexuality in relation to their societal and cultural framework is important information that will help researchers and clinicians to provide the necessary support and attention to these issues.

In this chapter, we examine the role of race, ethnicity, and culture and how these variables play out in the self-acceptance, views of sexuality, partner selection, and type of sex chosen or expected among 250 HIV-positive gay and bisexual men participating in the Seropositive Urban Men's Study (SUMS; see chap. 1, this volume, for a full description of study methodology). Focusing on the responses to a series of open-ended questions, the chapter will also examine personal attitudes and perceptions about why men of color are more likely than their White counterparts to become infected. This information provides insight about the types of racial and ethnic stereotypes that still exist and that could lead to increased sexual risk practices.

GENERAL EFFECTS OF CULTURE

In the course of describing their life experiences, many men commented on their cultural backgrounds and how these affected their behaviors and views as HIV-positive men. They often described the influence of ethnicity and culture as an internal dynamic that influenced their ability to cope with their HIV status and influenced their own sense of self:

> Well, I think sometimes that gay Latino men, even though they could be flaming queens, they still feel that they're macho. You know that's still very ingrained; and being HIV-positive, it's something that they don't want to see or face. (Latino male, age 43, New York)

> Well, certainly in the Black community, I find it to be more homophobic than in other communities, and therefore, in the Black community there may be more self-hatred as a result. And out of that self-hatred comes irresponsible behavior. (Black male, age 45, New York)

In addition to the internal dynamics, many men described their ethnic and cultural worlds with regard to how they were accepted as gay men:

> A lot of my friends are Asian, and they have all of the discrimination; their families can't stand us. . . . I had one Asian friend, when he told his mother he's gay, his mother said, "Oh, you know, maybe we should move out of here and go to another state." Then he explained to his mother; he says, "No, I have been gay ever since I was in high school. I like men. But I never tell you because I was in fear of shame." Shame is one of the biggest issues in the Asian culture because Asian people has a different religion. They worship their ancestor. They want to show the best of themselves out in public. Then their ancestor will be in peace, ancestor spirit will be in peace. If you make something bad or if you do something bad, then your whole ancestor is going to be very disappointed. (Asian or Pacific Islander male, age 45, San Francisco)

For some men, sexuality of any kind was embedded in a broader context and cultural taboo:

> Well, first of all, I didn't ever tell my parents I'm gay. It didn't matter what the sex was. All sex was bad, equally so, in Irish Catholic households. (White male, age 34, New York)

For most men, particularly men of color, their racial and ethnic heritage was a source of disapproval, a reference point from which they had diverged, which left many feeling rejected, judged, and shamed by their families and cultures of origin. Being HIV-positive simply added to this rejection and, for some, reinforced their own internal sense of low self-worth:

> One very sad Native American I was talking to recently . . . his family has nothing to do with him. His tribe doesn't want anything to do with him. He was born and raised on the reservation, and that's his world. So here, he is a fish out of water in San Francisco because he doesn't know where else to go or what else to do, and all the people important to him have tossed him out. (Alaska Native male, age 64, San Francisco)

Some men also reflected on the role of religious beliefs and how these interacted with the reality of their lives:

The whole thing of getting HIV was like a punishment, a sin, you know. So I had a lot of things with that, a lot of problems with that. Like especially when I got AIDS, I figured, "Oh well, this is my punishment," you know. . . . Well, it was sort of almost the same thing as the church that you're not a man because as a Black man you're supposed to, you know, the whole thing of father and manhood. . . . being a leader, you know, being a warrior. You're not tough and you're not macho, you know; a football player, you know, all that kind of stuff. (Black male, age 43, New York)

When you find out you're gay or HIV-positive, you think on two different levels. Like, "Oh, is this a curse from God. And are we the bad people?" . . . God knows I was born this way so my Catholic upbringing must be wrong. And then if your Catholic upbringing is wrong, it means your whole family is wrong. . . . So, I mean, it kind of shakes your foundation. (White male, age 34, New York)

Many men reported being instilled with negative ideas about sex throughout their upbringing, which seemed to oppress any sense of healthy sexual development and identity and gave impetus to misunderstanding, confusion, and insecurities. As noted in chapter 14 (this volume), however, many men resorted to self-created networks of "family" among their friends and connected to religious and spiritual organizations that accepted them for who they were, which resulted in a great deal of social support and self-acceptance. Sadly, few men expressed any sense of empowerment or pride originating from their cultural and ethnic origins, although many longed for that acceptance and sense of belonging:

It's enormous. Um, first my personal relationship with my family and friends changed. . . . I lost friends . . . some of the members of my family never accepted [it]. So I believe, ah, the term, that isolation, that I tried to break it through painting and writing and participating in community services and doing volunteer work, helping people. (Latino male, age 39, New York)

Then you have a culture, you know, African American community, sometimes they upset me because they're not—it's all right to march there for one right but not for the other; you know what I'm saying? I'm Black and gay and sometimes transgender; you know what I'm saying? Three things are affecting me, you know. And it's just like people only want to see that one thing. (Black male, age 45, New York)

EFFECTS OF CULTURE ON SEXUALITY

The range of responses regarding the meaning of sex has been presented in an earlier chapter (chap. 2, this volume). In this chapter we highlight how men's descriptions of sex, and who they were having it with, took on overarching meanings that were connected to how race, culture, religion, family history, and HIV serostatus each influenced their outlook and experiences in life. The meaning and importance of sex varied. Some men described sex on more of a personal or individual level, whereas other men, particularly men of color, described sex in a manner that tied in elements such as cultural history and norms, religious beliefs, upbringing, and barriers to sexual communication. By further examining how all of these factors influence the sexual lives of HIV-positive gay and bisexual men, a greater understanding of the interplay between race, culture, and sex can be achieved.

> To me, sex with a Black man or maybe a Hispanic man is just the best because we share a common history; we share just certain things on a basic historic level that being with a White person, I just—certain things are intrinsic. I don't want to have to teach and explain every time we get into bed. (Black male, age 39, New York)

INFLUENCE OF RACE AND ETHNICITY ON SEXUAL PARTNERSHIPS

For some men, the tension of being with a partner of the same race and ethnicity versus a partner of different race and ethnicity was fueled by assumed expectations of how men wished to be perceived within a sexual encounter:

> [As a Latino man] I think it's easier for White and Latino to date than it is for Latinos to date. I don't know. It's very difficult. It's really nice to be able to eat the same food, enjoy the same movies; the culture's the same, but when it comes to sex, it's difficult. Because we don't—we don't want to show how nasty we can get. And with a White man, I have no problem getting nasty with a White man, but with a Latino man I hold back. I think we try and hide how dirty we can get by trying to portray ourselves, you know, the Latino culture as Catholic, with rules, and we try to present that to the other person, you know—I was taught these things. And actually, behind your head, you're thinking, "Well, I hope we get nasty." With a White man, I never think I have to hide my addiction to sex. (Latino male, age 38, San Francisco)

> And I think African Americans ... culturally ... are different. And they come from a different place and understanding about sex, what one does or doesn't do; and even then, when you talk about sex, I'm

not sure we communicate evenly. Even though I think we understand the words, our meanings and definitions are different. I think culture always enters into it, yes I do. (White male, age 64, San Francisco)

I do have this one fantasy of every once in a while being over the—being dominated by a man who is White, which I assume is terribly taboo in our community, you know. I mean, I'm a Black person. I have a history of slavery that my ancestors went through. So if I'm going to like, you know, have sex with a White guy and then I'm going to let him dominate me, I can just see them saying, "What the hell are you doing? We went through 400 years of this, and now you're willingly giving up." (Black male, age 45, New York)

Previous research on sexual behaviors of gay and bisexual men has not focused on the racial and ethnic characteristics of partnerships and how these may influence behaviors. For these HIV-positive men, their responses about how race and ethnicity may interact in their own sexual lives provided a much deeper and more complex picture of these internal dynamics and underscored the importance of addressing such factors in discussing sexual risk.

The sexual partnership preferences of HIV-positive gay and bisexual men encompass a gamut of physical attributes and personality types. The meaning behind these preferences can be even more varied and diverse. When asked specifically about what they looked for in a sex partner, men made it evident that the race or ethnicity of their partner was important in determining sexual attraction, desirability, and the type of sexual behavior that they would engage in. Most, if not all, men described their ideal sexual partner in terms of race. Although many stated a variety of preferences unrelated to race, most men clearly defined sexual attraction to their partner based on a range of racial and ethnic groups they perceived to be desirable (and undesirable). Some indicated the race of their partner as a preference or determinant before describing other physical attributes such as height, age, body type, or hair color:

I like all different races of men, but there are certain types of Northern European men that I really like. I like Dutch men and German men, Scandinavian men; and one of the things that I like about them, in general is that they all have big legs. I like big calves and thighs and big legs. (Latino male, age 39, New York)

I'm not attracted to ethnic types. I mean, there are some that have physical attraction to them, but it just really kind of takes something different to make me go any further with them. It's just not my first choice. (White male, age 27, New York)

Other men said, "I only really enjoy sex with other Black men or Latin men. But brown Latin men" (Black male, age 56, New York). And "I get along with everybody. Could be White, Puerto Rican; could be Black, African; could be anything" (Latino male, age 28, New York).

When asked what they found attractive in a sexual partner, men in New York City responded differently than men in San Francisco. Despite the great racial and ethnic diversity of both cities, men in New York responded that they preferred and had sexual experiences with a wider range of partners that were not of their same race or ethnicity more often than did men in San Francisco. White men in New York indicated interracial sexual partnering with Latino, Black, and Asian men more commonly than did White men in San Francisco, who more often indicated a preference for other White men.

This difference was similarly evident among men of color. Although many, if not most, men of color in New York indicated a preference for other men of color (or no preference at all), men of color in San Francisco more often stated preferences for White men. In some instances, men of color from San Francisco indicated a lack of sexual attraction toward men who shared their racial or ethnic background or who were not White, "I don't like no men darker than me. They gotta be light, damn near white. That's a must" (Black male, age 37, San Francisco). "I wouldn't have been with him if he was Black or Latino. I'm not really attracted to people of color" (Latino male, age 34, San Francisco).

In addition to racial and ethnic preferences, men in New York and San Francisco described other characteristics they found to be desirable in a sex partner. Many men offered descriptions of necessary personality traits such as honesty, trustworthiness, having a sense of humor, and being "a nice guy." Other men described their partner in terms of a specific image or look. In some instances, men used terms such as "trucker," "lumberjack," "b-boy," "trade," "bear," "hustler," and "leather man," to describe the types of men they found to be attractive. Similarly, more than any other characteristic, masculinity was a quality that men stated was an integral determinant of sexual attractiveness and desirability. Particularly among Black and Latino men, the ability to appear and act "macho," "butch," or "like a man" was clearly important for their sex partners. For most men, regardless of race, a feminine appearance or mannerisms was not regarded as appealing or desirable, "Sort of macho. Yes, I like them macho. They can be a little queeny too, but they'd have to be macho" (Black male, age 45, New York). Others described their ideal partner as, "A person like myself. Very masculine. I like the masculinity. I like the challenge. The aggressiveness" (Black male, age 34, New York). And "I like real butch boys, you know. I don't like very feminine men. If you're very feminine, get out of my face. I like a man that's more masculine" (Latino male, age 40, New York).

In a race-conscious society such as the United States, one's racial/ethnic classification can have a profound impact on daily life experiences

(Jones, 2000). In many situations, these social classifications can have a direct influence on how one is perceived. Similarly, it is safe to assume that HIV-positive gay and bisexual men would exhibit and subject themselves to a parallel belief system commonly held by mainstream culture. Although some men stated a desire for a variety of types of men, others expressed preferences for certain races or ethnicities on the basis of sexual and nonsexual stereotypes. Some men specifically sought out sex partners on the basis of race and the perceived attributes associated with that racial or ethnic group:

> I like Asians. I just get turned on by that, and it's just more than just good bodies; it is the way they carry themselves. They are very silent. I guess I connect with that. They keep things in, you know; I just connect with that. (White male, age 42, New York)

> I love Black people; they're so sensitive and they have hair all around their ass. I find that very sexy. (White male, age 62, New York).

INFLUENCE OF RACE AND ETHNICITY ON SEXUAL BEHAVIORS

Racial and ethnic perceptions often had a clear influence on the type of sexual behavior that men desired and would engage in. In several instances, men's personal preference or bias dictated the types of sex they sought out and had with specific racial and ethnic groups: "Very seldom will I blow somebody and let them come in my mouth, unless it's hot. Unless they're somebody Hispanic or Black" (White male, age 36, New York).

> I have had sex in the last 6 months with White guys, but it's been very infrequent and it's been a guy that I perceive to be, as I would say, "freaky," meaning that he's more willing to do some of the things to me sexually that a Black guy may not be willing to do. (Black male, age 50, New York)

> I found certain things that I like; Black men have a certain smell of their balls that's really like, kind of—it's really, like, musky, and this unusual smell that I kind of like. So therefore, I like to suck Black men. If they have big dicks, it's an influence too. If I see a Black man who's real built, then he may also have a big dick, and it makes me want to suck it. (White male, age 46, New York)

> I think Caucasian men are much more open sexually. They like to do this; they like to do that. They talk about it easily. Asians do not. We're very quiet about it, very private about it. That's why I find Caucasians more interesting. They're very open. I don't have to hide and I love that. I don't have to pretend, and that's the kind of lover that I like to have. (Asian or Pacific Islander male, age 45, San Francisco)

Contrary to men in the preceding examples, some men described their aversion or unwillingness to have sex or date certain men because of reasons related to their particular racial or ethnic background:

I'll have sex with anybody, but not Black. And that's not a racist comment. It is not. I don't care what you think . . . it's not racist. It's just I probably got scared by some man who happened to be Black when I was a child or something simple like that. (White male, age 39, San Francisco)

I had an experience with a Puerto Rican, and it was totally insane. I still don't believe it, but they're wonderful for sex; so if you see them at the tubs and you want to do sex, fine. You just don't get caught up in their craziness. (White male, age 33, New York)

Other men commented, "I don't do Asian guys and I don't do Black guys. I just choose not to sleep with them. I just don't like them" (Latino male, age 20, San Francisco).

I can say that the only people that I'm not attracted to—and I would say 99% of them I'm not attracted to—is Oriental people. Otherwise, I don't have any problems. (Latino male, age 49, New York)

A few men had concerns within their own racial group:

I don't date Black men. I think Black men have a lot of . . . they carry around a lot of excess, unnecessary baggage that I don't have to have in my life. And I find that other nationalities don't carry around as much baggage as Black men do. (Black male, age 32, New York)

EXPERIENCES OF STEREOTYPING, REJECTION, AND OBJECTIFICATION

Almost exclusively reported by men of color, sexual stereotyping, objectification, and rejection were an important part of navigating through sexual decision making and establishing partnerships. These forms of stereotyping were not only indicative of the particular sexual roles and behaviors that men themselves engaged in, but the sexual roles and behaviors that were expected of them by their partners as well. Many men of color spoke candidly about certain sexual situations in which they felt their race or ethnicity was an issue:

He kept calling me Chocolate Boy, his little Mandingo; and this is a White guy, you know . . . I felt humiliated by some of the comments he made; even when he fixed me dinner that night, he made some pasta patina [phonetic]—it's an Italian dish—and he made a little joke.

He thought it was funny; I found it offensive. He said wouldn't I rather have collard greens. (Black male, age 30, New York)

Other men internalized feelings of sexual objectification because of their race or ethnicity and were able to discuss how their own sexual behavior, as well as their choice in partner, has been affected:

[My cultural background] has contributed more to the vengeful part of the sex that I have because being Hispanic with a big uncut dick, it's like, you know, you're a little piece of meat on the street, you know, and so I use that sometimes, and that's when the sex is like more vengeful. I'll be like, "Fuck you. I'll fuck your ass good and then, you know, treat you like shit after," you know, that kind of thing. I think that's how that has affected me culturally because of the backlash that I get from it, you know, and it also has affected my choice in sexual partners. If I'm feeling vengeful, or if I'm feeling like angry, which happens a lot, I would rather have sex with a White person than with a person of color because that's how I wanted to get back, you know. You don't get your vengeance doing it to a person of color because, you know, they are the same as you. (Latino male, age 33, New York)

Some men of color expressed uncertainty about whether men were genuinely interested in them as individuals or interested in specific attributes based on sexual stereotypes. This uncertainty, in some instances, also influenced their choice of partner and sexual behaviors:

But I always have this issue with my—I always think that a White man, does he want me for me, or does he want me because I am Black. I always have those issues going on in my head; so I just don't deal with it, I just don't. Because I don't know, I just don't, I don't know. (Black male, age 34, New York)

I think in general I look for Black men. But I like people from other groups as long as I don't sense any racism. I mean, I think there's racism among most people. And I can tolerate a certain level, because that's just the way we've been brought up. But if its not, if it's too—I am not going to be the Black buck for people. (Black male, age 47, New York)

PERCEIVED EFFECTS OF RACE, ETHNICITY, AND CULTURE ON RISK FOR HIV

To learn how HIV-positive men understood the current course of the HIV pandemic, we asked them why they thought Black and Latino men who have sex with men are getting infected with HIV more often than

White men who have sex with men. Men of all racial and ethnic groups described poor economic status, substance abuse, lack of education, and poor self-esteem as factors contributing to this racial disparity:

> Because when it comes to sex and HIV, those are not the top things for men of color to deal with. We deal with housing, discrimination, disbarred from our family, not accepted by our religions, our cultures. We have a lot of other barriers and baggage that we haven't dealt with, or we are dealin' with, that come before dealin' with that. (mixed race/ ethnicity male, age 36, San Francisco)

Some men were much more likely to describe some stereotypes related to race and ethnicity even within their own groups as reasons for the overrepresentation of men of color among people living with HIV:

> Well, they're [Latino men] very promiscuous and there's a lot of drugs around them, drug related poverty. And that goes all hand in hand. (Latino male, age 33, New York)

> I think—I'm not prejudiced, okay, but I do believe that the darker the skin, the higher the sex drive. . . . I think Latino men are a little more promiscuous because sex is very important to these people. . . . They have to have sex every day. I know a lot of Black men that have to have sex every day, once a day. (White male, age 55, San Francisco)

Discrimination, low self-esteem, and consequent apathy regarding sexual risk were expressed by many as important contributors to the disproportionate effects on men of color:

> My belief as a Caucasian is that Latin Americans, men of color, have been marginalized by the White society; and because of that, their sense of self-esteem is not what it should be, and they don't value themselves enough. (White male, age 39, San Francisco)

> I think predominantly because of drug use and depression. Yes. I seriously believe that depression is at epidemic levels within our community. And when I say "our," I do mean specifically men of color, particularly African American men, Latino American men, and immigrants. . . . I mean, depression addresses—it tends to address some of the self-esteem issues. So, you know, and hopeless, you know. So there's less concern about, you know, self-care, positive movement, positive growth. So they're very complacent about it. Apathetic about their lives. And, you know, certainly apathetic about their approach to sexual relief. (Black male, age 51, New York)

The role of cultural beliefs was also offered as an explanation for the larger rates of HIV infection among men of color:

I think Latinos tend to have a certain fatalistic streak that's really . . .
in our culture, you believe in destiny, or God's will, a lot more than
you believe in personal power. (Latino male, age 47, San Francisco)

DISCUSSION

The role of race and ethnicity in the sexual behaviors, attitudes, and
beliefs of the HIV-positive gay and bisexual men in this sample was significant and evident at many levels. Men's sense of self-worth and how they
contextualize their lives is largely affected by their feelings of acceptance
or rejection from their cultures of origin, particularly for men of color. These
findings are consistent with findings of previous studies of social support
and psychological stress among HIV-positive men from different racial and
ethnic backgrounds (Gant & Ostrow, 1995; Siegel & Epstein, 1996) and
continue to suggest the importance of addressing racial and ethnic issues
with regard to the ability to cope and engage in health-seeking behaviors.

The sexual choices made by men in this sample were often linked to
the men's internalized cultural expectations. For some men this included
decisions about the type of sex they would have, depending on the racial
or ethnic characteristic of their partners or their own preferences regarding
the race or ethnicity of sex partners. For others, a strong emotional dynamic
emerged in situations in which a shared ethnic background could be a barrier
or a facilitator of sexual satisfaction or in situations in which racial and
ethnic differences sometimes brought about concerns of objectification or
rejection. For most men, these racial and ethnic influences seemed to predate
their becoming infected with HIV; however, for many men, HIV status
became yet another layer of dynamic in sexual encounters (see chap. 7,
this volume).

Finally, views about why Black and Latino men are disproportionately
infected with HIV included both individual and social responsibility. The
perceptions of racial and ethnic stereotypes suggested a certain level of
blame placed on men of color, even among men of color themselves. This
type of characterization is not unlike that often applied to victims of rape,
in which individuals are perceived as partly responsible for their own plight.
Assuming that it is mainly a matter of individual irresponsibility of a particular race, ethnicity, or gender ignores the contribution of social and cultural
norms in determining behaviors. Many men were able to attribute the
consequences to social inequities that do result in lower education, lack of
access to health care, substance use, and poor mental health, which can
affect HIV transmission.

The role of race, ethnicity, and culture in the sexual lives of HIV-
positive gay and bisexual men cannot be underestimated and must be incor-

porated into any type of program that supports sexual behavior patterns that promote health. One can argue that our whole concept of sexuality is driven by social influences. Gregersen (1994, p. 1) noted, "Sex began as a biological adaptation, but in all human cultures it has become a focal point for social and moral codes." In a society that puts so much emphasis on racial, ethnic, and cultural differences, this dynamic will be present in most sexual interactions and sexual choices. For HIV-positive gay and bisexual men, the importance of being accepted and supported by cultures and families carries a special significance in the face of coping with a life-threatening illness; it can greatly influence their ability to maintain psychological and physical well-being that affects their sexual lives. In the sexual lives of HIV-positive gay and bisexual men, culture matters.

REFERENCES

Alonzo, A. A., & Reynolds, N. R. (1995). Stigma, HIV and AIDS: An exploration and elaboration of a stigma trajectory. *Social Science Medicine, 4,* 303–315.

Choi, K.-H., Kumekawa, E., Dang, Q., Kegeles, S. M., Hays, R. B., & Stall, R. (1999). Risk and protective factors affecting sexual behavior among young Asian and Pacific Islander men who have sex with men: Implications for HIV prevention. *Journal of Sex Education and Therapy, 24*(1–2), 47–55.

Crawford, I., Allison, K. W., Zamboni, B. D., & Soto, T. (2002). The influence of dual-identity development on the psychosocial functioning of African-American gay and bisexual men. *Journal of Sex Research, 39,* 179–189.

Díaz, R. M. (1997). Latino gay men and psycho-cultural barriers to AIDS prevention. In M. P. Levine, P. M. Nardi, & J. H. Gagnon (Eds.), *Changing times: Gay men and lesbians encounter HIV/AIDS* (pp. 3–13). Chicago: University of Chicago Press.

Díaz, R. M. (1999). Trips to fantasy island: Contexts of risky sex for San Francisco gay men. *Sexualities, 2,* 89–112.

Díaz, R. M., & Ayala, G. (2000). The impact of social discrimination on health outcomes: The case of Latino gay men and HIV. In A *Monograph of the National Gay and Lesbian Task Force* (pp. 8–17). San Francisco: Center for Community Research Institute on Sexuality, Inequality and Health.

Díaz, R. M., Ayala, G., & Marin, B. V. (2000). Latino gay men and HIV: Risk behavior as a sign of prevention. *FOCUS: A Guide to AIDS Research and Counseling, 14,* 1–4.

Gant, L. M., & Ostrow, D. G. (1995). Perceptions of social support and psychological adaptation to sexually acquired HIV among White and African American men. *Social Work, 40,* 215–224.

Gregersen, E. (1994). *The world of human sexuality: Behaviors, customs, and beliefs.* New York: Irvington.

Herek, G. M. (1991). Stigma, prejudice, and violence against lesbians and gay men. In J. C. Gonsiorek & J. D. Weinrich (Eds.), *Homosexuality: Research implications for public policy* (pp. 60–80). Newbury Park, CA: Sage.

Herek, G. M. (2002). Thinking about AIDS and stigma: A psychologist's perspective. *Journal of Law, Medicine and Ethics, 30*, 594–607.

Jones, C. P. (2000). Levels of racism: A theoretic framework and a gardener's tale. *American Journal of Public Health, 90*, 1212–1215.

Manalansan, M. F. I. (1996). Double minorities: Latino, Black, and Asian men who have sex with men. In R. C. C. Savin-Williams & M. Kenneth (Eds.), *The lives of lesbians, gays, and bisexuals: Children to adults* (pp. 393–415). Ft. Worth, TX: Harcourt Brace.

Myers, H. F., Javanbakht, M., Martinez, M., & Obediah, S. (2003). Psychosocial predictors of risky sexual behaviors in African American men: Implications for prevention. *AIDS Education and Prevention, 15*, 66–79.

Pares-Avila, J. A., & Montano-Lopez, R. (1994). Issues in the psychosocial care of Latino gay men with HIV infection. In S. A. Cadwell, R. A. Burnham, & M. Forstein (Eds.), *Therapists on the front line: Psychotherapy with gay men in the age of AIDS* (pp. 339–362). Washington, DC: American Psychiatric Association.

Siegel, K., & Epstein, J. A. (1996). Ethnic–racial differences in psychological stress related to gay lifestyle among HIV-positive men. *Psychological Reports, 79*, 303–312.

Stokes, J. P., & Peterson, J. L. (1998). Homophobia, self-esteem, and risk for HIV among African American men who have sex with men. *AIDS Education and Prevention, 10*, 278–292.

7

I HAVE SOMETHING TO TELL YOU: HIV SEROSTATUS DISCLOSURE PRACTICES OF HIV-POSITIVE GAY AND BISEXUAL MEN WITH SEX PARTNERS

MICHAEL J. STIRRATT

Decisions about disclosing serostatus to romantic and sex partners can constitute a significant challenge for HIV-positive gay and bisexual men. The potential difficulty associated with disclosing one's HIV infection grows largely from the stigma that surrounds HIV/AIDS. Prejudice against people living with HIV/AIDS remains pervasive, even within gay communities that have been fighting the epidemic for more than two decades (Herek, Capitanio, & Widaman, 2002; Hoff, McKusick, Hilliard, & Coates, 1992; Zierler et al., 2000). As a result of this climate, HIV-positive gay and bisexual men often bring three understandings to sexual encounters: the knowledge of their own serostatus, the recognition that sexual contact can result in HIV transmission if precautions are not taken, and the awareness that some partners may be uncomfortable with these facts. These concerns can culti-vate serious questions among HIV-positive gay and bisexual men about whether, when, and how to inform their romantic and sex partners about their serostatus.

A growing body of research has examined the serostatus disclosure practices of HIV-positive gay and bisexual men. Studies have found that HIV-positive men commonly disclose their serostatus to primary romantic partners but infrequently disclose to casual sex partners (Hays et al., 1993; Mansergh, Marks, & Simoni, 1995; Mason, Marks, Simoni, Ruiz, & Richardson, 1995; Mason, Simoni, Marks, Johnson, & Richardson, 1997; Wolitski, Rietmeijer, Goldbaum, & Wilson, 1998). Men who have greater numbers of sex partners also report less serostatus disclosure than men with fewer sex partners (De Rosa & Marks, 1998; Marks, Richardson, & Maldonado, 1991; Stein et al., 1998). These findings are likely interrelated because individuals with one or few partners are more likely to be participating in close relationships, whereas individuals with many partners are more likely to be having sex in the context of casual or anonymous encounters.

Prevention research has investigated whether serostatus disclosure practices are related to sexual risk behavior. Although the results of these studies are mixed, some suggest that partner serostatus affects the relationship between serostatus disclosure and sexual risk practices. Disclosure between HIV-serodiscordant partners (one HIV-positive and one HIV-negative) is often associated with reduced-risk sex practices, whereas disclosure between seroconcordant partners (both HIV-positive or both HIV-negative) may facilitate unprotected sex (Dawson et al., 1994; De Rosa & Marks, 1998; Ekstrand, Stall, Paul, Osmond, & Coates, 1999; Marks et al., 1991; Niccolai, Dorst, Myers, & Kissinger, 1999; Wolitski et al., 1998). These findings must be interpreted with caution, however, because many of these studies were unable to analyze disclosure and sexual risk behavior on a per-partner basis (Marks & Crepaz, 2001), and factors such as partner type (primary or casual) may be more predictive of sexual risk taking than either disclosure or partner HIV status (Dawson et al., 1994).

This chapter examines how HIV-positive gay and bisexual men negotiate the challenges of serostatus disclosure issues with romantic and sex partners. The themes reported emerged from a two-stage content analysis of the 250 study interviews. A subsample of 36 interviews contributed to the development of the initial themes, which were then extended through examination of the remaining interviews. (See chap. 1, this volume, for a description of the Seropositive Urban Men's Study [SUMS] methods.) The analysis centered on four primary issues: (a) contexts for disclosure practices, (b) the significance of disclosure issues, (c) strategies used to address issues of disclosure, and (d) the relationships between serostatus disclosure and sexual risk behaviors.

CONTEXTS FOR DISCLOSURE PRACTICES

The serostatus disclosure practices of HIV-positive men cannot be adequately understood without first considering the social contexts and interpersonal concerns that give shape to these practices. In the interviews, men spoke of three primary themes that framed and influenced their disclosure practices with sex partners: fear of prejudice and rejection, perceived norms and sexual scripts, and catalysts for disclosure.

Prejudice and Rejection

When asked generally about issues that come up when dealing with disclosure to sex partners, men of all ages and backgrounds often began their response with a single word: rejection. For example, one participant noted that disclosure raised the prospects of "being accepted or rejected, loved or scorned, getting laid or not getting laid" (White male, age 46, New York), and another added that "there's always a chance that when you open up to tell them ... that you are HIV-positive, that relationship is gonna end" (Black male, age 29, San Francisco). Many men referred to personal experiences with rejection, such as the following:

> Several years ago I had met someone in—in the neighborhood. And he was out looking for sex, bumped into me, and I brought him home. And we were having safe sex. And he had asked me if I was HIV-positive or -negative. I said, "Positive." And he just stood back and slugged me. Wouldn't touch anything. Just put on his clothes and walked out. (White male, age 51, New York)

Rejection from partners following disclosure took many forms, including refusal to have sex, unwillingness to engage in particular sex practices, emotional distancing, abrupt or longer term relationship dissolution, and even (although rarely) acts of violence. In addition to being the recipient of rejection, a small number of men recalled being the rejector of other HIV-positive individuals before they knew they were HIV-positive themselves.

Some men found that anxiety about the outcome of disclosure was not warranted because many of their partners had greeted their HIV-positive status with acceptance or indifference. Acceptance after disclosure was often attributed to one's partner being either HIV-positive or educated about HIV/AIDS. Some men stated that their strong expectations of rejection frequently outweighed their actual experiences of rejection. One man commented, "In the past, a lot of the time I felt like damaged goods and that nobody would want me, but it turns out that that has not been the case" (White male, age 33, New York), and another stated, "They usually really,

really respect it, and it's amazing that, you know, the rejection has not really been there" (Native American male, age 29, San Francisco). The theme of rejection was generally stronger in men from New York than in those from San Francisco, which was reflected in the comments of one man who had disclosed his serostatus to men in both cities: "You know, on the East Coast that tends to scare people away. Out here [in San Francisco] you're most—90% of the reactions that I've gotten have been, 'well, so am I'" (White male, age 24, San Francisco). However, at both sites, men who found acceptance from partners after disclosure often reported a sense of relief, underscoring their recognition of the potential for rejection (see chap. 3, this volume, for more on concerns regarding rejection).

Norms and Sexual Scripts

Another theme that set the context for men's disclosure practices concerned their perceptions of disclosure-related norms and sexual scripts. One perceived norm was a general understanding that serostatus disclosure was uncommon with casual and anonymous sex partners. Men made comments such as, "It is something that just never comes up—they don't bring it up and I don't bring it up" (Black male, age 34, New York), and "I've never met one person that has ever told me first, before I've told them" (mixed race/ethnicity male, age 35, San Francisco). One participant explained that his past efforts to disclose his serostatus often resulted in disbelief: "Before when I tried to say something to people they were like, 'Why are you even telling me this?' It seemed strange to them" (White male, age 46, New York). Serostatus disclosure with casual sex partners was less of a norm for men interviewed in New York than those in San Francisco; more men in San Francisco seemed to believe that disclosure was an accepted practice with casual partners. At both sites, however, men added that perceived sanctions against verbal serostatus disclosures were particularly strong in the context of public sex environments. One man explained that in these contexts "nobody really discusses [laughs] anything—you know, there's virtually no talking at all" (mixed race/ethnicity male, age 46, New York; see chap. 5, this volume, that further describes the lack of verbal communication in these contexts).

In addition to representing serostatus disclosure as an uncommon practice, men also described disclosure as antithetical to scripts for casual sexual encounters between gay and bisexual men. Men noted that serostatus disclosures serve as a reminder of the possibility and reality of HIV infection and, as a result, can disrupt the desire for sex:

> Well, sometimes when you reveal a status or even bringing the HIV up, I guess the whole mind gets into a different set. It leaves the sex and it goes to sickness, death, friends me or him have had in the past.

It changed the whole atmosphere. It's not negative; it just gets more serious and more nonsexual as opposed to, you know, "Let's enjoy each other for the day . . . let's have some fun. Let's enjoy each other's body." (mixed race/ethnicity male, age 41, New York)

Other SUMS participants echoed this sentiment, noting that "Actually talking about it, it ruins everything, it is not sexy, it is not romantic, you are taken away from the moment" (Black male, age 34, New York). The representation of serostatus disclosure as disrupting sexual desire provided an impulse to avoid disclosure during casual encounters. One man commented that the norm was therefore, "a lot of just not wanting to think about it, and so, 'Please don't bring it to my attention—let's not talk about it, and you know, we'll be fine'" (White male, age 46, New York).

Catalysts for Disclosure

Men identified three primary catalysts that strongly compelled them to disclose their serostatus to partners: romantic relationships, the embodiment of serostatus within their lives, and moral mandates to disclose.

Men consistently described how the development (or prospects) of a romantic relationship would foster serostatus disclosure. Many men felt that serostatus disclosure early in the course of relationship development was critical for cultivating trust and emotional intimacy, such as the following:

The reason to let them know is that there is a possibility that there will be a long-term relationship. And there's a possibility of having trust established in a relationship, is the main reason to let them know. And I found from experience that I've lost somebody who I was falling in love with for not having told him at first. (White male, age 46, New York)

Some also mentioned the inverse of this dynamic in that the ongoing development of trust and intimacy with a romantic partner encouraged serostatus disclosure through mutual discussions of personal and private concerns. Men therefore represented disclosure as both a product and a facilitator of the emotional intimacy found in serious relationships.

A second disclosure catalyst was the embodiment of HIV serostatus within the daily lives of the men. Men pointed to a broad constellation of daily practices and life situations that could reflect their seropositive status, such as medications, regular doctor visits, symptoms of illness, medication side effects, subscriptions to HIV/AIDS publications, being on disability, participating in HIV/AIDS support programs, working for HIV/AIDS service organizations, and living in an HIV/AIDS residence. Participants felt that it would be difficult to mask these potential markers of their serostatus from partners with whom they had personal or repeated contact:

If you're very close to somebody, he will find out sooner or later, even if you don't live together. Because you have to take drugs, you have to go see doctors. If you won't tell him, he's going to find out sooner or later; he gets suspicious, why you going to see a doctor . . . and why you need to go pick up prescription drugs every month. (Asian or Pacific Islander male, age 38, San Francisco)

Some men felt that certain objects and practices could communicate their serostatus without the need for verbal disclosure, such as leaving their medication bottles out in the open. Some also reported that they used HIV-related signifiers to help initiate verbal serostatus disclosure. In this regard, men said they used events such as taking a dose of medication or mentioning an upcoming doctor's appointment as a means of introducing their serostatus to their partner:

I tell them that I have a doctor's appointment that I can't miss on the day that they tell me that I have to go out with them . . . that's how I actually find out a way of telling them that I'm sick. (Latino male, age 35, New York)

Moral mandates represented a third important catalyst for serostatus disclosure. From a partner-related standpoint, many men felt a powerful ethical obligation to disclose their serostatus because of feelings of responsibility for protecting their partners from HIV transmission (see chap. 10, this volume). These men perceived an ethical obligation to inform their partners of their serostatus because of the potential risk of HIV transmission through sexual contact, "Because, you know, the condom can break, you know, the—I just want them to know what they're dealing with, you know?" (Native American male, age 29, San Francisco). Men also wished to let their partners make an informed choice about their sexual conduct; as one man explained, "You give the person an option also to decide. This is life, you know, it's a person's life. Mine is fucked up already because maybe somebody didn't tell me (Latino male, age 33, New York). From a personal perspective, some men also felt compelled to disclose their serostatus so they could feel honest or avoid feeling dishonest with their partners:

As scared as I am of being rejected, I just know what it's like to live in my own skin with myself and having that—keeping secrets and all of that stuff. I hate that even more. So it's like the lesser of two evils. (Black male, age 44, New York)

In informing their sex partners of their serostatus, men therefore sought to protect themselves from the guilt they associated with nondisclosure and to protect their partners by letting them make an informed decision about their sex practices.

THE SIGNIFICANCE OF DISCLOSURE

Many men viewed disclosure of HIV-serostatus as a significant challenge because of overlapping and competing concerns about the contexts mentioned earlier: rejection, norms and sexual scripts, and catalysts for disclosure. The intersection of these varied concerns prompted many men to feel anxious and troubled regarding serostatus disclosure:

> I think it changes the dynamic for me in that, you know, up until 1989 if I met somebody I liked, I didn't have to think about telling them, "Excuse me. I have this virus, you know." I didn't have to worry about that and now I do. Or, "worried" might be a strong word. Yeh, "worried" works. (Black male, age 44, New York)

> It's put up fences. It's been an obstacle . . . if I meet someone and if there looks like there's any indication that we might end up playing, I feel very strongly that he should know up front my HIV status, that I'm HIV-positive. That can turn off a lot of people. It's kind of an iffy situation. I feel like I should say it, but at the same time I almost hate to. It's never a pleasant thing. (White male, age 50, San Francisco)

Many men who viewed serostatus disclosure as a significant challenge also had questions about how to best address this issue. Men made comments such as, "I still don't know how, if I meet somebody, how do I do that; how do I talk, tell them I have the virus" (Black male, age 34, New York). One participant noted how disclosure was a significant concern for him and his friends:

> I understand from a lot of my friends that this is a really big issue, because the big talk among most of my circle of friends is, at what point do you tell somebody? When do you approach it? How far do you let things go? You can call or meet a date. Where along this line do you say, "Listen, here's the deal"? (White male, age 36, New York)

Men therefore commonly requested programs that would help them with disclosure, such as "learning how to deal with telling people or not telling people" (White male, age 28, New York). They also sought services that would broadly promote the development of resilience and pride in the face of HIV/AIDS stigma and prejudice:

> One that advocates the all rightness around it and to accept it. You know, and to be proud of it, not to run around and brush it under the table. Not to be so paranoid about it. You know what I mean—one that advocates, "Say, listen, this is what you got; wear it," you know. (Latino male, age 32, New York)

Although many men viewed serostatus disclosure as a recurrent dilemma, some noted that they had become more comfortable with disclosure issues over time and through the accumulation of experience, "As time has gone on, it's become easier and easier, and now it's very easy" (Native American male, age 64, San Francisco). A large number of men were therefore able to transcend fears of partner rejection and other concerns about serostatus disclosure, effectively arriving at a point where they had developed the strength to reject the rejectors:

> At the beginning, it was like, "Oh, well, he rejected me," and I'd call my friend and tell him, "He rejected me." Now it's like, "Excuse me? Fuck you! Goodbye," and just keep walking and, "Next?" [Laughter]. "Okay, you're next. Come over here." That's it. (Latino male, age 33, New York)

The significance of disclosure was another element in which a difference emerged between the New York and San Francisco sites. In general, San Francisco respondents were less likely than New York respondents to report experiences with partner rejection after disclosure or concerns about disclosure leading to partner rejection. The theme of disclosure as a significant challenge or obstacle within one's sexual life was stronger among men from New York. Nonetheless, many men in both cities feared potential rejection from partners after disclosure.

DISCLOSURE STRATEGIES

Most men elaborated specific strategies or approaches they had adopted for addressing disclosure issues with their sex partners: *tell before sex, play it safe, it all depends, stay positive, avoid intimacy,* and *be indirect.* These strategies were often formulated in response to awareness of HIV/AIDS stigma and past experiences with disclosure, and they served as rules of thumb that guided their ongoing and future disclosure practices. Although the strategies are considered separately in this chapter, it is important to note that any one individual may use a combination of different disclosure strategies and may shift strategies over time and across different interpersonal contexts.

Tell Before Sex

Some men had adopted a policy of disclosing their HIV-positive serostatus to their partners before having any sexual contact with them. One participant summarized this approach succinctly, "If they are going to be a sex partner, they automatically find out—it is that simple" (Latino male, age 20, New York). Men who pursued this strategy commonly connected it to strong moral beliefs about protecting their partners from HIV:

> There's nothing—there's nothing that can come up or nothing that can happen to make me not want to tell somebody I'm HIV-positive because I made my mind up to always protect the next person. Because, see, if somebody would have had that same outlook about me, then I wouldn't have it; so I refuse to allow myself to harm someone like I was harmed, you know. (Black male, age 37, San Francisco)

Men who elected to disclose their serostatus before sex established a type of informed consent with their sex partners by alerting them to any possible risk and allowing them to decide whether they were willing to assume that risk. Serostatus disclosure before sexual contact therefore became a route for men to share responsibility for any risk of HIV transmission with their partner.

Men who chose to disclose their HIV serostatus before having sex reported doing so with all types of partners, from potential one-night stands they had just met in a bar or nightclub to men they had dated (platonically) for months. However, this strategy was often emphasized as being particularly important with partners who had romantic potential. Men felt that disclosure before sex was essential to cultivating a trusting relationship:

> You can't fall in love with a guy unless you establish a trust. You can't establish a trust unless you're honest. And if you're positive and—and you're making an investment with a guy in some of his time and, in terms of a relationship, you have to say it up front, whether you like it or not. If you don't do it and you—you bond with him, and then he finds out later on, and you weren't—you weren't honest about it, your relationship is down the tubes, and all the time and energy you put into it is for nothing. You have to say it up front. (Latino male, age 38, New York)

Although men noted that they risked rejection by disclosing their HIV-positive serostatus before having sex, they felt rejection was preferable to feeling dishonest by not disclosing or prolonging the anxiety of disclosure. Men also noted how disclosure up front was an important way to screen out undesirable partners:

> I don't want to be a part of anybody's life who can't accept me for who I am. Being HIV is a part of who I am. So if they don't want to be with me because I'm HIV-positive, then they don't need to be. Period. (mixed race/ethnicity male, age 37, New York)

Some men who chose to disclose their serostatus before sex therefore came to view rejection as a two-way street, feeling that partners who could not accept them were unacceptable as prospective sex partners or boyfriends.

Play It Safe

Another strategy was forgoing serostatus disclosure as long as safer sex was practiced. Men who used this strategy stated that there was no need to disclose their HIV status if their sex practices presented little or no risk for HIV transmission:

> Until there's a law saying that you got to tell somebody that you're positive before you fuck 'em . . . I don't feel I have to tell anybody, as long as we take all the precautions to make sure we're safe, you know. (White male, age 24, San Francisco)

Men who used this strategy articulated a slight modification of the informed consent approach to sex practices and disclosure. They argued that men who consent to participate in safer sex should already have a clear understanding of the (relatively small) risks involved, so disclosure should only be required if one ventured beyond the bounds of safer sex practices. From this perspective, men used condoms to protect others from HIV transmission and to protect themselves from concerns about disclosure. Some men noted that practicing safer sex helped preserve the option to disclose their serostatus in the future:

> Thank god I made the decision about not having sex without a rubber because then it will be the time that I have to tell him I'm HIV . . . he won't have to get upset and I will not get upset because I didn't expose him to anything. (Latino male, age 33, New York)

This play it safe approach to sex and serostatus disclosure was sometimes paired with the idea, "I treat everybody like they're HIV-positive" (White male, age 51, New York). Assumptions that any partner could be HIV-positive contributed to a perspective that serostatus disclosure was irrelevant and safer sex was essential for preventing HIV transmission among gay and bisexual men.

It All Depends

Men further evidenced a set of approaches in which disclosure was contingent on particular interpersonal situations or characteristics of their sex partners. The most prominent of these conditional approaches was to reserve serostatus disclosure for romantic partners and men who had the potential to become boyfriends. Participants commented, "If it's like I want them to be there for the long term, then I'll disclose my status to them" (Black male, age 39, San Francisco), and, "If I really believe there is an emotional future, a real tie, I have no choice. I have to tell him, because you can't have a relationship if there are walls of secrecy" (White male, age 43, San Francisco).

Another common conditional approach was to make disclosure contingent on a partner's observed and apparent attitudes toward people with HIV/AIDS. Men described a process of testing the waters by monitoring their partners' responses to both general statements and direct references regarding HIV/AIDS:

> I had a guy that I really liked, and you hear them talk about—you just—you know, you start conversations, and, "Oh man, I saw this program on television about this HIV guy that had a lover and he was dying and he was falling apart," and then the conversation starts and you see their reaction or what the person says about the person. (Latino male, age 35, New York)

Men who took this approach would disclose to partners who appeared accepting but would avoid disclosure with partners who appeared prejudiced. If it seemed that their partner may not accept their HIV-positive status, men said that they would often seek to end the relationship without disclosing their serostatus.

A third conditional approach was disclosing serostatus if the partner asked about it or if the partner disclosed his own serostatus. Men often commented that they felt a moral mandate to respond truthfully to partner inquiries regarding serostatus, such as, "I believe that if they have the responsibility enough to ask, then I believe they have the right to know, especially if I'm their sexual partner" (White male, age 32, San Francisco). Men also tended to reciprocate partner disclosures of serostatus (and similarly, situations in which the respondent initiated disclosure often resulted in partner disclosure). One man stated, "I'm not letting nobody know about it unless I just happen to feel comfortable because they told me first" (White male, age 34, New York). Men further underscored that the inverse relationship frequently held true, in that "If they don't ask, I won't tell" (Black male, age 44, New York). In these ways, men described both disclosure and nondisclosure as a mutual process, and some made disclosure contingent on partner serostatus disclosure or related inquiries.

Men also voiced several other conditional strategies. Some men reported that their disclosure was dependent on the context in which men met or had sex with their partners—in other words, public sex environments or other locations. Men commented that norms of nondisclosure in public sex environments led them to reserve disclosure for partners whom they encountered outside of these contexts. Another conditional approach centered on the specific sexual behavior, in that some men disclosed only if they were going to have anal sex or if their partner sought unprotected anal sex. In this approach, men reserved disclosure for circumstances that presented the highest risk for possible HIV transmission. Finally, another conditional strategy was to disclose serostatus with undesirable sex partners, to deflect men in whom they had no sexual or romantic interest. One participant explained, "Quite often I've brought up my status with people with whom were—who were attracted to me but with whom I was not attracted and in the hopes that it would turn them off" (Black male, age 45, New York).

Stay Positive

Men described seeking HIV-positive peers to meet, date, and have sex with as another strategy for addressing the challenges associated with serostatus disclosure (see chap. 3, this volume). Partnering with HIV-positive men helped men to circumvent the difficulties of disclosing their status. One man described, "For the past 4 years, when I tell people that I might have been sexually involved with, then I seem to lose those people . . . so I decided to get with a person who already has it" (Black male, age 29, San Francisco). The principal advantage of this strategy was that it eliminated fears of partner rejection as a result of HIV-positive serostatus: "You don't have to worry about how they're gonna react to what you have because they have it as well" (Latino male, age 38, New York). Another man elaborated:

> I originally stated that I wanted to be in the HIV community. I would only date in the HIV. I didn't want to have to deal with the question of, telling someone that I'm HIV, for the rejection of, "I'm sorry, I can't handle that." I felt that in the HIV community . . . it was easier. It's like a comrade, a camaraderie. So I—in the HIV community there was no problem. (White male, age 51, New York)

In addition to defusing disclosure dilemmas, men noted that having HIV-positive partners would help reduce their concerns about HIV transmission. One participant remarked, "It's also easier, um, being that, you know, you can't infect a guy because he's already infected—you don't—you don't have to have that on your mind and always wonder" (Latino male, age 34, New York). The pursuit of HIV-positive partners to circumvent disclosure concerns raised the challenge of finding avenues for meeting peers. Men tried to meet HIV-positive partners in many ways, including social events for HIV-positive men, HIV/AIDS support groups and agencies, personal ads, and "this new [chat] room on AOL" (White male, age 46, New York). Men also voiced a desire for more opportunities and venues where HIV-positive men could meet.

Avoid Intimacy

One of the most striking themes to emerge from the interviews was the resolve with which some men stated that they chose to avoid emotionally intimate relationships that might foster expectations, pressure, or desires to disclose one's HIV-positive status. By avoiding intimate relationships, men divorced themselves from interpersonal contexts that invited disclosure and consequently sidestepped the potential for rejection. Some men spoke of how disclosure concerns and rejection fears had led them to withdraw from seeking boyfriends:

> I really don't go out all that often. I mean I'm not looking for anybody. Because you always have to deal with that, telling them that you're HIV. You don't want to develop feelings for somebody and then have to tell them that you're positive. (White male, age 28, New York)

Others said they occasionally began relationships but would withdraw from them before the level of emotional intimacy deepened to the point where they would feel compelled to disclose their serostatus:

> Well, on occasions, if I care about this person and I believe that I can get to know this person, I'll just end the relationship. I will tell them we can't be together, or that I have a girlfriend, or something. So this person will be angry, be more angry and will leave, so I wouldn't have to tell this person [my status]. (Black male, age 29, San Francisco)

Men who shunned romantic relationships frequently paired this approach with a strong preference for anonymous and casual sex partners. Reliance on these types of partners allowed the men to participate in norms of nondisclosure and avoid rejection:

> It [being HIV-positive] makes me not want or not consider looking for—it steers me away from looking for a serious relationship, you know; it makes me feel like I just want to go and have sex real quick, get it over with and not deal with all that trauma that goes along with like, you know, revealing your status and talking about it and then the rejection that comes along with it and all that kind of crap. (Latino male, age 33, New York)

A number of men stated that sex clubs, bathhouses, and other commercial and public sex environments provided the ideal context for meeting sex partners without the entanglements of disclosure and intimacy:

> Experiences like that [partner rejection] make you tend to not want to pursue anything anymore. And since I discovered these sex clubs, you know, sexually I can go and take care of, you know, that, without getting emotionally involved with anybody . . . so it's sort of become like a—a sexual little refuge for me. (mixed race/ethnicity male, age 46, New York)

In addition to visiting these locales, some men mentioned other ways they avoided emotionally intimate relationships that may invite disclosure, such as relying on masturbation, maintaining a set of strictly sexual "fuckbuddies" and, in one instance, using male prostitutes or street hustlers.

Be Indirect

A final strategy for addressing serostatus disclosure was to be indirect about the ways that one conveyed or represented one's serostatus to sex partners. These methods are indirect because they rely on nonverbal communication, partner assumptions, and even obfuscation of one's serostatus. A number of men used their medications and other embodiments of their serostatus as tools for nonverbal disclosure:

> Uh, it shouldn't be too hard to find out. I left traces all over my apartment. I don't put my medications away. So, it's just sitting on the table. [Laughter]. Yeah. And, you know, and sometimes I feel it's a better way, to do it like that, instead of going through the awkwardness. (Asian or Pacific Islander transgender, age 32, San Francisco)

Other men believed that they conveyed their serostatus to their partners by mentioning or exhibiting various embodiments of their serostatus: that they received disability payments, worked in HIV/AIDS services, lived in an HIV/AIDS residence, or had visible HIV/AIDS symptoms (a detailed discussion of how men made assumptions about partner serostatus is provided in chap. 8, this volume).

Some men felt that their participation in bathhouses, sex clubs, and other public sex environments should signify their HIV-positive status to partners whom they met in those environments (see also chap. 12, this volume):

> If it's in a sex house, I don't feel that it's necessary that I tell them. I'm just assuming they are and that that's why they're there. And I'm assuming that they know I am or I wouldn't end up there. (White male, age 46, New York)

In addition to participation in public sex environments, a few men who avoided verbal serostatus disclosures felt that their willingness to have unprotected sex signified their HIV-positive status. Men who took this perspective believed that unprotected sex reflected a lack of concern about acquiring HIV and that this lack of concern should convey to others that they were HIV-positive. One participant therefore explained, "The willingness for me to have sex without a condom—that's how I try and tell my sex partner" (Latino male, age 33, New York). The association between unprotected sex and being HIV-positive was magnified within the context of public sex environments:

> I look at it as though I'm in San Francisco or New York and you're in the bath house, something like that, and somebody drags you into a

room and they're having sex and they don't even ask or pull out a condom or ask you about anything. But I'm assuming that that's their willing consent to contract anything that they might get from you, that they're already HIV-positive or worse. And, you know, you don't go to a place like that and exhibit that behavior and not be that way. (White male, age 34, New York)

Under this perspective, men believed that their (or their partner's) willingness to have unprotected sex effectively served as an indirect form of serostatus disclosure, particularly within public sex environments.

A few men discussed ways that they obfuscated the fact that they were HIV-positive, using statements that were designed to create ambiguity about their serostatus. One man reported that he sometimes responded to partner queries about his serostatus by stating that he just had an HIV test and was still waiting to receive the result:

Or you give him, you know, the whole story: "I just went for the test. I'm waiting—oh, my god, what day is today? I'm supposed to be getting—I'm supposed to go for the test results [laughter], and I'm afraid because I did things," and you start telling him you're HIV-positive if you see him another day. "Hey, guy, I'm sorry. The test came out positive. [Laughter]. I'm HIV-positive," and you just like wait. (Latino male, age 33, New York)

This approach allowed him to skirt initial acknowledgments of his HIV-positive status while preserving the option of future disclosure with the partner. A different man commented that he once replied to partner inquiries about his serostatus by simply stating that he didn't know:

I mean, once in a while people will say, "Are you positive?" you know, and I'm sorry, but you don't ask somebody who's a stranger, "Are you positive?" when you're just about to go down on them in some back room or something, you know, or in a sauna, in a bath house; it just doesn't make sense to me, so I always said I didn't know. I didn't want to say, "No, I'm not positive" and maybe let them think that. I always said, "I don't know" because I didn't want to deal directly with the issue. (Latino male, age 33, New York)

These obfuscation practices appeared to grow from powerful and conflicting desires to neither lie nor tell.

Combined, Shifting, and Unplanned Strategies

It was uncommon for any one man to use a single approach for addressing issues of serostatus disclosure. More often, participants described a synthesis of approaches, such as the following mix of play it safe, it all depends, and tell before sex:

I think I've come up with an uneasy solution for myself, which is that if it's going to be casual sex, which I know is going to be safe sex—I mean I'll make it safe sex— I don't feel I need to tell. If it's going to be a relationship—if it's somebody I have a feeling that it's going to be a relationship with, then I'll hold off on sex, and I'll tell them before we have sex. (White male, age 33, New York)

It was also common for men to rely on one or more disclosure strategies at the same time that they professed a preference for HIV-positive partners for sex and dating (in other words, staying positive). Many men in addition indicated that, regardless of their approaches to disclosure, they would honor partner inquiries about their serostatus (it all depends—if they ask).

Some men further discussed how they made ongoing shifts in their disclosure strategies as they grew in their acceptance of their illness and acquired experience with disclosure over time. It was rare for men to state that they did not have a strategy for addressing serostatus disclosure issues with romantic and sex partners. However, even for those who did not, the disclosure practices that they described usually fit into one of the identified strategies (e.g., play it safe or forms of it all depends). The relative lack of spontaneity in men's approaches to disclosure reflected the strong significance and forethought that many men invested in the issue.

RELATIONSHIPS BETWEEN SEROSTATUS DISCLOSURE AND SEXUAL RISK BEHAVIORS

In general, men described an indirect relationship between serostatus disclosure practices and sexual risk taking, which was strongly moderated by knowledge or assumptions regarding partner serostatus. This relationship contained two important elements. First, serostatus disclosure practices often determined whether a man was aware of his partner's serostatus. As noted earlier, disclosure practices were usually mutual, in that verbal disclosure (or an inquiry) from one partner was often reciprocated through disclosure (or a corresponding inquiry) from the other partner. Conversely, if neither partner raised the issue of HIV serostatus, then mutual nondisclosure typically occurred. Second, men described their knowledge (or assumptions) about partner serostatus as an important influence on their sexual risk practices. The HIV-positive men in this sample were generally extremely cautious about practicing safer sex, particularly with known HIV-negative partners, whereas some were more amenable to having unprotected sex with partners who were either known to be HIV-positive or assumed to be HIV-positive within the context of nondisclosure (see chaps. 3 and 4, this volume). Sexual risk behavior was consequently influenced by serostatus disclosure practices, primarily through their ability to engender awareness of partner serostatus. Additional discussion of the influence of serostatus disclosure and assumptions on sexual risk practices can be found in chapters 8 and 10 (this volume).

DISCUSSION

The interviews evidenced how HIV-serostatus disclosure practices are more complex than a simple dichotomous formulation of whether to verbally disclose one's serostatus to a romantic or sex partner. Men pursued broad behavioral strategies that specified not only whether to disclose their serostatus but also when, where, how, and to whom they would disclose. Some men also pursued strategies that aimed to circumvent the need for disclosure, such as meeting peers through HIV/AIDS services or avoiding close relationships entirely. Furthermore, some men used a set of indirect disclosure strategies that relied on nonverbal communication and partner assumptions as a route toward serostatus disclosure, and some discussed ways that they obfuscated their serostatus with their partners. These examples demonstrate that it may be better to conceptualize serostatus disclosure as a diverse range of practices rather than as a singular act of telling or not telling.

The themes articulated in this chapter contain important implications for HIV prevention with seropositive gay and bisexual men. First, programs should address serostatus disclosure as a significant and ongoing concern of many men. Men were interested in discussing the challenge of disclosure with peers and professionals, and this opens an important opportunity to bring men into wider conversations about their sexual lives and practices. Second, programs should help men consider a range of disclosure practices that will simultaneously meet personal needs and address prevention goals. For example, men who told before sex noted how this practice helped them to feel honest, build trusting relationships, and avoid rejection from partners after having establishing a relationship. Those who played it safe or stayed positive felt that these strategies helped avoid anxiety associated with disclosure. Third, it is important that programs provide men with multiple skill sets for addressing disclosure issues. This not only includes the skills to disclose their serostatus to sexual partners but also strategies for dealing with rejection and the acumen to implement complex, context-sensitive disclosure practices.

This analysis pointed to some differences between participants in New York and San Francisco, which indicated that in general, men in San Francisco had fewer concerns about partner rejection and viewed disclosure as less challenging than did men in New York. This difference most likely reflects differing social climates and responses regarding HIV/AIDS in the two cities. Because stigma and prejudice are the key factors that render serostatus disclosure a recurrent dilemma for many men, this difference also highlights the importance of addressing the "epidemic of stigma" (Herek & Glunt, 1988). Efforts to help HIV-positive gay and bisexual men address the challenge of serostatus disclosure with romantic and sex partners should be coupled with initiatives to fight HIV/AIDS prejudice and should in addition consider the role of serostatus disclosure by HIV seronegative individuals.

The interviews also showed that the serostatus disclosure practices of HIV-positive gay and bisexual men are intimately connected with their sex practices. Complex and competing personal, situational, and ethical considerations prompted many men to view serostatus disclosure as a recurrent challenge in their sexual and romantic lives. The regularity with which men found themselves at the difficult intersection of these issues led many to adopt specific strategies to guide their ongoing serostatus disclosure practices. These strategies were closely connected with the men's sexual and romantic lives in multiple ways: they determined whether men pursued romantic relationships, affected the course of romantic relationships, dictated the partners with whom the men had sex, guided where and how men met partners, and shaped men's sexual risk practices. As a result of these intertwined connections, it is difficult to speak of the men's disclosure practices without discussing their sex practices. Concerns and practices regarding serostatus disclosure therefore exerted a powerful influence over the substance of men's sexual and romantic lives.

REFERENCES

De Rosa, C. J., & Marks, G. (1998). Preventive counseling of HIV-positive men and self-disclosure of serostatus to sex partners: New opportunities for prevention. *Health Psychology, 17,* 1–8.

Dawson, J. M., Fitzpatrick, R. M., Reeves, G., Boulton, M., McLean, J., Hart, G. J., et al. (1994). Awareness of sexual partners' HIV status as an influence upon high-risk sexual behavior among gay men. *AIDS, 8,* 837–841.

Ekstrand, M. L., Stall, R. D., Paul, J. P., Osmond, D. H., & Coates, T. J. (1999). Gay men report high rates of unprotected anal sex with partners of unknown or discordant HIV status. *AIDS, 13,* 1525–1533.

Hays, R. B., McKusick, L., Pollack, L., Hilliard, R., Hoff, C., & Coates, T. J. (1993). Disclosing HIV seropositivity to significant others. *AIDS, 7,* 425–431.

Herek, G. M., Capitanio, J. P., & Widaman, K. F. (2002). HIV-related stigma and knowledge in the United States: Prevalence and trends, 1991–1999. *American Journal of Public Health, 92,* 371–377.

Herek, G. M., & Glunt, E. K. (1988). An epidemic of stigma: Public reactions to AIDS. *American Psychologist, 43,* 886–891.

Hoff, C. C., McKusick, L., Hilliard, B., & Coates, T. J. (1992). The impact of HIV antibody status on gay men's partner preferences: A community perspective. *AIDS Education and Prevention, 4,* 197–204.

Mansergh, G., Marks, G., & Simoni, J. M. (1995). Self-disclosure of HIV infection among men who vary in time since seropositive diagnosis and symptomatic status. *AIDS, 9,* 639–644.

Marks, G., & Crepaz, N. (2001). HIV-positive men's sexual practices in the context of self-disclosure of HIV status. *Journal of Acquired Immune Deficiency Syndromes, 27,* 79–85.

Marks, G., Richardson, J. L., & Maldonado, N. (1991). Self-disclosure of HIV infection to sexual partners. *American Journal of Public Health, 81,* 1321–1323.

Mason, H. R., Marks, G., Simoni, J. M., Ruiz, M. S., & Richardson, J. L. (1995). Culturally sanctioned secrets? Latino men's nondisclosure of HIV infection to family, friends, and lovers. *Health Psychology, 14,* 6–12.

Mason, H. R. C., Simoni, J. M., Marks, G., Johnson, C. J., & Richardson, J. L. (1997). Missed opportunities? Disclosure of HIV infection and support seeking among HIV+ African-American and European-American men. *AIDS and Behavior, 1,* 155–162.

Niccolai, L. M., Dorst, D., Myers, L., & Kissinger, P. J. (1999). Disclosure of HIV status to sexual partners: Predictors and temporal patterns. *Sexually Transmitted Diseases, 26,* 281–285.

Stein, M. D., Freedberg, K. A., Sullivan, L. M., Savetsky, J., Levenson, S. M., Hingson, R., et al. (1998). Sexual ethics: Disclosure of HIV-positive status to partners. *Archives of Internal Medicine, 158,* 253–257.

Wolitski, R. J., Rietmeijer, C. A. M., Goldbaum, G. M., & Wilson, R. M. (1998). HIV serostatus disclosure among gay and bisexual men in four American cities: General patterns and relation to sexual practices. *AIDS Care, 10,* 599–610.

Zierler, S., Cunningham, W. E., Andersen, R., Shapiro, M. F., Bozzette, S. A., Nakazono, T., et al. (2000). Violence victimization after HIV infection in a U.S. probability sample of adult patients in primary care. *American Journal of Public Health, 90,* 208–221.

8

GUESSING GAMES: SEX PARTNER SEROSTATUS ASSUMPTIONS AMONG HIV-POSITIVE GAY AND BISEXUAL MEN

ANN O'LEARY

The HIV epidemic among gay and bisexual men in the United States has been ongoing for 22 years, indicating sustained transmission. It might be argued that the epidemic would have been eliminated, or at least greatly reduced, if all men were tested and disclosed their HIV status to all partners, as serodiscordant disclosers are unlikely to practice risky behaviors together (Dawson et al., 1994). As discussed in chapter 7 (this volume), disclosure of HIV infection is difficult because men may fear rejection or even violence on disclosure. In the absence of disclosure, men must use whatever means are available to make decisions about engaging in sexual behaviors on the basis of the partner's HIV status. Many seropositive men, while loathe to engage in behavior that might put a seronegative partner at risk, are less

This chapter was authored by an employee of the United States government as part of official duty and is considered to be in the public domain. Any views expressed herein do not necessarily represent the views of the United States government, and the author's participation in the work is not meant to serve as an official endorsement.

concerned about their behaviors with a partner who is already infected (Gómez, 1999). Although such behaviors between two seropositive men carry the risk for infection with other sexually transmitted diseases or even superinfection with a medication-resistant strain of HIV, these outcomes are perceived as less serious than the transmission of HIV infection.

One reason for assessing risk before engaging in sex with a partner is to avoid using condoms. Research has shown that most, if not all, men find condom use to substantially reduce the pleasure, intimacy, and spontaneity of sex (Dilley et al., 2002). Thus, to the degree that motivated reasoning (Kunda, 1990; see also Kaplan & Shayne, 1993, for a general discussion of motivated reasoning about HIV risk) may influence behavior, the tendency should generally be for men to assume that their partner or potential partner is seroconcordant so that condom use is unnecessary (or less important). That is, seronegative men should be motivated to believe that their partners are seronegative, and seropositive men (such as the respondents in the Seropositive Urban Men's Study [SUMS]) should wish to believe that their partners are seropositive.

Research has shown that gay men hold stereotypes about men who are and are not HIV-infected (Gold & Skinner, 1993, 1996; Gold, Skinner, & Ross, 1992). In one study, men were asked to describe recent sexual encounters and were then given a checklist of possible justifications that they might have used for engaging in risky behavior without incurring excessive guilt or fear (Gold et al., 1992). Some of the justifications had to do with assumptions about the partner's HIV status (e.g., that he must already be infected).

In another study, men were presented with descriptions of hypothetical gay men and asked to rate the likelihood that these men were infected (Gold & Skinner, 1996; Gold, Skinner, & Hinchy, 1999). Assessment was affected by physical attractiveness, intelligence, healthy appearance, and personality of these hypothetical men (Gold & Skinner, 1996). In a subsequent study that included more possible characteristics (Gold et al., 1999), ratings were affected by preferred haunts (such as public sex environments), preferred role in sex, clothing style (e.g., leather), occupation at an AIDS service organization, and sexual orientation (straight men were rated as less likely to be infected).

As suggested by the retrospective endorsements of assumptions in Gold's work, it appears that men use their assumptions in their sexual decision making. Work conducted by the author before beginning work on SUMS revealed two startling sets of experiences, as reported by HIV-positive men in a focus group: On the one hand, they received angry reactions from HIV-negative partners to whom they disclosed their own status only after having sex (the HIV-negative men clearly believed that HIV-infected men have a duty to disclose that fact beforehand); but on the other hand, they assumed that HIV-negative partners would make their status known before sex and that if they did not, they too must be HIV-positive (O'Leary, 1996). This apparent tendency for men to assume partner seroconcordance, whether negative or positive, seems potentially dangerous.

Two hundred and fifty gay and bisexual participants in SUMS (see chap. 1, this volume, for a full description of the study) were asked whether they had made serostatus assumptions about sex partners and if so on what they had based those assumptions. Narrative responses that described assumptions were identified, and the assumptions were found to adhere to several general themes with regard to the partner: physical appearance, sexual behavior, venues frequented, personal characteristics such as age, medical evidence, and instinct or "sixth sense."

PHYSICAL APPEARANCE OF PARTNERS

Many men with whom we spoke based their assumptions about serostatus on aspects of their partner's appearance. For the most part, an unhealthy physical appearance led them to believe that the partner was infected. Symptoms of wasting or lipodystrophy (a side effect of highly active antiretroviral treatment or HAART) were given as the basis for assuming a partner was infected:

> And I think the guy who was—who lives in Palm Springs—he and his partner are HIV-positive, because you have—the body takes some shape, the people with AIDS, in some time of your illness. (Latino male, age 32, San Francisco)

> It's just a certain look that I know, I think I know when somebody has the virus . . . It is a face and it is in their eyes, you could just see it . . . I know once I was walking in Hoboken and . . . I had passed a man who looked very—the virus had really taken its toll, and it is a very drawn face, very thin. . . . So I kind of know, I guess, by now. (Black male, age 34, New York)

Conversely, men who did not have "the look" were presumed to be seronegative: "Yes, I assumed he was negative because I could—I didn't see any visible symptoms" (Latino male, age 31, New York).

For some SUMS participants, actual symptoms (which might or might not indicate HIV illness) may be disregarded on the basis of overall physical appearance.

> Well, he didn't have the look, meaning he didn't look too sickly. I mean, people who are real, real sick with AIDS have a strange look to

them. And he didn't have that look that I could tell. He did have these weird sores, but he seemed a little bit overweight. He didn't look gaunt or emaciated. And you know, that's what I mean. (Black male, age 48, New York)

For this respondent, the perception that the partner was HIV-negative was not associated with a decision to engage in safer behavior. "Well, he let me fuck him without a condom" (Black male, age 48, New York). Often these assertions were qualified by recognition of the fallibility of the strategy of using physical appearance to assume serostatus:

Well, that's, you know, it's—it's impossible to judge by the looks of somebody, but of course by the looks of them I—he looked pretty healthy to me. Because somebody that—good-looking, looks healthy, that—the chances are that they're they are healthy as opposed to somebody that's . . . not looking well. (mixed race/ethnicity male, age 47, New York)

One is reminded of the work by Howard Leventhal and colleagues about "common-sense" theories of health, specifically the study in which people with hypertension reported knowing that hypertension is asymptomatic but believing that they had learned to detect when their own blood pressure was elevated (Meyer, Leventhal, & Gutmann, 1985).

Sexual risk behavior was generally influenced by serostatus assumptions. Indeed, this latter respondent did not put his presumed-negative partner at risk for infection, "I think it was, a lot safer for him than it was for me . . . there was no oral sex, no anal sex, on his part" (mixed race/ethnicity male, age 47, New York).

However, assumptions that a partner is HIV-seropositive and decisions to engage in risky behavior were more common. One respondent insisted that his partner was HIV-positive on the basis of his appearance despite having been told the contrary. When asked why he didn't believe that the partner was really HIV-negative, this respondent replied:

Okay, why? Because he's too skinny, and I think I realize sometime he have problem with his stomach, you know. He's very sensitive to certain food. . . . His skin is not the normal color; the color is kind of pale. (Black male, age 35, New York)

In summary, assumptions were made about partner serostatus on the basis of whether the partner looked healthy or ill. It is arguably true that looking ill is a better indicator of HIV-positive status than looking healthy is of HIV-negative status. HIV-infected individuals generally look healthy for much more time than they look ill. However, more of our respondents used the former strategy than the latter. This strategy often resulted in willingness to engage in transmission-risk behavior.

SEXUAL BEHAVIOR OF PARTNERS

Many men formed assumptions about partner serostatus primarily on the basis of the sexual behavior that the partner was willing to engage in with the respondent. Indeed, sexual behavior was commonly the basis for assumptions. Partners who appeared to be unconcerned for their own safety were presumed to be infected, or presumed likely to become infected eventually, regardless of whether they engaged in risk behavior with the respondent:

> I guess I'd have to say I assumed he might be [positive], the way he charged into it and didn't ask anything, didn't do anything to make me think otherwise. (White male, age 28, New York)

> Well, if he's out there, you know, and he's sleeping around that easily, and I have to tell him to put the rubber on, I'm pretty much sure if he wasn't positive at the time, it's just a matter of time before he is. (Black male, age 45, New York)

> I assume that he's positive, because of, we have unsafe sex. He's never mentioned the use of a condom. And he wants me to come in his ass. (White male, age 34, New York)

The previously mentioned finding that HIV-negative partners would make their status known before sex and that if they did not, they too must be HIV-positive was confirmed by some of the SUMS respondents. The seropositive men in SUMS also assumed that HIV-negative men would speak up before engaging in sex:

> I assumed that since he didn't ask, that his situation was probably the same as mine. Usually people who are not positive, you know, are negative, will ask. That's mostly what I—mostly what I find. (White male, age 44, New York)

Of course, this belief may well be made on the basis of the respondent's having assumed HIV-positive status for many partners who did not speak up but who in fact were HIV-negative. In one instance, a partner assumed the respondent to be HIV-negative: "He said, 'We're both [negative].' Assuming that I was" (White male, age 35, New York).

> Some respondents assumed that their partners were HIV-negative because they used condoms, "I assume because he wore a condom that he was probably . . . negative, so to protect himself." (White male, age 29, New York)

On the other hand, other measures to protect the respondent were seen as implying that the partner was infected:

I certainly got the impression that he might be HIV-positive based on a couple of things that he said. First of all, he asked me where I wanted him to come. And he sort of implied to me that he wanted me to fuck him. And some other stuff like that. (White male, age 35, New York)

Although most respondents endorsed making some assumptions, one denied having assumed the serostatus of a recent partner, saying:

That's why I said I couldn't. I couldn't. I couldn't at all. I mean, somebody that will not use a rubber, you'd think that he will have— that he'll do it with everybody, but that doesn't mean anything because he maybe not do it with everybody and not be HIV, but you would think that somebody who's—I would think it's more ignorance than anything else . . . because I look healthy. That's the trick;, that's the bad part. A lot of people think because people who are HIV, you don't have to look it. If you take care of yourself, you don't have to look no different than you. (Latino male, age 32, New York)

Public sex venues were seen by some respondents as being frequented predominantly by HIV-positive men:

I assumed that he was HIV, and he did too. I mean, the way I see this is if you're in a bookstore, and you pick somebody up, or you're having sex in a bookstore, then you might as well assume that somebody you're playing with is HIV-positive. You know? And if it turns out that you're not HIV-positive and you're fuckin' around with somebody who didn't tell you they were HIV- positive, then it's your own fuckin' fault for being in the bookstore to begin with. You know? I mean, everybody knows what kind of sex goes on in those places, and it's not usually safe sex. So, if you run into somebody who is HIV-positive, then you did it to yourself. (Latino male, age 35, San Francisco)

PERSONAL CHARACTERISTICS OF PARTNERS

A variety of personal characteristics were thought to convey information regarding a partner's serostatus. One was age, with older men being seen as more likely to be HIV-positive because they had had more opportunities to become infected:

He's 43, okay? So, he done it all and done been there. Like I told him this morning, "You may as well . . . go down to the AIDS Foundation and get your number off the shelf. (Black male, age 35, San Francisco)

Residing in neighborhoods popular with gay men was also seen as being associated with HIV-positive status, "I assume everybody in the Castro's HIV-positive. In one way, shape, or form" (Native American male, age 41, San Francisco).

Other personal characteristics, such as failure to plan for the future, were seen as being associated with HIV-positive status and possibly impending death: "He strikes me as a perfect profile of somebody who's positive. Not saving money for anything. He's not working" (Latino male, age 35, San Francisco).

Even avoidance of the topic of HIV led to the assumption of HIV-positive status:

> I kinda assumed that he was because he didn't want to bring it up. He was—it was like one of those topics where it was—when it was mentioned, it was quickly, you know, taken somewhere else. (Black male, age 36, San Francisco)

Surprisingly, one respondent's willingness to discuss the topic led to the assumption that the partner was seronegative, rather than as a possible entree to disclosure of an HIV-positive status:

> And then he said, "Well, most people my age are dead." And I said, "I assume you mean from AIDS." He goes, "Yes." He goes, "Almost all my friends have died." . . . I just assumed that he is probably negative. I mean, if he's saying that, but I don't know. (White male, age 34, New York)

Partners who were believed to be heterosexual or bisexual were seen as less likely to be infected:

> Well, I met him at—when he came out—he said he came out of a relationship, his wife just died. And he's got sons. And he doesn't look like he goes out to bars. He just doesn't dress like a gay man. He dresses like a straight man. So I'm just assuming he's HIV-negative through that. (Black male, age 32, New York)

Sexual inexperience with men was taken to indicate heterosexuality and thus HIV-negative status: "I assumed he was hetero because of his lack of experience, which is not necessarily a good assumption" (White male, age 46, New York). One respondent paired sexual behavior with bisexuality to assume HIV-negativity:

> Because he is married with a child. And also the condom. He also wore a condom. Also wanted the condom. So just like I make the assumption that if people don't want the condom, they are HIV-positive; and if they do want the condom, they are HIV-negative. (White male, age 46, New York)

MEDICAL EVIDENCE

Observing medical evidence that a person is being treated for HIV/AIDS can also be the basis for assuming that person to be HIV-positive.

Evidence of HIV infection was used to assume a partner was infected and to assume a partner knew the respondent's HIV-positive status:

> I think the only thing that I could say about the whole experience was that I knew he was HIV-positive, even though he never told me. And the only reason I say that is I—I'd—like from here to the end of that desk, we were next to his bed, and he was taking these pictures. And I looked over and there's this medicine thing that I'm—I know what they are. And if this was his bedroom, it could only mean to me that he was HIV-positive, even if he didn't want to say it. (Native American male, age 41, San Francisco)

> The other one is in my calendar, you know, sometimes you know about certain agencies, that would be HIV doctors, psychiatrists at the IVC clinic. . . . Oh, I have another one . . . and it's [an] HIV project, and I have another one say, "Latinos against HIV" or something like that, but these are little posters I have to in the kitchen. (Black male, age 35, New York)

Partners who frequented HIV-related venues or engaged in HIV-related activities were often believed to be infected themselves: "But he did make some mention of the fact that he was at GMHC. So I guess he was—he is positive, but it never came up" (Black male, age 30, New York).

> I saw him in the past, and he [was] involved with some AIDS agency. And when I was working at Wellness Center, he did come over and give out some brochures and fliers like that, so I'm pretty sure he's HIV-positive. (Asian or Pacific Islander male, age 38, San Francisco)

"SIXTH SENSE"

Finally, some respondents seemed to believe that HIV-positive men exuded some vague, nonspecific quality that could be detected, that was shared by themselves as well as potential partners:

> Not verbally, no. But there's a certain energy that you exude about it. You know what I mean. Hell, I do anyway. I know it—it's clear that I'm positive. I mean, I've been handed the cards [invitations into SUMS, which were given to everyone, irrespective of perceived HIV status] by you people all the time. (Latino male, age 32, New York)

> I kind of had the feeling that he was, also. You know, for people who are HIV, you kind of get that sense. It's just like, you know, you're gay, you—it takes one to know one. And I got that sense, that vibe from him. You know? (Latino male, age 29, San Francisco)

DISCUSSION

Many SUMS participants reported having assumed the serostatus of sex partners. Consonant with motivated reasoning theory, most assumed that partners were HIV-positive (seroconcordant) and used this assumption in deciding to have unsafe sex. Assuming seroconcordance of sex partners may justify unsafe behavior and may also alleviate guilt associated with having risky sex with partners of unknown serostatus and thus be a form of motivated reasoning.

Some of the assumptions about partner serostatus that emerged in this study were similar to those identified by Gold and colleagues (Gold & Skinner, 1993, 1996; Gold et al., 1992, 1999). Indeed, almost every justification described in the Gold studies emerged in the SUMS study. As with participants in Gold's studies, SUMS participants used physical appearance to determine partner serostatus, with healthy and good looks implying HIV-negative status. Heterosexual identity, although associated with HIV-positive status in Gold's work, was thought by SUMS participants to connote negative status. Like the participants in Gold's studies, SUMS participants believed frequenting public sex environments to establish HIV-positive status. SUMS participants, like Gold's, believed association with AIDS service organizations to indicate HIV-positive status.

These data suggest that men engage in complex thought processes when deciding whether disclosure of serostatus is necessary, one of which involves using whatever information is available to guess the status of a partner or potential partner. Similarly, SUMS participants reported many complex strategies for reducing sexual risk, including "gray-area behaviors" (Wolitski & Branson, 2002) such as withdrawal before ejaculation and taking known partner serostatus into account in deciding safe positions for anal sex—in other words, insertive (top) or receptive (bottom). Little research has been conducted to document these thought processes or to determine how best to integrate them into risk-reduction interventions.

Risk-reduction interventions, whether designed for HIV-negative or HIV-positive individuals, should attempt to discourage the tendency to make assumptions about serostatus and to use them to justify unsafe behavior. A notable example is a campaign sponsored by the San Francisco AIDS Foundation, called "How do you know what you know?" Campaign materials included posters, billboards, and GoCARD postcards that read: "I'm positive. I assumed he was too. How do you know what you know?" Materials typically showed two men, each thinking a different thought. For example, one was thinking, "He'd tell me if he was negative," while the other thought, "He'd tell me if he was positive." Assumptions regarding gray-area behaviors were also addressed in this campaign (e.g., "He came inside me. He must be negative," and "I came inside him. He must be positive"). Unfortunately, this campaign has not been evaluated.

Gold and Rosenthal (1995, 1998) have conducted two intervention studies testing the approach of encouraging close examination of serostatus assumptions and other so-called self-justifications. In the first study (Gold & Rosenthal, 1995), men were asked to think back to a recent risky sexual encounter and identify justifications that they had used; then they were asked how reasonable those justifications had been. Gold and Rosenthal found that assumptions about partner serostatus were composed of a subset of justifications. Men receiving the intervention reported fewer lapses to unsafe sex than did men in receiving a standard type of HIV education. A subsequent study (Gold & Rosenthal, 1998) was designed with two objectives: (a) to establish that the earlier result had not been simply a result of revivifying a risky experience and (b) to test a different type of intervention, one using mass media elements to present self-justifications. This intervention was similar to the "How do you know what you know?" campaign. In one condition, participants vividly imagined recent sexual encounters but did not identify or evaluate self-justifications, demonstrating that the earlier effect had indeed been a result of the self-justification component of the intervention. However, the mass media intervention was not effective. The investigators attributed the difference between the two self-justification intervention formats to the fact that the earlier one had had more personal relevance, causing deeper cognitive processing of the self-justification. This finding suggests that the "How do you know what you know?" campaign may not have been effective in changing men's behavior, although men in San Francisco during this campaign were exposed to much more information.

Perhaps the most pressing research need is the development and evaluation of interventions and programs that directly encourage serostatus disclosure, particularly by individuals who are already infected, but also by those who believe themselves to be uninfected. Because disclosure does carry some risks, no HIV-positive person can be expected to disclose with every partner. It may be easier to encourage HIV-negative men to disclose their status to partners, but as noted earlier, they may not be believed. In addition, seroconversion may have taken place since the person was tested, and people who have been recently infected are more infectious (e.g., Brandt et al., 1996). However, under some conditions, disclosure of HIV-negative status may be reliable—for example, if status has been determined on the basis of a negative antibody test result received at least 2 months in the past and the person has engaged in only safe behavior since testing.

The assertion by Gold and colleagues that serostatus assumptions are self-justifications cannot be addressed in this study because we did not collect data relevant to this issue. However, in no narrative did any indication emerge that the participant had such an insight. Indeed, one is struck by the fact that many of these bases for partner serostatus assumptions are often likely to yield accurate assessments. For example, noting the partner's HIV medications should work to confirm positive serostatus most of the time (although in the example given, the respondent was not certain about whether the room he was in was indeed his partner's bedroom, leaving some doubt about the effectiveness of the strategy in this instance). The appearance of lipodystrophy may be quite an effective identifier of men who are HIV-positive, as long as it is clearly understood that the converse— that absence of lipodystrophy does not imply HIV-negative status—is not true. The use of a partner's sexual risk behavior to assume HIV-positive status appears to be more problematic, if it is indeed common for both HIV-positive and HIV-negative men to assume seroconcordance.

In summary, these results suggest the importance of interventions that address assumptions about serostatus and other related assumptions, as well as interventions that encourage disclosure of serostatus before sex. In this way, individuals will be encouraged to make sexual decisions based on information rather than on assumptions that may or may not be accurate.

REFERENCES

Brandt, C. D., Sison, A. V., Rakusan, T. A., Kaufman, T. E., Saxena, E. S., O'Donnell, R. M., et al. (1996). HIV DNA blood levels in vertically infected pediatric patients: Variations with age, association with disease progression, and comparison with blood levels in infected mothers. *Journal of Acquired Immune Deficiency Syndromes and Human Retrovirology, 13*, 254–261.

Dawson, J. M., Fizpatrick, R. M., Reeves, G., Boulton, M., McLean, J., Hart, G. J., et al. (1994). Awareness of sexual partners' HIV status as an influence upon high-risk sexual behavior among gay men. *AIDS, 8*, 837–841.

Dilley, J. W., McFarland, W., Woods, W. J., Sabatino, J., Lihatsh, T., Adler, B., et al. (2002). Thoughts associated with unprotected anal intercourse among men at high risk in San Francisco 1997–1999. *Psychology and Health, 17*, 235–246.

Gold, R. S., & Rosenthal, D. A. (1995). Preventing unprotected anal intercourse in gay men: A comparison of two intervention techniques. *International Journal of STD and AIDS, 6*, 89–94.

Gold, R. S., & Rosenthal, D. A. (1998). Examining self-justifications for unsafe sex as a technique of AIDS education: The importance of personal relevance. *International Journal of STD and AIDS, 9*, 208–213.

Gold, R. S., & Skinner, M. J. (1993). Desire for unprotected intercourse preceding its occurrence: The case of young gay men with an anonymous partner. *International Journal of STD and AIDS, 4*, 326–329.

Gold, R. S., & Skinner, M. J. (1996). Judging a book by its cover: Gay men's use of perceptible characteristics to infer antibody status. *International Journal of STD and AIDS, 7*, 39–43.

Gold, R. S., Skinner, M. J., & Hinchy, J. (1999). Gay men's stereotypes about who is HIV infected: A further study. *International Journal of STD and AIDS, 10*, 666–605.

Gold, R. S., Skinner, M. J., & Ross, M. W. (1992). Situational factors and thought processes associated with unprotected intercourse in young gay men. *AIDS, 6*, 1021–1030.

Gómez, C. A. (1999). *Sexual HIV transmission risk behaviors among HIV positive injecting drug users and HIV positive men who have sex with men: Implications for interventions*. Paper presented at the National HIV Prevention Conference, Atlanta, GA.

Kaplan, B. J., & Shayne, V. T. (1993). Unsafe sex: Decision-making biases and heuristics. *AIDS Education and Prevention, 5*, 294–301.

Kunda, Z. (1990). The case for motivated reasoning. *Psychological Bulletin, 108*, 480–498.

Meyer, D., Leventhal, H., & Gutmann, M. (1985). Common-sense models of illness: The example of hypertension. *Health Psychology, 4*, 115–135.

O'Leary, A. (1996). [Experiences of HIV-seropositive men in public sex venues]. Unpublished data.

Wolitski, R. J., & Branson, B. M. (2002). "Grey area behaviors" and partner selection strategies: Working toward a comprehensive approach to reducing the sexual transmission of HIV. In A. O'Leary (Ed.), *Beyond condoms: Alternative approaches to HIV prevention* (pp. 173–198). New York: Kluwer Academic.

9

CAUSE AND EFFECT: ATTRIBUTIONS ABOUT BECOMING HIV-POSITIVE AND SAFER-SEX DECISION MAKING AMONG GAY AND BISEXUAL MEN

DAVID S. BIMBI AND JEFFREY T. PARSONS

Assigning responsibility for an individual's behaviors, such as initiating condom use, has its basis in attribution theory (Heider, 1958). According to this theory, individuals in social situations use the information available to them to make moral or causal judgments for events occurring within that situation. Attributions help individuals assign responsibility and blame for events (Kelley, 1967) and are self-protective against negative effects such as lowered self-esteem, blame, or guilt.

Attempting to explain events is a fundamental part of human nature. Social psychologists have also suggested that attributions serve a defensive function (Shaver, 1975). When individuals take responsibility for adverse events, they protect themselves from the thought that accidents happen and that negative events can occur randomly; thus, they feel as if they

The authors thank Vita Rabinowitz for her insight and Gideon Feldstein and Florian Fessel for their assistance in preparing this chapter.

133

have more control over their lives and feel more secure. Conversely, when individuals assign blame to others, they can avoid feelings of guilt and shame for the event in question.

Much research on attribution theory over the past several decades has focused on the attributions that people make regarding who is responsible for a particular event or behavior (Fiske & Taylor, 1991). Psychologists have rarely focused, however, on the attributions that individuals may make for their own behavior and how these attributions relate to future behaviors or other attitudes. Ingledew, Hardy, and Cooper (1996) have commented that applications of attribution theory to the examination of health behaviors have been surprisingly few.

Given the effect of HIV infection in terms of medical issues (difficult medication schedules and opportunistic illnesses) and the potential for personal loss (facing rejection and stigma), becoming HIV-positive certainly may be viewed as an event that will be attributed to someone or something. HIV-positive individuals may seek to make sense of becoming infected by making attributions to themselves or their sex partners for who is at fault for their seroconversion. As one man in the Seropositive Urban Men's Study (SUMS; see chap. 1, this volume, for full description of the study) observed, "We have a tendency as human beings to kind of blame things on people . . . Oh, they ask me all the time, 'Who infected you?'" (Latino male, age 32, San Francisco).

Attribution theory has been used in a few studies to understand safer sexual behaviors of gay and bisexual men. Some HIV-positive men will assign responsibility for their infection, and this may influence their attitudes toward safer sex practices and reported behaviors. In the case of HIV-negative gay and bisexual men, for example, those who placed the blame on themselves for previous episodes of unsafe anal sex were more likely to report unsafe sex in the future (Curtin, Stephens, & Roffman, 1997). In a study of HIV-positive men, it was found that those who blamed themselves for their infection engaged in more unsafe sex (Taylor et al., 1992). Conversely, another study of HIV-positive men found that attributing the blame for their HIV infection to others was related to unprotected anal insertive intercourse (Bingman, Marks, & Crepaz, 2001). These findings support the notion that investigations using an attributional framework may provide new approaches to HIV prevention for HIV-positive men (Cohen & Hubert, 1997).

Given the empirical support for the connection between attributions for seroconversion and unprotected sex (Bingman et al., 2001), HIV-positive individuals' attributions about their seroconversion may be related to attitudes about protecting others from infection, which then will lead to condom use or nonuse. The theoretical models of helping and coping by Brickman et al. (1982) could provide some insight into the relationship between such attributions and attitudes. This theory focuses on prosocial behavior (helping and coping with problems) and the attributions that individuals make for responsibility for initial problems and subsequent solutions. Seroconversion is clearly a problem, and protecting others from infection with HIV is just as clearly a prosocial behavior (taking responsibility for protecting others or making attributions about who is responsible for safer-sex decisions); therefore, this theory may be applicable in seeking to understand the sexual behaviors of HIV-positive individuals.

In the SUMS study, 250 HIV-positive gay and bisexual men were interviewed in depth about their sexual lives and behaviors as well as living with HIV. Of these, 50 men spontaneously mentioned attributions about their seroconversion (the interview protocol for the SUMS study did not include questions on this topic). In this chapter, the attributional statements made by this subset of 50 men regarding their seroconversion are examined for common themes. Many of the men's statements included a connection between their attribution for their seroconversion and their attitudes about protecting their sex partners from HIV. Therefore, this relationship is also explored for themes and patterns.

BLAMING ONESELF FOR HIV INFECTION

Of the 50 who made attributional statements about their HIV infection, 23 men clearly assigned responsibility to themselves. Four themes emerged from a review of statements made regarding self-blame for infection with HIV: promiscuity, inconsistent safer sex practices, drug and alcohol use–abuse, and various forms of self-punishment.

Sexual Promiscuity

There were men who clearly lay the blame for their HIV infection on their promiscuous sexual pasts, for which they take full responsibility. For example, "Then I was told I had HIV and it didn't flip me out . . . I know my promiscuous life" (Black male, age 40, New York City). Similarly,

> It hasn't involved me one bit. First it did. But I wasn't surprised, because when I first came to New York, I was very promiscuous. So it wasn't nothing I didn't expect. So it wasn't a surprise to me. So it didn't bother me. (Black male, age 34, New York City)

Others tied their promiscuity specifically to a sense of fatalism that they had about becoming HIV-positive: "There was never any doubt in my mind that I was going to end up with it" (Latino male, age 33, New York City), and "Given the history of my sexual partners, I pretty much concluded that I was going to be HIV-positive. I purposely didn't take the test for seven years" (Latino male, age 34, New York City).

Others attributed their infection to their sexual promiscuity but refused to be fatalistic in terms of their reactions:

> In a sense it didn't surprise me, but then I didn't react like most people would, pronounce a death sentence, because I know and I believe that all sickness is not unto death and I prayed about it. And I said well, you know, this is the recompense I brought on myself for my sexual promiscuity, so therefore I have to deal with this. (Black male, age 37, San Francisco)

Safer Sex Practices

The men in SUMS also clearly attributed their HIV-positive status to their practice of unsafe sexual behaviors. Some men attributed their seroconversion to the previous absence of any safer sexual behaviors or strategies, and others discussed this notion in terms of inconsistent safer sex practices. One man stated, "But there have been times I've been unsafe and, you know, otherwise I wouldn't be sitting here now" (Black male, age 45, New York City). Said another,

> Except there were times—obviously, there were times when I wasn't safe, and that's when I was infected. So my general philosophy was to practice safer sex, except in situations where it just got out of hand and I let myself go. (Asian or Pacific Islander male, age 36, San Francisco)

Attributing seroconversion to inconsistent safer sex practices rather than to the number of past sex partners avoids the emotionally and morally laden minefield of attitudes regarding the stigma-laden term *promiscuity*. Attributing HIV infection to unsafe sex becomes a matter of a lapse of judgment and not necessarily a character defect or deficiency. However, one man connected this theme of unsafe sex directly to the previous theme of sexual promiscuity, "I knew I was being highly promiscuous, and, even though I was safe most of the time, most of the time doesn't cut it" (White male, age 28, New York City).

Substance Use and Abuse

All of the men who mentioned substance use as part of their self-blame directly attributed engaging in unprotected sex to impaired judgment (see chap. 11, this volume, for more about substance use among the men in SUMS). "That's how I got sick, from getting drunk one night and going out and using and having sex without condoms. It's my own fault; that's why I have nobody to blame but myself, you know" (Latino male, age 40,

New York City). This was most clearly stated by one man, who said, "I didn't think, you know? See, the thing is that when you drink and have recreational drugs, it really impairs you" (Asian or Pacific Islander male, age 51, San Francisco).

The emphasis on drug and alcohol use–abuse could be conceptualized as a distancing strategy. Although these men have clearly taken some level of personal responsibility for their initial HIV infection, the underlying subtext is that the drugs and alcohol were the causative factor. Implicit in this strategy of self-blame is the assumption that had they not been using drugs or drinking, perhaps they would not be HIV-positive today.

> It was Valium. I used to take Valium years ago. And I'll tell you, if it wasn't for Valium, I don't think I wouldn't have gotten AIDS. I think Valium got me AIDS. . . . And, you know, like I want to sleep alone, but I took the Valium that night and I stayed over their place. I didn't want to go back to my place. And I woke up in the morning with a penis in my butt, literally. And it turns out that was the guy that gave it to me. (White male, age 39, New York City)

Thus, although these men attribute blame to themselves, there are some indicators of contextual blaming, in terms of the context of being high or unable to assume full responsibility because of alcohol and drug use. Some of the men clearly indicated that they were addicts at the time of initial infection, which could further exacerbate this idea of self-blame with underlying tones of blaming the addiction, "I wish I was not positive and still had gotten the message or the awakening that I had to change [referring to his drug addiction]" (mixed race/ethnicity male, age 37, New York City).

Self-Punishment

Some men spoke of HIV as a form of punishment that they brought on themselves, as in the following three comments: "The whole thing of getting HIV was a punishment, a sin [for being gay]" (Black male, age 43, New York City); "I became very rageful and angry [after being rejected by a potential sex partner], and I went out to look for someone who was obviously HIV positive (mixed race/ethnicity male, age 43, San Francisco); and, "My HIV infection was around the issue of depression and not caring about myself" (Black male, age 37, New York City).

Although these three comments are seemingly disparate, the internalized homophobia, sexual rejection, and depression within each statement, respectively, speak to the issue of punishment, whether inflicted by a deity or the self because of some perceived inherent deficit. The blame is clearly directed at the self and is, in fact, heightened by the corresponding belief that they became HIV infected in part because something is or was wrong with them. Ironically, these same three men also indicated that they do not initiate condom use and therefore fail to protect their sex partners from HIV infection, an issue that is addressed later in the chapter.

BLAMING OTHERS FOR HIV INFECTION

Blaming someone or something other than oneself also emerged spontaneously in some of the interviews. Many men blamed former sex partners, and this blame was expressed in several specific ways. A few men blamed someone or something other than a sexual partner for not protecting them from initial infection. As a result, four themes arose from a review of statements regarding other blame for infection with HIV. Of these, three focused on former sexual partners (victimization, coercive sex, and nondisclosure of HIV status) and one focused on blaming someone other than a sex partner.

Victimization

Some men made statements in which the underlying message or self statement was that "this was done to me, I was not a willing participant in the sexual act that led to my seroconversion," such as

> I'm basically a top . . . of course, I mean that's why I got HIV because I wasn't a top all the time. And probably because of that, because I knew that I got HIV because somebody fucked me. (Latino male, age 42, New York City)

Rather than say, "I got fucked," this man stated, "somebody fucked me," the passive language implying that he was unwilling or perhaps acquiescing to his sexual partner's request for insertive anal sex and therefore victimized by the sex act. Through the lens of attribution theory, this is a distancing strategy that protects the individual from faulting himself. This passive strategy then permits the individual to put himself in the place of the victim regardless of the situation.

"There is always a bad memory, but you go through your head and say, 'who gave it to me? Maybe it was him'" (Latino male, age 32, New York City). This statement, and similar ones made by other men, suggests that the speaker places the blame for his seroconversion on someone else. The reference to searching his memory for an answer may indicate that this individual had numerous episodes of unsafe sex before finding out he was HIV-positive because he cannot ascertain who "gave it to him." If this is indeed the case, attributing the cause of HIV infection to someone else permits the avoidance of any feelings of guilt or shame, again representing a victim stance.

However, for some men, the theme of passive infection via victimization was readily clear, because of HIV infection by a romantic partner. One man, in addition to being infected by his partner, which alone could result in focusing blame on the partner, faced the added burden of infection by a partner who was dishonest, thus enhancing his sense of victimization:

> I know how I contracted it, who I contracted it from. I knew for many years. Probably 1982 was when I became infected. . . . I also found out towards the end, that he [the man's romantic partner] hadn't been monogamous and that he was shooting drugs with these guys and hanging out with them at periods when I was away on business and stuff. And that is most certainly the path of infection. (mixed race/ethnicity male, age 40, New York City).

Coercive Sex

Unfortunately for some men, the sense of victimization was very real and legitimate, enabling the individual to make attributions without any distancing:

> He's [the man's brother] basically the one that—that caused my whole HIV status, my whole homosexuality to my HIV status by sexual molestation, physical abuse, um, sexual abuse, verbal abuse. So if certain factors like that hadn't happened, I wouldn't be sick today. (Black male, age 30, New York City)

Other men also stated that they were infected through sexual coercion, typically sexual abuse or rape. These men were quite clear about attributing their HIV infection to sexual coercion:

> I've been sexually abused all my life, since I was 18. When I was 19 I was raped. That's how I got the HIV virus. And, sometimes it plagues me and I can't be with anyone. I can't be touched. And it has affected my behavior and having sex. (Black male, age 32, San Francisco)

Some men stated that they were intending to have protected sex and, in fact, believed that they were having sex with a condom but found out later that a condom had not been used. "I feel that I know when I became infected, and that experience made me sadder but wiser in the sense that I thought he was using a condom and I found out that he was not" (White male, age 51, New York City). Another man reported a similar experience; in this case however, sex began with a condom:

> I think . . . I got it—was from a friend doing that to me [anal sex], but I think the rubber broke and he didn't tell me about it. I knew the

rubber was going on, but later it didn't come out of me. I was goin' . . .
I go "uh oh" in my head, and I was thinking "uh oh, you should have
told me . . . you should have said something right away, but you didn't
say anything, and I didn't know. (Asian or Pacific Islander male, age
39, San Francisco)

Nondisclosure of HIV Status by Former Partner

Several men explained that they discovered that the sex partners who
infected them knew of their HIV status but failed to tell them at the time
or actually lied about their status.

And then we ran out of condoms. I was bottom, and we fucked and
fucked and fucked until we both came and then were lying there in
the afterglow. And 5 minutes later he tells me that he's positive. You
know, he didn't tell me 5 minutes before we stopped using condoms;
he told me 5 minutes after we're done. (Native American male, age
29, San Francisco)

Sadly, many of these cases involved romantic or long-term partners
rather than one-night stands. "This is one of the things that broke us up—
he said he already had a test done. And then I said, 'Well, why didn't you
tell me about it?' He just told me that he was scared" (White male, age 42,
San Francisco). Another told a similar story: "He had told me he was getting
checked. Great. He didn't tell me he had it, but he said he was being—
checking for it" (White male, age 24, San Francisco).

Blaming Someone Other Than a Sex Partner

Some men blamed an institution, such as this man who attributed his
seroconversion to the gay community at large:

Yeah, my anger is directed at the, ah, community or whatever it's called,
that—the established gay health community that has told people certain
things are safe [oral sex] when it's not safe . . . and, as I told you, the
reason I am HIV-positive is because I accepted this. (White male, age
46, New York City)

Other men attributed blame to authority figures under the premise
that these individuals should have done more to educate and protect them
from HIV infection. The age of the following man and the target of his
blame offer a classic example: "I blamed my mother. I cussed my mom out.
'It's all your fucking fault; you never talked to me about safe sex and you
knew this was out there'" (White male, age 24, New York City).

One man blamed his HIV infection on an apparent transfusion he
received at a hospital. However, it is unclear if this was actually the reason

for his infection, because this person also expressed that he assumed he would contract HIV anyway:

> And when I was diagnosed, you didn't get no counseling or nothing. I was at [a hospital], and they're the one that had infected me, 'cause when I went there, I wasn't HIV-positive. They operated on me, and a few months when I was coming back from my periodic visit at the clinic, they tell me that I'm HIV-positive. . . . But then with my lifestyle that I had lived, I understood that there was a good chance that I would, you know, this would happen to me. (Latino male, age 44, New York City)

Perhaps it was easier for this man to attribute blame to the hospital as a way of distancing himself from any sense of self-blame because of his previous history of unprotected sexual encounters.

ATTRIBUTIONAL EFFECTS ON SEXUAL RISK BEHAVIORS AND DECISION MAKING

In the interviews men did discuss their decision making about HIV sexual risk practices in terms of their attributions for their seroconversion. (See chap. 10, this volume, for another exploration of decision making about safer sex unrelated to attributions for seroconversion.) These men clearly articulated that they did not want to be responsible for transmitting HIV to a sex partner. This was particularly evident among those men who attributed blame for seroconversion to a sex partner who did not disclose his HIV-positive serostatus.

> I'm not going to do what my lover did to me to anybody else. . . . You know, he knew he was positive and he never told me. He outright told me that he was negative. (Black male, age 22, New York City)

This link between the attribution about seroconversion and current safer sex attitudes clearly arose, either directly, as in the previous statement, or within the context of the whole interview. "I feel like, you know, I allowed this to happen to me, you know, by not practicing safe sex when I knew, you know, I knew and I don't want to infect anyone else" (Black male, age 35, New York City).

The men in SUMS also specifically talked about their perceptions of morality and expressed strong feelings and statements that to potentially infect another person with HIV was morally wrong.

> And I personally don't like spreading, you know, diseases onto other people because it has been done to me . . . In the Bible, God—God

wrote, "Thou shall not kill." And I want to live like that, although I was infected by another man, which was morally wrong. (Black male, age 28, New York City)

But if he knew when he did it, he's a murderer. I just hope this is—you know, maybe they'll show mercy up there, but I hope they separate the murderers from the non-murderers that they know and they give people AIDS. (White male, age 39, New York City)

The themes described suggest that HIV-positive gay and bisexual men do make attributions for past sexual behavior that resulted in their infection with HIV and that these attributions appear to be linked to their current attitudes about protecting their sex partners. This linkage appears to take four different forms. These combinations of attributions and attitudes are strikingly similar to the models of helping and coping theorized by Brickman et al. (1982). As stated in the introduction of this chapter, this theory posits that individuals attribute the cause of their problems to themselves or to someone else and also attribute responsibility for finding a solution to the self or someone else. The end result is what Brickman et al. (1982) called four orientations: moral, compensatory, enlightenment, and medical. The nomenclature for the orientations was meant to capture the essence of the attitudes within each (Rabinowitz, personal communication, August 5, 1998). For example, in the compensatory model, the judgment is made that the responsibility for the problem does not lay within the individual in question, however there is the belief that people should find their own solutions to the problem. Individuals may be born into economically disadvantaged situations by no fault of their own; however, they are responsible for improving their own lot in life. The "American dream" is a concept that clearly encompasses this orientation.

The themes that emerged from the interviews presented could be viewed through an adaptation of the orientations in Brickman and his colleagues' (1982) models of helping and coping. Thus, it is proposed that there may be four orientations regarding seroconversion and safer sex attitudes. The following orientations for coping with seroconversion and responsibility for safer sex have been labeled in a similar manner to the Brickman model to reflect the emotional and psychological essence of each.

Sympathetic Orientation

The individual attributes responsibility for initial infection to himself but demonstrates compassion toward others and attributes responsibility for protection to himself as well. Individuals with this orientation are demonstrating compassion or altruism toward their sex partners, "I feel like I took the risks, I knew the consequences, and at least I am a responsible enough person to get checked and then not to infect other people" (White male, age 28, New York City).

Empathetic Orientation

The individual does not attribute responsibility for infection to himself and subsequently is able to place himself in the position of an uninfected person and attributes responsibility for protection to himself. The compassion demonstrated within this model is based on the fact that an HIV-positive person views his sexual partners as being in the same vulnerable position that he was at the time he became infected. "'Cause the person who infected me just had no concept of morality or decency, because he told me everything else except for that he was positive. . . . So I just refuse to do this to someone else (mixed race/ethnicity male, age 33, San Francisco).

Antipathetic Orientation

The individual takes responsibility for initial infection but not for protecting others. Individuals with this orientation do not appear to be demonstrating compassion or empathy for their sex partners:

> But I can tell you that [my] sex practices have changed practically immediately since I found out. And maybe I should blame myself for just letting things happen [seroconverting] and not taking more control over my life. But since I found out that I was positive . . . I have had unprotected sex since I found out . . . I used to insist. If I didn't see a condom, I used to insist on it, and I don't do that anymore. (White male, age 32, New York City)

Apathetic Orientation

Individuals attribute no responsibility to themselves for being infected or for protecting others. This orientation is characterized by the absence of feelings of self-blame and no empathy for sex partners:

> Actually, when I found out [about getting HIV from a non-disclosing partner], I just like—I was like—I didn't even care anymore about living. I just—I was like more—I've gotten more promiscuous. . . . It's like, okay, so I got it now; let the whole world get it too . . . So sometimes I might agree to use a condom and sometimes I just wouldn't. (West Indian male, age 28, New York City)

DISCUSSION

These attributional analyses demonstrate that HIV-positive gay and bisexual men in the SUMS study did have definite ideas about how they seroconverted. One note of caution: The analyses presented in this chapter were based on spontaneous comments made by some of the men in SUMS for whom making an attribution regarding their seroconversion was a salient issue. The men in SUMS were not directly asked the question "How were you infected with HIV?" Therefore, the analyses should be viewed as preliminary. However, for those men who did mention their attributions for seroconversion, there does appear to be a relationship between those attributions and attitudes and decision making about safer sexual behaviors. One hopes that future research interviews with HIV-positive gay and bisexual men will explicitly explore this making sense of becoming infected and all its implications.

However, the attitudes and behaviors of making an attribution for seroconversion may be mediated by other factors. Bernard Weiner (1990) has suggested a general attribution–affect model of helping behavior under various circumstances that may add additional depth to the analyses and results presented. Weiner stated that the initial attribution for an event leads to an emotional response, which is in turn then related to subsequent behavior. Marks (1998) has adapted Weiner's theory to be specific to seroconversion and safer sex. In this situation, according to Marks, blaming someone else for becoming infected with HIV leads to negative affects, such as anger. This emotional response then may result in attributing responsibility for safer sex to one's sexual partners. Therefore, the adapted Brickman model presented herein, if used in future research, should include the affective component to ascertain if specific emotional responses are unique within each orientation of attributions for seroconversion and attitudes toward protecting others.

The results of this chapter and the usefulness of the theories presented demonstrate the importance of addressing attributions for seroconversion and the emotions surrounding that event in sexual risk reduction interventions as well as in clinical settings and future empirical investigations. One hopes that researchers, pubic health officials, and clinicians will recognize that they have an obligation to examine and address this phenomenon to prevent the further spread of HIV among gay and bisexual men. The public health consequences of not taking any action or failing to ask questions may already be upon us in the dog eat dog urban gay ghetto. As one SUMS participant emphatically pointed out, "Like I said before, that [anyone who] doesn't have protection for themselves deserves to get infected because they know what's out there. And if you don't know what's out there, honey, you'd better wake up!" (White male, age 36, New York City).

REFERENCES

Bingman, C. R., Marks, G., & Crepaz, N. (2001). Attributions about one's HIV infection and unsafe sex in seropositive men who have sex with men. *AIDS and Behavior, 5,* 283–289.

Brickman, P., Rabinowitz, V. C., Karuza, J., Coates, D., Cohn, E., & Kidder, L. (1982). Models of helping and coping. *American Psychologist, 37,* 368–384.

Cohen, M., & Hubert, M. (1997). The place and time in understanding sexual behaviour and designing HIV/AIDS prevention programs. In L. Van Campenhoudt, M. Cohen, G. Guizzardi, & D. Hausser (Eds.), *Sexual interactions and HIV risk: New conceptual perspectives in European research* (pp. 196–222). Bristol, PA: Taylor & Francis.

Curtin, L., Stephens, R. S., & Roffman, R. A. (1997). Determinants of relapse and the rule violation effect in predicting safer sex goal violations. *Journal of Applied Social Psychology, 27,* 649–663.

Fiske, S. T., & Taylor, S. E. (1991). Attribution theory: Theoretical refinements and empirical observations. In *Social cognition* (pp. 57–96). New York: McGraw-Hill.

Heider, F. (1958). *The psychology of interpersonal relations.* New York: Wiley.

Ingledew, D. K., Hardy, L., & Cooper C. L. (1996). An attributional model applied to health behavior change. *European Journal of Personality, 10,* 111–132.

Kelley, H. H. (1967). Attribution theory in social psychology. In D. Levine (Ed.), *Nebraska Symposium on Motivation: Vol. 15. Perspectives on motivation* (pp. 192–238). Lincoln: University of Nebraska Press.

Marks, G. (1998, August). *Theoretical underpinnings of behavioral interventions: Attribution-affect-behavior model of sexual risk in HIV-positive persons.* Paper presented at the 96th annual meeting of the American Psychological Association, San Francisco.

Shaver, K. G. (1975). *An introduction to attribution processes.* Boston: Little, Brown.

Taylor, S. E., Kemeny, M., Aspinwall, L., Schneider, S. G., Rodriguez, R., & Herbert, M. (1992). Optimism, coping, psychological distress, and high-risk sexual behavior among men at risk for acquired immunodeficiency syndrome (AIDS). *Journal of Personality and Social Psychology, 63,* 460–473.

Weiner, B. (1990). On perceiving the other as responsible. In R. A. Dienstbier (Ed.), *Nebraska Symposium on Motivation: Vol. 38. Perspectives on motivation* (pp. 165–198). Lincoln: University of Nebraska Press.

10

IT TAKES TWO TO TANGO: HIV-POSITIVE GAY AND BISEXUAL MEN'S BELIEFS ABOUT THEIR RESPONSIBILITY TO PROTECT OTHERS FROM HIV INFECTION

RICHARD J. WOLITSKI AND CAROLINE J. BAILEY

Concern that some individuals living with HIV would purposefully and recklessly attempt to infect others is reflected in our popular culture, mass media, and the law. The urban legend of AIDS Mary tells the tale of a man who, after a casual sexual encounter, finds a lipstick-scrawled note on his bathroom mirror that ominously proclaims, "Welcome to the World of AIDS" (Mikkelson, 2000). In the real world, a small number of AIDS Marys and AIDS Harrys have been the focus of news reports that have

This chapter was coauthored by an employee of the United States government as part of official duty and is considered to be in the public domain. Any views expressed herein do not necessarily represent the views of the United States government, and the author's participation in the work is not meant to serve as an official endorsement.

The chapter is based on Wolitski, R. J., Bailey, C. J., O'Leary, A., Gómez, C. A., & Parsons, J. T. (2003). Self-perceived responsibility of HIV-seropositive men who have sex with men for preventing HIV transmission. *AIDS and Behavior, 7*, 363–372. In the public domain.

drawn national attention to HIV-seropositive individuals who have been accused of placing others at risk for HIV infection without their knowledge or consent. One of the most widely reported stories came to light in 1997. This case centered on Nushawn Williams, a young man who is believed to have infected 10 teenage girls and young women in upstate New York (Centers for Disease Control and Prevention, 1999). The publicity associated with this case and others like it spurred many states to consider laws that criminalize the sexual practices of people living with HIV. Statutes that place criminal penalties on acts that result in HIV transmission (or place others at risk for exposure to HIV) were on the books in 27 states in 2000 (HIV Criminal Law and Policy Project, 2001).

These events and the legislation they inspired have sparked considerable debate about the responsibility that individuals living with HIV have to protect others. Some advocates have worried that emphasizing the responsibility of HIV-seropositive people represents an erosion of the rights of individuals living with HIV that will further stigmatize an already vulnerable group, discourage at-risk individuals from being tested or seeking medical care, and create a false sense of security among individuals who are not infected. This perspective has profoundly affected the development of HIV prevention messages. Until recently, most prevention messages were focused almost exclusively on encouraging uninfected individuals to protect themselves and paid little attention to the sexual practices of individuals living with HIV (Bayer, 1996; Janssen et al., 2001; Wolitski, Janssen, Onorato, Purcell, & Crepaz, 2005).

Once the rhetoric of this debate is peeled away, it becomes surprisingly clear that it is not based on empirical data. There has been almost no research on how people living with HIV view their responsibility for protecting others or how prevention messages for this population may be received. Only a few researchers have studied issues related to personal responsibility. Nimmons and Folkman (1999) interviewed 36 gay men about their reasons for practicing safer sex and found that both HIV-seropositive and HIV-seronegative men were motivated by concern about the effects that their sexual behavior may have on others. In a study with 15 HIV-seropositive gay men (Crosby, 1998), some men believed it was their responsibility to either disclose their HIV status or use condoms. Other men thought that taking these steps was the responsibility of HIV-seronegative men and left it to the partner to raise HIV-related issues. We have examined this issue in two quantitative studies and found that HIV-seropositive gay and bisexual men's beliefs about personal responsibility are associated with risky sexual practices. Men with higher levels of perceived personal responsibility, compared with men whose levels are lower, are less likely to engage in unprotected anal sex with uninfected partners (Wolitski et al., 2002; Wolitski, Gómez, Parsons, Ambrose, & Remien, 1998).

In this chapter, we describe what participants in the Seropositive Urban Men's Study (SUMS) had to say about their own and their partners' responsibility for preventing HIV transmission. Chapter 1 (this volume) provides a complete description of the research methods used in SUMS and the characteristics of study participants. In this chapter, our primary aims are to illustrate the various views of responsibility, identify factors that affect perceived responsibility, and examine the association between perceived responsibility and the sexual practices of HIV-seropositive gay and bisexual men. Responsibility for preventing the sexual transmission of HIV was spontaneously mentioned by 72% (180/250) of SUMS participants. The information in this chapter is based on the comments of these 180 men who talked about issues related to responsibility. The men's comments reflect three main themes: (a) their personal responsibility for preventing HIV transmission to their sex partners, (b) their sex partners' responsibility for protecting themselves from becoming infected, and (c) their own and their partners' mutual responsibility.

PERSONAL RESPONSIBILITY

Nearly two thirds of the participants who mentioned responsibility (114/180) did so in terms of their desire to protect sex partners from becoming infected and expressed concern about the possibility that they could transmit the virus to others:

> I do feel a certain sense of responsibility, and I don't want to be exposing someone who is negative. That, I feel, is just simply being stupid. (White male, age 37, New York)

> If you don't [have safer sex], you are at a detrimental risk of endangering the person's life to the point of death, and it's like murder. . . . I am a responsible person, and I have chosen this for myself and those that I am in contact with. (White male, age 33, New York)

An especially strong sense of perceived responsibility was apparent among the men who refused the requests of HIV-seronegative partners to engage in behaviors that could transmit HIV. This subgroup of men described numerous situations in which they had acted against their partners' wishes and refused to engage in specific sexual activities that they considered unsafe:

> I have to think within myself, this person may not know what's good or not good for them. They may not know the reasons, or they may not care, but that doesn't mean that I can't care for them. (White male, age 41, San Francisco)

> I've run into a couple of people out there who were HIV-negative and wanted to play around still, wanted me to fuck 'em still. And I said, "I

can't do it. I'm sorry." They're like, "Oh, come on. I don't care." Well, I do care . . . it's like someone who wants to commit suicide giving you a gun and saying, "Shoot me. I can't do it myself." (mixed race/ethnicity male, age 35, San Francisco)

For some men, personal responsibility was associated with a deep fear that they might unintentionally transmit the virus to others. This fear seemed to be greatest among men in an ongoing relationship with an HIV-seronegative partner. Stress associated with the fear of transmitting HIV led to the premature termination of some sexual encounters and negatively affected ongoing sexual relationships. Men who were in a relationship with a seronegative partner reported that differences between their own and their partners' perceptions about the risk from oral sex and other sexual practices (and their level of comfort with these risks) were common sources of tension. Although protecting oneself from the emotions associated with putting others at risk was commonly mentioned, a few participants mentioned a desire to avoid possible legal action and physical harm:

> Sometimes it happens that some individual wants to have unsafe sex, and I don't want it. I don't want it to protect that person and to protect myself . . . protect himself in the physical way and even the emotional way . . . and myself in the legal way, because he could sue me. He'll say, "This guy had sex with me, and he didn't tell me he had AIDS." (Latino male, age 45, San Francisco)

Some men dealt with their concerns about transmitting HIV to an uninfected partner by choosing to have sex only with other HIV-seropositive men. A participant who reported having sex only with HIV-seropositive men described his decision:

> If they're not HIV, I won't have sex with them. I will not get involved with them. We'll be friends or whatever, but I don't want to feel responsible for possibly infecting anyone because condoms are not 100%. And I don't want to take that chance. (Black male, age 32, San Francisco)

Personal responsibility for protecting others seemed to be motivated by several factors, including altruism, personal standards, and self-interest. For example, some participants expressed altruistic motivations that reflected a desire to safeguard the health of their sex partners, the health of others that their partner might have sex with in the future, or the gay community:

> I'm very cautious—very cautious—because I wouldn't want someone to do what has happened to me. Having HIV is not a fun thing because you think about it on a daily basis. Even though you may not want it to, it does overwhelm your life in every aspect. Believe me, every aspect from employment to—to, you name it . . . it's a terrible thing to have to go through the day like that. (Black male, age 40, San Francisco)

I don't want to feel responsible for this person to give it to other people. I don't want people to go through what I went through. (Latino male, age 44, New York)

Well, you have a responsibility to not make people like where you are. It's an awesome responsibility . . . we can't procreate as gay people but we can keep what's already here living . . . and the only way we can keep doing that is by keeping our species alive. And we can't do that if we're giving everybody a disease that's going to kill them. (White male, age 34, New York)

Personal ethical, moral, and religious standards also seemed to be powerful factors that positively influenced some men's beliefs about their responsibility to protect others. These men said that having unprotected sex with uninfected partners would violate their own ethical beliefs or conflict with the teachings of their religion. This perspective was illustrated by the words of a participant who described how these beliefs helped him avoid behaviors that could transmit HIV:

[I] just keep thinking in the back of my head that it's wrong . . . the way I was raised, that it would, it would just be wrong. . . . And I don't think my God would be able to forgive me on Judgment Day. That's what keeps me from not doing it. (White male, age 42, San Francisco)

Adopting responsibility for preventing HIV transmission also represented an effort by some HIV-seropositive men to protect themselves from experiencing negative emotions (such as guilt or sorrow) that they believed they would feel if they inadvertently transmitted HIV to a sex partner:

When he said that he was negative, I just, you know, I almost said, "Well, forget it . . . I don't want to be the one who is going to infect you." Basically, I don't want that guilt trip on myself. I don't want to carry that baggage with me. (White male, age 40, San Francisco)

I have a conscience, and I do experience guilt. And I, I like to be able to live with myself . . . so I try to do, do things that are morally correct, sexually. (Black male, age 30, New York)

PARTNERS' RESPONSIBILITY

About 1 of 8 participants who talked about responsibility (22/180) described this responsibility as resting with their sex partners, not themselves. One participant who had difficulty maintaining safer sex practices expressed this perspective, "It's very difficult. You're tempted all the time. If the other person says yes [to unprotected sex], then why not? They have made the decision at that point" (White male, age 41, New York). This sentiment was also expressed by another participant, who described his belief that his partner should be aware of the potential risks associated with having sex without using condoms:

> Because this is a grown man. Maybe he's like in his late 30s or like 40. I said, "Hey, he knows." I said, "If he wants to do it without it, hey fine!" I had no problem, you know. I mean, I guess I felt kind of guilty that I wasn't just telling him [about my HIV status], but at the same time I figured it's his responsibility. (Black male, age 43, New York)

Many of the men who ascribed responsibility to their partners emphasized the ability of consenting adults to make informed choices that balance a basic human desire for sexual intimacy against the potential risk of contracting HIV and other sexually transmitted infections. Some men also talked about the need for adults to be able to choose a level of risk that they are willing to accept along a continuum that ranges from behaviors that pose no or little risk to those that pose high risk:

> For me, it's important to let them know [that I am HIV-seropositive]. But everybody's responsible for their own . . . bodies and their lives and the risks that they put themselves under. Everybody has different opinions of what's safe and what's not safe. (Latino male, age 37, San Francisco)

Most of the men who believed that their partners were responsible for protecting themselves discussed this issue in terms of respecting their partners' autonomy and did not communicate a malicious desire to infect others. A lack of concern for the health of others was evident, however, in comments made by a small number of participants. For some, this lack of concern reflected a transient state of mind that was associated with accepting and coping with their own HIV diagnosis:

> One time I had the philosophy of, "Well, I'm dying anyhow. I might as well live it up." And I left the responsibility in my partner's hands— the person that I was with—in their hands. Well, if they really don't care, then it's not up to me to take care of them. (White male, age 32, San Francisco)

For some men, the belief that responsibility rested with their partners was associated with a fear of being rejected by HIV-seronegative partners. This motivation caused some men to avoid disclosing their HIV status to new partners and increased their willingness to engage in sexual practices that could transmit HIV. In some instances, previous experience with rejection by HIV-seronegative partners influenced participants' current disclosure practices:

> And for a while I was, like, watching them run as I was telling them I was positive. And then I got to that point where now I am: it's like

it's not my responsibility to inform you of my status, but if you ask me, I'm not going to lie to you about it. But I'm not going to lay it on the table. (Black male, age 36, San Francisco)

SHARED RESPONSIBILITY

About one quarter of participants who discussed responsibility (44/180) described it as something shared by HIV-seropositive and HIV-seronegative partners in a sexual relationship. These men perceived that they had a responsibility to protect uninfected partners and that these partners also had a responsibility to protect themselves. Both individuals in a sexual encounter were described as having a mutual role in deciding which sexual practices carry an acceptable level of risk:

Whatever happens between the two of you, you both allow that to happen. Whether I want someone to penetrate me anally or not, that I care whether they use a condom or not, that's up to me, and that's up to them. Each person has to take individual responsibility as to how far they'll go, or what they'll do, with either a safe or an unsafe practice. (White male, age 41, San Francisco)

I follow safe sex, as I understand it for me. They follow safe sex as they understand it for them. I'm not—I don't have sex with the mentally retarded or the insane. I think the responsibility to protect yourself is on each person. (White male, age 43, San Francisco)

Men who talked about shared responsibility often raised this issue when discussing a sexual encounter that they believed was unsafe. The perception that both partners share responsibility seemed to help some participants cope with the negative emotional (e.g., guilt, depression) and interpersonal consequences (e.g., rejection, angry reaction from partner) that sometimes followed unsafe sexual encounters. In these situations shared responsibility led to a diffusion of responsibility in which the HIV-seropositive partner viewed himself as only partially responsible for the actions he and his partner had engaged in. A participant who was the receptive partner during unprotected anal intercourse described how this point of view helped him deal with his own emotions about this experience:

I mean, I didn't rape the guy, didn't have a gun to his head, forcing him to fuck me. You know, he also has to be responsible for his actions. You know, he was the one that was being a little bit—you know, he was the one who was more aggressive. He was the one doing the fucking. You know, it was his decision as well not to use a condom, so it takes two people to make that decision. So that alleviates, a little bit, that sense of guilt. (White male, age 40, San Francisco)

In addition to influencing the ability of HIV-seropositive gay and bisexual men to cope with their own emotions, a shared sense of responsibility helped another participant address his partner's reaction to a sexual encounter that neither considered safe:

> We wound up getting carried away, and we wound up not having not too safe sex . . . and he basically blamed me for it, and I turned around and I told him. I said, "Look this is a two-way street. I'm not taking all the blame for it." I said, "I'm only taking half the blame because you were just as much at fault as I was." (Latino male, age 39, San Francisco)

FACTORS THAT INFLUENCE PERCEIVED RESPONSIBILITY

Four main factors seemed to affect whether participants described responsibility as resting with themselves or their partners or as something that was shared: (a) characteristics of the participants, (b) characteristics of the sex partners, (c) disclosure of HIV status, and (d) environmental influences.

Characteristics of Participants

Several characteristics of participants seemed to influence HIV-seropositive gay and bisexual men's beliefs about their own and their partners' responsibility. One was participants' mental and emotional state. Some participants described how negative moods, such as depression or loneliness, reduced their sense of personal responsibility and made them more willing to have unprotected sex. Similarly, sexual arousal seemed to affect some participants' beliefs about their responsibility to protect others. A participant who normally sought to protect his HIV-seronegative partners from becoming infected described how his desire for sexual gratification affected his decision making:

> I don't want to be unsafe with them because then I could be the carrier . . . and then there's some times when you kind of throw that out of your mind because you're so horny that it—like, it's not going to matter, and you decide to place all the balance on them. (White male, age 41, San Francisco)

The participants' use of alcohol or drugs was also described as causing some men to feel less responsibility for preventing HIV transmission to their sex partners. Substance use was described as compromising the motivation to protect their partners, shifting the focus to the immediate sexual experience, and limiting the ability to exercise control over sexual behavior:

You just get high. You just don't care. You just think about yourself. You don't think about anyone else. You could give two shits about anybody else. (Latino male, age 31, New York)

I just, I wish that I would have been able to have been a little bit more responsible with the sex. Being that I was under the influence of alcohol and drugs. And that sort of affected my ability to make a decision to have safer sex. So hopefully in the future I could sort of experience sex without the uses of alcohol and drugs. And I could be a little bit more— a lot more—responsible. (Latino male, age 31, New York)

Men's beliefs about the relative risk from specific sexual practices and their own infectiousness seemed to influence perceived responsibility. Men who believed that there was little risk of transmitting HIV through a given sexual activity were less likely to believe that they had a personal responsibility to disclose their HIV status or protect their partner from potential risk. For example, some men believed that they had less responsibility for safer sex when they were the receptive partner during anal intercourse because they viewed the risk to an uninfected insertive partner as much lower than the risk if the partner had taken the receptive role.

Characteristics of Partners

Perceived and actual characteristics of sex partners also seemed to influence beliefs about the responsibility to prevent HIV transmission. Some men expressed a greater sense of personal responsibility when they knew that the partner was seronegative than when they did not know their partner's HIV status. When HIV status was not discussed, some men made assumptions about the partner's HIV status that influenced perceived responsibility (see chap. 8, this volume). Some of the participants who assumed that the partner was already infected believed that responsibility for reducing the risk of HIV transmission rested with the partner:

I assume everybody's positive. And unless they tell me otherwise, I just assume that they are. And if they don't bring up the issue of safe play, then I assume that it's not an issue with them. (White male, age 35, San Francisco)

If you don't say a word to me then I'm not saying a word to you. . . . I'm just going to assume [that you are HIV-seropositive]. I'm assuming that you're assuming the same thing. And if I'm wrong, then it's your life. (White male, age 34, New York)

Beliefs about responsibility were also affected by the characteristics of the partners that participants thought were associated with increased HIV awareness or previous risk for infection. Age, sexual orientation, and perceived level of sexual activity were three such factors. Some men seemed to have a greater sense of responsibility for protecting younger partners than those who were older:

> If I find out they're young, they're in their 30s or their 20s, they can beg me to not put the condom on and I still will put it on . . . because you are too young to be going through what I'm going through. (Black male, age 45, New York)

A few men whose sex partners did not identify themselves as gay seemed more concerned about infecting these partners than partners who identified as gay. Non-gay-identified men were perceived as less informed about HIV than gay men, and some participants expressed concern that these men might unknowingly transmit HIV to their female partners if they became infected. One participant whose boyfriend occasionally brought a third partner home for sexual encounters described how the sexual orientation of these partners affected his behavior:

> Like he might pick up a straight, a closet straight . . . and I'd have to have safe sex with them. But, you know, people I know that are gay and in the life and know what's goin' on, I wouldn't worry about having safe sex with them. (Black male, age 42, San Francisco)

This participant also described how he was more willing to have unprotected sex with men he perceived to be promiscuous, or "ho-ish":

> I fucked him, you know, without a rubber. I didn't really feel guilty about it cuz he's kinda ho-ish anyway. . . . Knowin' that he is ho-ish, you know, I endangered myself of catchin'. Cuz he goes to bookstores and shit like that. And, you know, there's a lot of STDs out there . . . but he got me at the right moment, and I said, "Okay. Let's do it right quick." (Black male, age 42, San Francisco)

For some men, their sense of personal responsibility increased if their partner's decision-making ability was impaired by alcohol or drug use. These men indicated that they did not want to take advantage of men who were willing to engage in behaviors that they might otherwise avoid. One participant, who had started to engage in unprotected anal intercourse with an intoxicated partner, described his experience:

> [He] was obviously drunk out of——drunk as a skunk . . . and, although I wanted to go through with it, as far as to get my rocks off, I didn't. My conscience came through and it was like . . . he's obviously in a state not to make a complete, you know, decision on his own. (White male, age 41, San Francisco)

The participant's relationship with the partner also seemed to influence beliefs about responsibility. HIV-seropositive men with a main, or primary, partner were more likely to perceive a special responsibility to protect this partner compared with one-time or casual partners, who were often seen as having the responsibility for protecting themselves from infection. This differentiation is evident in the words of a participant who discussed his thoughts about sex with his primary partner: "I was so careful with him. . . . If you're making love with somebody who you love, I mean, it's great, it's wonderful . . . having caring, loving, responsible sex is beautiful sex" (Latino male, age 31, San Francisco). This same participant expressed a different perspective when he spoke about his sexual relationships with casual partners:

> I say, "Well, it's half-and-half responsibility." Right? It doesn't mean that you want to be a murderer, you know. It's just that in a casual encounter, it's just to relieve all the sexual potential or sexual energy. And sometimes it doesn't matter how you are going to release it. The point is just to get rid of it, but you're not involved in feelings or nothing else. (Latino male, age 31, San Francisco)

Disclosure of HIV Status

The disclosure of HIV status to a potential sex partner (see chap. 7, this volume) appeared to affect participants' beliefs about responsibility. Although disclosure did not seem to influence the beliefs of all men, in many instances, disclosure shifted perceived responsibility from the participant to his partner. The effects of disclosure were succinctly described by one participant who said, "And I told him, but he still didn't want to use a condom. So, like that's you, that's on you. I mean, I told you. I did my part. You know? So, we had unprotected sex" (Black male, age 25, San Francisco).

Environmental Influences

The setting in which participants met sex partners also seemed to influence perceived responsibility (see chap. 12, this volume). Men who met partners in public sex environments, where anonymous sexual encounters take place (e.g., bathhouses, sex clubs, adult bookstores) commonly perceived these partners as responsible for protecting themselves from HIV infection and often assumed that the men they met in these settings were already infected:

> If you're in a bookstore, and you pick somebody up or you're havin' sex in a bookstore, then you might as well assume that somebody you're playin' with is HIV-positive. And if it turns out that you're not HIV-positive, then it's your own fuckin' fault for being in the bookstore to begin with. I mean, everybody knows what kind of sex goes on in those places, and it's not usually safe sex. So if you run into somebody who

is HIV-positive, then you did it to yourself. (mixed race/ethnicity male, age 35, San Francisco)

I don't insist on it [condom use] in the baths, for example, where I assume everybody is taking responsibility for themselves, their own risk, their own level of risk that they'll accept. (White male, age 46, New York)

DISCUSSION

Personal responsibility seems to be an important and salient factor that shapes the sexual decision making of HIV-seropositive men. Most of the men spontaneously discussed issues related to responsibility when asked to talk about their sexual relationships and the effect that HIV has had on their lives. Most of the men believed that they had a responsibility to protect their sex partners from HIV infection and had adopted risk-reduction practices that were consistent with this belief. Despite this belief, these men faced numerous challenges in maintaining safer sex practices. Some men reported that they had even had to turn down requests by HIV-seronegative partners for unsafe sex. These findings are consistent with those from earlier reports describing HIV-seropositive gay and bisexual men's use of multiple strategies to manage the risk of HIV transmission (Flowers, Duncan, & Frankis, 2000) and further illustrate the ongoing challenges in adopting and continuing safer sex practices that confront gay and bisexual men living with HIV.

A sense of responsibility for protecting others seemed to be motivated by several factors, including altruism, personal standards, and self-interest, which qualitative research has shown to motivate the adoption of safer sex practices among HIV-seropositive and HIV-seronegative gay men (Nimmons & Folkman, 1999). Tapping these motivations may enable therapists and HIV prevention programs to increase a sense of responsibility among HIV-seropositive gay and bisexual men and reduce transmission risk. Our findings suggest that appeals to altruism should focus both on the potential consequences of unprotected sex for one's own sex partners and the indirect effects that may be experienced by later partners, friends and family members, and the gay community as a whole. By appealing to personal standards, it may be possible to build on personal beliefs and values that facilitate efforts to protect sex partners from infection. Messages that appeal to self-interest and communicate the personal benefits of protecting others may also increase a sense of responsibility among some HIV-seropositive gay and bisexual men. A combined approach that addresses altruism, personal standards, and self-interest may be the most successful strategy. This type of approach might reduce potential negative reactions from HIV-seropositive gay and bisexual men who feel that messages that address only the protection of others reflect a lack of concern about their own welfare or are based on values that they do not share.

Some men's beliefs about responsibility seem to be relatively stable. The beliefs of others are more mercurial, shifting in accord with the characteristics of the person with whom they are having sex. Some participants were more willing to engage in unprotected anal sex with partners they assumed were already HIV-seropositive and those who "should know better." More specifically, they expressed greater willingness to have unprotected sex with partners who were older, identified themselves as gay, had large numbers of male sex partners, and met partners in public sex environments. These findings are consistent with those from earlier research on gay men's use of nonverbal cues to guess the serostatus of their partners (Gold & Skinner, 1992, 1996; Suarez & Miller, 2001). These findings hint that the processes that lead some members of the general public to place blame on some groups of HIV-seropositive individuals may also influence the perceptions of HIV-seropositive gay and bisexual men (Crandall, 1991; Herek & Capitanio, 1999; Mannetti & Pierro, 1991; Schellenberg & Bem, 1998). These HIV-seropositive men seemed to be less willing to risk infecting naive or vulnerable partners in much the same way that some members of the general public are less willing to blame or stigmatize "innocent victims" who are perceived as less culpable for having contracted HIV. Considered as a whole, these findings indicate a critical need for a deeper understanding of the many personal, interpersonal, and environmental factors that may influence personal responsibility among people living with HIV.

A key concern for those who work with HIV-seropositive men is the finding that disclosure of HIV status sometimes led to a shift in responsibility from the participant to his partner. After disclosure, some participants indicated that they would be more willing to have unprotected sex if the partner requested or allowed it. In part, this shift in responsibility reflects a belief that unimpaired adults should have the freedom, and an obligation, to make informed decisions about the level of risk that they are comfortable taking. One may argue that this is a reasonable position to take. Unfortunately, however, it is a perspective that places the ultimate responsibility for HIV prevention on the shoulders of those who cannot intimately know the physical and psychological burdens that those living with HIV must bear. These findings provide important insights that may partly explain why research on disclosure and transmission risk has produced inconsistent results (De Rosa & Marks, 1998; Marks & Crepaz, 2001; Wolitski, Rietmeijer, Goldbaum, & Wilson, 1998). Together, this study and earlier research on disclosure raise important questions about the role that encouraging serostatus disclosure should play in prevention programs for gay and bisexual men living with HIV. Although HIV-seropositive individuals may have an ethical obligation to disclose their HIV status to potential sex partners, it cannot be assumed that disclosure will decrease the risk for HIV transmission. Counselors should stress the need to protect the health of all sex partners who may be HIV-seronegative (including those whose HIV status is not known), regardless of whether the person who is HIV-seropositive has disclosed his status.

The responsibility of people living with HIV to protect their sex partners cannot be considered without emphasizing the responsibility that all sexually active men and women have to protect themselves and others. It also cannot be discussed without careful examination of the social or collective responsibility that public health agencies and society as a whole have to remove barriers to the maintenance of safer sex practices among infected and uninfected adults and adolescents. As described by Marks, Burris, and Peterman (1999),

> collective responsibility emphasizes that all of us, infected or not, low risk or high, bear a responsibility to change our attitudes and behaviors that may promote HIV infection. Without this balance, calls for personal responsibility become almost indistinct from those of blaming the victim and are likely to be counterproductive to prevention efforts. (p. 301)

Acting on this collective responsibility to limit the spread of HIV infection not only will require the development of prevention programs to promote behavior change among people living with HIV but will also necessitate efforts to enact changes in the legal infrastructure, social attitudes, and public policy (Marks et al., 1999). Increased recognition of the need for collective responsibility will ensure the development of prevention programs and public health policies that work with HIV-seropositive people to help them adapt to the myriad challenges of living with HIV and maintaining safer sex practices for a lifetime.

REFERENCES

Bayer, R. (1996). AIDS prevention—Sexual ethics and responsibility. *New England Journal of Medicine, 334,* 1540–1542.

Centers for Disease Control and Prevention. (1999). Cluster of HIV-positive young women—New York, 1997–1998. *Morbidity and Mortality Weekly Report, 48,* 413–416.

Crandall, C. S. (1991). Multiple stigma and AIDS: Illness stigma and attitudes toward homosexuals and IV drug users in AIDS-related stigmatization. *Journal of Community and Applied Social Psychology, 1,* 165–172.

Crosby, G. M. (1998, July). *Whose responsibility is it to stop the spread of HIV—Is it mine, is it his, is it ours?* Paper presented at the XII International Conference on AIDS, Geneva, Switzerland.

De Rosa, C. J., & Marks, G. (1998). Preventive counseling of HIV-positive men and self-disclosure of serostatus to sex partners: New opportunities for prevention. *Health Psychology, 17,* 224–231.

Flowers, P., Duncan, B., & Frankis, J. (2000). Community, responsibility and culpability: HIV risk-management among Scottish gay men. *Journal of Community and Applied Social Psychology, 10,* 285–300.

Gold, R. S., & Skinner, M. J. (1992). Situational factors and thought processes associated with unprotected intercourse in young gay men. *AIDS, 6,* 1021–1030.

Gold, R. S., & Skinner, M. J. (1996). Judging a book by its cover: Gay men's use of perceptible characteristics to infer antibody status. *International Journal of STD and AIDS, 7,* 39–43.

Herek, G. M., & Capitanio, J. P. (1999). AIDS stigma and sexual prejudice. *American Behavioral Scientist, 42,* 1130–1147.

HIV Criminal Law and Policy Project. (2001). *HIV-specific criminal transmission laws.* Retrieved August 29, 2002, from http://www.hivcriminallaw.org/laws/hivspec.cfm

Janssen, R. S., Holtgrave, D. R., Valdiserri, R. O., Shepherd, M., Gayle, H. D., & De Cock, K. M. (2001). The serostatus approach to fighting the HIV epidemic: Prevention strategies for infected individuals. *American Journal of Public Health, 91,* 1019–1024.

Mannetti, L., & Pierro, A. (1991). Health care workers' reaction to AIDS victims: Perception of risk and attribution of responsibility. *Journal of Community and Applied Social Psychology, 1,* 133–142.

Marks, G., Burris, S., & Peterman, T. A. (1999). Reducing sexual transmission of HIV from those who know they are infected: The need for personal and collective responsibility. *AIDS, 13,* 297–306.

Marks, G., & Crepaz, N. (2001). HIV-positive men's sexual practices in the context of self-disclosure of HIV status. *Journal of Acquired Immune Deficiency Syndromes, 27,* 79–85.

Mikkelson, B. (2000, September 20). AIDS Mary. *Urban legends reference pages.* Retrieved July 26, 2002, from http://www.snopes.com/horrors/madmen/aidsmary.htm

Nimmons, D., & Folkman, S. (1999). Other-sensitive motivation for safer sex among gay men: Expanding paradigms for HIV prevention. *AIDS and Behavior, 3,* 313–324.

Schellenberg, E. G., & Bem, S. L. (1998). Blaming people with AIDS: Who deserves to be sick? *Journal of Applied Biobehavioral Research, 3,* 65–80.

Suarez, T., & Miller, J. (2001). Negotiating risks in context: A perspective on unprotected anal intercourse and barebacking among men who have sex with men. *Archives of Sexual Behavior, 30,* 287–300.

Wolitski, R. J., Bailey, C. J., O'Leary, A., Gómez, C. A., & Parsons, J. T. (2003). Self-perceived responsibility of HIV-seropositive men who have sex with men for preventing HIV transmission. *AIDS and Behavior, 7,* 363–372.

Wolitski, R. J., Gómez, C., Parsons, J., Ambrose, T., & Remien, R. (1998, July). *HIV-seropositive men's perceived responsibility for preventing HIV transmission of HIV to others*. Paper presented at the XII International Conference on AIDS, Geneva, Switzerland.

Wolitski, R. J., Janssen, R. S., Onorato, I. M., Purcell, D. W., & Crepaz, N. (2005). A comprehensive approach to prevention with people living with HIV. In S. C. Kalichman (Ed.), *Positive prevention: Reducing HIV transmission among people living with HIV-AIDS* (pp. 1–28). New York: Kluwer Academic.

Wolitski, R. J., Rietmeijer, C. A. M., Goldbaum, G. M., & Wilson, R. M. (1998). HIV serostatus disclosure among gay and bisexual men in four American cities: General patterns and relation to sexual practices. *AIDS Care, 10,* 599–610.

11

UNDER THE INFLUENCE: ALCOHOL AND DRUG USE AND SEXUAL BEHAVIOR AMONG HIV-POSITIVE GAY AND BISEXUAL MEN

DAVID W. PURCELL, GLADYS E. IBAÑEZ,
AND DEBORAH J. SCHWARTZ

Psychoactive drug and alcohol use has been observed across cultures for millennia (Westermeyer, 1999), and American culture is no exception to this pattern. Gay and bisexual men in the United States use substances for many of the same reasons that others do: to relax, to have fun with friends, to ease social anxiety, to increase positive feelings, to escape from life's pressures, to forget negative feelings, and to facilitate and enhance sexual interactions. Although this list is not exhaustive, it highlights some of the common reasons why different people use substances. However, there are also important influences in the lives of gay and bisexual men that differ from those of other people which affect their mental health (Purcell,

This chapter was coauthored by an employee of the United States government as part of official duty and is considered to be in the public domain. Any views expressed herein do not necessarily represent the views of the Unites States government, and the author's participation in the work is not meant to serve as an official endorsement.

Campos, & Perilla, 1996). Understanding substance use in the context of the lives of HIV-positive gay and bisexual men will help illustrate how substance use affects their sexual practices and their risk for acquiring other sexually transmitted infections or for transmitting HIV.

In general, when asked about recent substance use, gay and bisexual men report using a wider variety of drugs than do heterosexual men; but like heterosexual men, they report infrequent use of most drugs other than alcohol and marijuana (Stall & Wiley, 1988; Woody et al., 2001). This same pattern is seen with gay and bisexual men who are HIV-positive; they report using a variety of drugs infrequently and drinking alcohol and using marijuana somewhat more frequently (Purcell, Parsons, Halkitis, Mizuno, & Woods, 2001; Sullivan, Nakashima, Purcell, Ward, & the Supplement of the HIV/AIDS Surveillance Study Group, 1998). Purcell and his colleagues (2001) recently reported on the substance use of 456 HIV-positive gay and bisexual men, including all of the men discussed in this chapter, as well as a second sample. Most men in the combined sample (71%) reported using a substance in the past 3 months: 64% drank alcohol and nearly half used noninjection drugs. The most commonly used noninjection drugs were marijuana (36%), inhalants (poppers) (27%), cocaine/crack (17%), and amphetamines (12%). The use of alcohol or drugs before or during sex also was common among the men. Half of the men reported drinking before or during sex in the past 3 months, and more than 40% reported drug use before or during sex. Among men who drank or used drugs, they commonly reported using alcohol or drugs in sexual situations: 80% of these men used one or more substances in conjunction with sex (Purcell et al., 2001).

The link between sex and substance use has been particularly close for gay and bisexual men because historically bars were one of the few places to meet sexual or romantic partners (Stall & Purcell, 2000). For some men, the link between sex with other men and substance use is established when they first become sexually active; thus, they have never had sex when they were not high or drunk. Substances also are used to enhance the sensual pleasures of sex and to help men expand their sexual boundaries and enjoyment (Freese, Miotto, & Reback, 2002). Drugs and alcohol have been used by gay and bisexual men to deal with unique internal stressors (e.g., anxiety or fear about sex with same-sex partners) as well as challenging external stressors (e.g., coming out to family and friends, homophobia). More recently, the link between sex and drugs has been glamorized by segments of gay culture, as represented by circuit parties, which are large, multievent parties that go on for days and focus on music, dancing, and connecting with other men socially, sexually, and spiritually (Lewis & Ross, 1995; Mansergh et al., 2001).

Since the emergence of HIV in the early 1980s, it has become more important to understand the relationship between substance use and sexual risk for gay and bisexual men. For HIV-positive gay and bisexual men, certain sexual behaviors now put them at risk for STDs and possibly superinfection with HIV and put their partners at risk for HIV and other STDs. In addition, drug and alcohol use may have adverse interactions with medications for HIV (e.g., Harrington, Woodward, Hooton, & Horn, 1999) and may adversely affect the immune systems of HIV-positive men. Sex, which for most men is a highly pleasurable activity, now comes fraught with potential danger. When men add substance use to the mix, the potential increase in sensual pleasure may be accompanied by an extra willingness to take risk or to ignore the potential risk (McKirnan, Ostrow, & Hope, 1996).

Among gay and bisexual men, some drugs appear to be more related to sex and sexual risk than others. A variety of specific drugs have been linked to sexual risk for this population, including ecstasy (Klitzman, Pope, & Hudson, 2000), cocaine (McNall & Remafedi, 1999), methamphetamine (Molitor, Truax, Ruiz, & Sun, 1998; Rawson, Washton, Domier, & Reiber, 2002), and poppers (Woody et al., 1999). Many of the substances related to unprotected sex are often used in combination, and they can provide enhanced sensations during sex and easier acceptance of penetration by the receptive, or bottom, partner.

Researchers have developed models that try to explain substance use in the context of sexual risk among gay and bisexual men. One particularly relevant model developed by McKirnan and his colleagues (1996) is the cognitive escape model. This model tries to explain why HIV transmission continues to be high among gay and bisexual men despite the belief that most gay and bisexual men know how to be sexually safe. This model proposes that many men have conflicting feelings because sex is a highly desired activity, but community norms tell them that they must be safe. This model proposes that people cognitively escape (e.g., through drugs and alcohol) from anxiety-provoking awareness about HIV so that they can satisfy their sexual desires, although this escape conflicts with community norms or their own general desires to be safe. The model indicates that internal and external factors make people more vulnerable to using a cognitive escape mechanism when they drink or use drugs. Internal factors are personal characteristics such as thoughts, feelings, and preferences, and external factors include the setting in which sex occurs, partner characteristics, and substance use (McKirnan et al., 1996). Thus, this model suggests that sexual risk is determined by many factors, one of which may be the use of substances to allow them to cognitively escape awareness of risk and norms.

In this chapter, we describe what the HIV-positive gay and bisexual men in the Seropositive Urban Mens' Study (SUMS; see chap. 1, this volume) had to say about substance use, and we discuss the intertwining of substance use and sexual behavior. We begin with a brief summary of prevalence of substance use during the two sexual narratives (one regarding the most recent sexual experience and the other regarding a sexual experience that was different from the most recent in terms of risk). If men did not spontaneously report that substances were used during the sexual encounter, they were specifically asked whether they drank or used other substances in the context of the sexual situation. Then, most of this chapter focuses on the men who reported that they drank alcohol or used another substance before or during at least one of the two sexual encounters described in their two sexual narratives. We looked for patterns in the data to help us understand the complex relationships between substance use and sex for these HIV-positive gay and bisexual men. We also read other sections of the interview in which the men indicated that drug or alcohol use was related to the sexual interaction. Approximately half way through the study, we added a question about why the men thought that Black and Latino men had higher rates of infection than other men, and some of these responses were also relevant to this chapter.

EXTENT OF DRUG USE DURING SEX

Of the 250 men in the sample, 106 (just over 42%) reported that they drank alcohol or used another substance before or during at least one of the sexual interactions described in their two narratives. Of these 106 men, about three fourths drank alcohol or used another substance during the encounters described in both sexual narratives. Regarding alcohol use, slightly more than a fifth of the men (21%) reported using alcohol before or during one of the two sexual encounters. More than a third (37%) reported using drugs before or during their sexual encounters. Whereas drug use before or during sex was more common than drinking, most men reported never drinking or using drugs before or during these two specific sexual encounters. Even for men who did use substances, in many cases, the amount of any particular substance they used was small (e.g., one or two drinks or one marijuana cigarette). Other than alcohol, the most common substances used during one of the two sexual narratives, by the participant or the partner or both, were marijuana (18%), poppers (9%), cocaine or crack (9%), and methamphetamine (6%).

ROLE OF SUBSTANCE USE IN SEX

In many narratives in which substance use was mentioned, substance use did not appear to be the primary factor affecting the sexual practices and level of risk in the encounters. It was, however, one of a variety of personal and contextual factors that influenced sexual practices, and some narratives suggested that in certain situations, substance use was a crucial factor that affected sexual risk. Overall, patterns that emerged from the data suggested that substance use and sex were affected by three personal factors—behavioral, cognitive, and emotional—and three contextual factors—setting, partner type, and ethnicity.

PERSONAL CHARACTERISTICS AFFECTING SUBSTANCE USE AND SEX

Substance use seems to serve several purposes in the sexual lives of men who have sex with other men (MSM), and we grouped them into three broad categories. Some men described and sought out the behavioral effects of substances and reported that specific drugs facilitated or enhanced specific sexual behaviors. Men also reported cognitive effects of substance use. Some men described immediate cognitive effects (e.g., how drugs affected their thinking, judgments, and decision-making processes). Other men reported cognitive processes that occurred during or after using substances that led to them deciding not to use substances to avoid the anticipated cognitive effects. Finally, substance use was also related to the men's emotional needs. Although these categories are useful for organizing what the men told us, some of them clearly overlap.

Behavioral Effects

Many men mentioned seeking out specific drugs that had particular effects during sex. Although it was common for the men to drink and use other drugs at the same time, they often focused on the effects that one or a few of the drugs had on their sexual behaviors. The drugs that were specifically mentioned most frequently were poppers, methamphetamine (usually called crystal), cocaine, and marijuana.

Poppers

Many men reported that poppers were used to enhance their sexual experiences and that they could "drive you crazy."

> Now, I don't take poppers any more, but I used to. When I had the poppers, the sex was just, you know, so good! Back then—it wasn't that long ago, really—condoms didn't matter. (Black male, age 43, New York)

Other men talked about how poppers eased penetration during anal sex or how they facilitated sexual acts that the men, if not high, would not normally do.

The poppers only, I only do them right before penetration because it is like—it opens; you know, if you are sniffing poppers, you can get a fist up there. It doesn't hurt; it just kind of goes in and feels really good. (White male, age 28, New York)

Another man reported a similar experience with poppers leading to engaging in sexual behaviors different from his usual practices.

I would have never initiated eating a guy's ass without the poppers. I know if I take the poppers, I'm not going to worry about eating the guy's ass. But if I didn't, I would be too tense to initiate that action. (White male, age 28, New York)

Some men specifically noted that poppers were directly related to unsafe sexual behavior.

I don't think [poppers are] safe because I believe that—well, I know for a fact that when I do poppers, I'm pretty much not really thinking about, you know, what I'm doing. Things get carried away. (White male, age 40, San Francisco)

Methamphetamine

Men reported that methamphetamine (crystal) use increased excitement and lowered inhibitions and led to men not thinking clearly and not caring about their actions.

We did some crystal meth. You know how that gets you really high and excited. The drug did have an effect, and it made me do some things that generally I wouldn't do . . . I had not had anal sex in years. (Black male, age 28, San Francisco)

Methamphetamine also was the most frequently mentioned drug associated with marathon sex (e.g., sex lasting for days), group sex, and with other less frequent or more extreme sexual practices, such as fisting. One participant described the sexual behavior that occurred when he and some friends smoked some methamphetamine.

I think it was five of us—kind of large orgy type thing . . . . And it was just a free-for-all, everybody was just doing everybody, and I don't think anyone was wearing a condom (Latino male, age 34, San Francisco)

Cocaine/Crack

To a lesser extent, cocaine and crack also were associated with increasing sexual excitement, and their effects were often compared with those of methamphetamine. Cocaine and crack also were associated with losing control.

The speedier drugs. Definitely crystal, coke, it just makes them so—at that point they could sit on a fire hydrant, and they don't care at that point. It becomes more about that immediate, they're so numbified [sic]. (Latino male, age 32, New York)

We was smoking crack, we were doing blow [cocaine], we were smoking reefer [marijuana], and we were drinking. When you are messed up like that, you don't know what the hell you're thinking. You're like—you're so dizzy that, "Okay, let's just do it and get it over with," you know. When I like get fucked up, I like to get fucked . . . it's why I don't get fucked up so much because I get horny, I want to get dick. (Latino male, age 40, New York)

Marijuana

Marijuana, or pot, also was associated with facilitating sexual moods and behaviors. Some men reported that, similar to what happened when they used some of the other drugs, they engaged in certain behaviors when they smoked marijuana that they would not have engaged in had they not been high. One man reported that marijuana enhanced his orgasms and overall sexual experience.

I've been using [pot] a lot more. To relax, to improve my erotic feelings. I also find that it enhances the quality of my orgasms. So I just enjoy it more, and I have a much better time when I'm stoned than when I don't. (White male, age 35, New York)

Cognitive Effects

Although some men discussed the behavioral effects of substance use, others discussed the various ways that substance use influenced their thinking with regard to sex. Three broad themes emerged: (a) substance use impaired thinking or judgment; (b) substance use led to denial, fantasy, or escape; and (c) substance use was specifically avoided because of its effects on thinking.

Impaired Thinking or Judgment

Many men reported that substance use impaired their thinking and made them not care about their actions, which sometimes led to risky sexual behaviors.

People do a hit of cocaine, and that's it. Their entire train of thought and thinking process just seems to go out the window. And they can care less. (Latino male, age 31, New York)

I think drugs—major drugs—I think really interferes. It affects you. You don't think; everything's skewed anyway. I used to do coke, and

I've done acid, and I've done NDA [MDMA or ecstasy], and you don't—you're not in a normal state of mind. (Latino male, age 40, New York)

Similarly, some men specifically mentioned that their judgment and capacity to make rational decisions was affected by substance use.

But I think that from my experience, I know that [alcohol] can really affect my judgment. Obviously, if I turned around at [the sex club] once and found a dick up my butt without a condom, that could happen again very easily. So while it helps me relax and play when I'm in the mood to play. . . . I also have to be really careful and I think that lots of other men with HIV do. (White male, age 50, San Francisco)

Because a lot of times when you're on—when you're on drugs, then their mind's not right. Your mind's not all there, you know. You'll say, "Fuck everything"; everything goes out the window. (Black male, age 31, New York)

That beer, it like do something to your brain, you mind; it be saying, "Well, you don't need no rubbers," you know. You don't think about using them. You don't want to use them. (Black male, age 37, New York)

In explaining how their sexual behaviors differed between the encounters described in the safe and unsafe sexual narrative, some men blamed substance use.

Well, the one that was unsafe was because we were using drugs and getting high. And when you are getting high and doing drugs, you just don't—you don't think about a condom. You're just outside yourself. (Black male, age 28, New York)

The ones where there was protection usually meant that there was some thought involved, some conscious thought, you know, where—and that—and that I was clear-headed. (Black male, age 37, New York)

Denial, Fantasy, and Escape

Some men reported that drinking or using drugs led them to denial, fantasy, or cognitive escape, which often led to riskier sexual behavior. For example, using substances allowed some men to deny facts about HIV in their lives or to deny that they were engaging in risky behavior. Some men talked about being in a denial stage in which they tried to forget or ignore the fact that they were HIV-positive.

The denial period was also an ecstasy era for me; okay, it was—was ecstasy and heroin era for me. So a lot of the sex that was going on during that time . . . it was just random; it was just out there, just being careless and being chaotic and not caring. (Latino male, age 26, New York)

We were both intoxicated. And . . . I had just found out [that I was HIV positive] and I was blocking it out. I wasn't even thinking about it . . . I was drinking. I started drinking more and using more substances after I found out. (Black male, age 36, New York)

Substance use also led to sexual risk by creating fantasies for the men, as illustrated by the following quotations:

The drug is doing all the talking and all that stuff, you know. . . . You know, I fantasize. You know, but that's the drug that's doing all the, you know, fantasies and stuff like that. (Black male, age 37, New York)

If I was in my right mind, I never have done it [unprotected sex]. . . . And the—once you're started—you see, once you start doing all those different things, drugs and stuff, then everything becomes absolutely what you say it is. (Black male, age 56, New York)

Men also reported that using substances often helped them to escape or get a break from their lives, although they also escaped the world of safer-sex norms.

I was definitely under the influence of [crystal], and that heightened my arousal and really affected my judgment and—see, I got to a point where like after a while it's like I just don't care. It's like all that pressure being built up with trying to be safe all the time. It was like it's so tiring. After a while it was like, you know, I just need a break. (Asian or Pacific Islander male, age 27, San Francisco)

There have been times in the past where I've gotten so stoned that it's just like I just want to go and do this and pretend like none of this is happening. I just want to escape for little while so I think there's an escapism going on at times. (White male, age 37, New York)

One man described how denial, fantasy, and escape all interacted together in his life to lead to unsafe sex.

I think that sometimes you just don't—you don't think about it. You want to go out there. And you're invulnerable. "I'm not positive. I'm not anything. There's nothing wrong with me" . . . You want to pick up the best man out there. You want to have a great time. You don't want to worry about the fact that, "Oh, I'm sick, I'm infected" . . . And especially after a few drinks you really began to think that. "It's a mistake. The tests are wrong. I can't be positive. I'm not sick" . . . And you honestly make yourself believe that for a while. But you are positive. And [laughs] you wake up the next morning with that person—if you do—with the person next to you. And you say, "I am positive, and what did I just do?" And you hope nothing's wrong. . . . And basically, you just want to lie to yourself for a while. You don't want to think about it. And if you do get away with it, you end up thinking about it later. You never just completely forget about it. You can ignore it for a while, but it always pops back up. (Black male, age 30, New York)

Avoiding Substance Use

Some men said that they chose to abstain from using drugs or drinking alcohol because they did not want to damage their immune systems or lose cognitive control in sexual situations. Some men reported abstaining from drugs and alcohol as a temporary strategy that they used in particular situations in which they were more likely to engage in risky behavior.

> Usually what I would do if I'm going out to have sex, I try to limit my use of alcohol or drugs so that I can make more responsible decisions when it comes to sex. So what I try to do is . . . I try to go to places where I know that—particularly, I won't visit bars. Or I won't go to a place where—cruising a place where there's . . . people coming out of bars. . . . Then I know that I'm probably dealing with someone who probably hasn't been drinking all night. Or, you know, that I haven't been drinking all night. (Latino male, age 31, New York)

Getting into treatment or recovery and permanently abstaining from drugs or alcohol was a longer term strategy that also helped men to be safer.

> Well, being that I'm not drinking and getting high like I used to, I can think more clearly about what I'm doing and that I should use one [a condom]. (Black male, age 28, New York)

> I think things more clearly now because I'm in recovery and I'm off the drugs and I think I can keep a level head. You know, and if ain't got no condoms or whatever, there ain't nothing happening. (Black male, age 30, New York)

Emotional Effects

Respondents spoke about several effects that substances had on their emotional lives or how their emotions affected their substance use and sexual behaviors. Themes that emerged were (a) improvement in positive emotions or good feelings when substances were used before or during sex, (b) substance use leading to behaviors that were later regretted, and (c) negative emotional states such as anxiety and depression leading to or being caused by substance use and sexual behavior.

Improvement of Positive Emotions

Men reported that substance use can heighten the thrill or the unique emotional high that sex itself provides and that they sought out enhancement of this sensation. In describing why he had engaged in unprotected insertive and receptive sex in an anonymous situation, one man said

Because it felt good. And I was somewhat stoned, and I was very, very high and I liked the guy. I liked what he was doing and I let him do that. (Black male, age 48, New York)

Other men reported that the high from sex or drugs caused them to ignore other factors in the sexual situation and focus on the sensation.

I think most of it is just—has to do with the powerful nature of sex and wanting the thrill that it provides and the ecstasy that it provided. And seeking to get high and being high—getting high from sex I think is the main thing that leads people to [have unprotected sex]. (White male, age 46, New York)

Even marijuana . . . or even just poppers. Are sufficiently disruptive of my judgment that what happens is I become focused on the sensation and a lot less focused on my brain. (White male, age 35, New York)

As long as I'm not drinking. As long as I'm not doing weed, you know, then I do have safer sex, to be totally honest with you . . . [with] weed or alcohol. . . . Then my walls come down a bit. . . . It's like I go for things I remember felt so good at one time, whether they're harmful to me or not. . . . It's basically that I go into this selfish mode. (Black male, age 39, San Francisco)

Regret After Sex

Some men reported that after the fact they felt bad about their lack of sexual safety when they were drunk or high but that at the time they might have used substances to try to feel better or to help rationalize an unprotected encounter.

I did kind of think, "Oh, my god, we don't have a condom, and we are doing this [unprotected insertive anal sex]," but I didn't stop it because it felt good. I just kept going. And I enjoyed it . . . [and afterward] I felt terrible, and awful, that since we didn't have a condom that—I kept thinking in my mind, "Oh, god, he could have had something," and this and that, and, "How come I don't—I need to stop drinking, I don't think anymore." I felt awful about myself. (Latino male, age 23, San Francisco)

When I get high, I get fucked, you know, and there was a lot of that going on and, you know, just having fun. My needs of being paid a lot of attention to were fulfilled. . . . [But] after the whole situation is done, when I took a look at it, I'm really depressed over relapsing, depressed over getting high, and most speed just brings me into a space where, "Why did I do that?" (Asian or Pacific Islander male, age 32, San Francisco)

One man described how regret about eating too much was similar to engaging in risky sexual behavior when you are high.

Being drunk or being impaired in some way with a drug, um, this is asking for trouble in sexual situations. . . . A lot of times, I sort of liken it to, ah, you eat that last piece of pie when you know you shouldn't have, when you really weren't hungry, but it looked good and you did it anyway, and afterwards you sort of regretted it. It's almost the same thing with sex, like, "Oh, I shouldn't have done that," you know. And afterwards, you know, when everybody is not high anymore, or when they've already come, you know, it brings a lot of clarity to certain situations. (Black male, age 29, New York)

Negative Emotions and Substance Use

A number of men reported that substance use and higher risk sexual behaviors were often linked for them during times when they felt depressed, anxious, less confident, needy for intimacy, or when their feelings were so overwhelming that they just did not care at the time about using condoms.

The alcohol is one of the factors of me having unprotected sex. . . . I get anxious and I get depressed 'cause things are not going right—this is falling apart, that is falling apart—and I will go out on a binge. I was a binge drinker. So I would go out on a binge with sex. . . . It's like the alcohol and the sex comes like right behind it, and its self-destructive behavior. (Black male, age 30, New York)

I had sex, unprotected sex; I smoked marijuana . . . [but] because it was depressing me. If I wasn't high, it wouldn't be bothering me, but when I was high things would just be magnified 50 times; if I felt lonely, then I would feel 50 times more lonely when I smoked marijuana. (Black male, age 34, New York)

Some men reported that substances took away their shyness or anxiety and allowed them to engage in behaviors that they would not have engaged in had they not been drunk or high. One man explained why he had unprotected anal receptive sex with someone in the park:

I was drunk and I was horny and I wanted some dick. . . . That's the only time I would go into the park, because if I'm sober, I'm very quiet and shy; I don't—I wouldn't talk to you if I did not know you. [Once in this situation] you mind goes off on you. . . . You know? You're not thinking about—you're not bringing a condom or doing—you just want to get busy, you know? (Latino male, age 40, New York)

Some men said that sex when they were sober made them more anxious but that sex when they had used drugs meant that safer sex was not even in the picture.

The only reason that . . . it [unprotected sex] would happen is because of being intoxicated. . . . Then, you know, it's just all safety goes out the window. It's like I don't give a fuck. . . . You just go for it, whatever you're going for. . . . I've had sex without drinking and using alcohol and stuff. . . . And it's, you know, a whole different experience. . . . Because, I mean, I don't know, it feels—you feel more nervous. (Black male, age 36, New York)

CONTEXTUAL CHARACTERISTICS AFFECTING SUBSTANCE USE AND SEX

Two contextual elements appeared to affect the sexual behavior of the substance-using men in our sample: the setting and the partner. In terms of settings, sex clubs, outdoor cruising areas, and private parties all have particular rules of conduct that may affect substance use and sexual behaviors. In some situations, these setting-based rules were more important in determining whether sexual behavior was safe than whether substances were used before or during a particular sexual interaction. (Sexual behavior in public and commercial sex environments is addressed in chap. 12, this volume, and thus it will not be discussed here.)

Regarding partner characteristics, the two primary themes that emerged in terms of affecting sexual behavior were the importance of (a) partner type (primary, casual, or paid/paying partner) and (b) substance use by the partner. A final contextual theme emerged regarding explanations that some men had for why there might be a link between higher rates of infection among men of color and substance use in those communities. (A more thorough discussion of ethnicity is addressed in chap. 6, this volume.)

Partner Type

For some men, substance use before or during sex depended on the type of partner they were with (see chap. 3, this volume). In almost a third of encounters described in the sexual narratives involving substance use, the HIV-positive gay or bisexual participant had sex with an HIV-positive partner, in some cases because it allowed him to worry less about using condoms. With long-term HIV-positive partners, with whom sex was reported to be less frequent, alcohol or drugs sometimes were used as an aphrodisiac or as a cue to indicate that sex was on the agenda, but the sexual script and condom use was decided in advance and not affected by whether substances were used.

> He's very cold; my lover's very cold. He doesn't like to be touched, doesn't want to be bothered; but when he gets a little tipsy, he's all over me . . . I said, "You only want sex when you're drunk." (Latino male, age 44, New York)

> Well, I can always tell when he wants to fool around because he puts a little bottle of poppers on his night stand on his side of the bed. (White male, age 36, New York)

For other men, substances were more likely to affect behavior with anonymous, or casual, first-time partners: "Had I been more sober, I probably would not have taken this guy home. So I'm sure the alcohol played a major role in that" (Latino male, age 41, San Francisco).

A few men reported that if they were using substances, they were more willing to be risky with partners who paid them for sex.

> When I was under the influence of drugs and when I was doing sex work and the trick insisted on not using a condom, to give me oral sex, and, oh, you know, occasionally I would look the other way. I wouldn't have much respect for some of the people who were doing it with me, anyway, so it makes it a little bit easier to deal with. (Asian or Pacific Islander transgender, age 32, San Francisco)

Substance Use by the Partner

Some men reported that they thought that if their partner was using drugs or alcohol, they were more likely to engage in risky behavior, sometimes because they let the partner decide whether to use protection.

> I prefer not to use any of that [any more], and I get nervous if the other person looks like he has been drinking or done some kind of substance. . . . Because I think that the intensity of the person wanting to do things that may make me uncomfortable or nervous would just kind of like ruin any chance of any kind of sexual release for me or make me want to leave once I'm aware. (White male, age 48, San Francisco)

> Not on my part anymore but on the other party's part. I found those that drink, or drug usually, defenses come down and they're open because they're not clear, you know. The clarity is not there. And I see it all the time. (Latino male, age 33, New York)

One man discussed that although men were willing to engage in unprotected receptive anal sex with him because of their own substance use, his partners tried to reduce their own risk by asking the participant not to ejaculate during anal sex.

> I don't think they're even really concerned because if you're doing poppers, plus, the majority of the times [inaudible] done marijuana, and you're drinking. And so, I don't know what they're thinking. . . . I'm enjoying whatever we're doing, and I know I'm not gonna come inside of them, you know. They do say stuff like that. "Don't come in me." (White male, age 31, San Francisco)

Substance Use in Communities of Color

The final theme emerged directly from a question asked to about half of the men about why the rates of HIV infection are higher among gay and bisexual men of color. Some men reported that they perceived a link between ethnicity and substance use and that substance use was a reason why Black and Latino communities have high rates of HIV infection. Drug use, and needle use in particular, was thought to be more common within minority communities than within White communities. Some men attributed in-creased availability of drugs to high HIV infection rates in communities of color.

> There's always the possibility of a lot of drug use involved, especially when there's a speed epidemic out there [in minority communities]. You know, sharing needles would be quite common. It won't surprise me a bit. (Asian or Pacific Islander transgender, age 32, San Francisco)

> But I heard like a—the use of drugs, needles, for instance. White people, they use needles, okay, but I think that minorities use it more. The Black people use a lot of heroin or speed, and Latinos use speed a lot, or cocaine; they inject cocaine nowadays. (Latino male, age 45, San Francisco)

Men also reported contextual factors such as poverty as possibly being related to substances use in minority communities, which in turn facilitates sexual risk.

> Like in minorities there's a lot of—a high percentage of people getting into drugs. The cheap kind of drugs, which is IVs and the crack and stuff like that. When people got money they go into cocaine and stuff like that, and that's harder for you to get an HIV infection that way. . . . A lot of people don't have money. They're minorities. They sell their bodies; they sell their sex to make money. Maybe to keep a habit of drugs . . . it's just more need in minorities. And by that reason, you know, the risk is higher. Money—money doesn't make you happy. But it keeps you away from many things. (Latino male, age 41, New York)

Another man thought drugs, sex, and family pressures might explain the ethnic difference.

> I think the drug use, sharing needles and stuff like that, and practicing unsafe sex. . . . Some people don't want to hear it, families are not supportive, and stuff like that, especially old traditional people. "Get out of here; you're gay," you know? (Asian or Pacific Islander male, age 39, San Francisco)

DISCUSSION

Drinking and drug use among the HIV-positive gay and bisexual men in our sample was common by itself and in conjunction with sex. More than 40% of the men used drugs or drank alcohol before or during the sexual encounters described in one of their narratives. The degree to which substance use accompanied sexual behavior is not surprising, given the historical link between sex and substance use among gay and bisexual men. However, there is not a simplistic association between substance use and sexual risk. Many narratives described the use of a small amount of alcohol or other drugs or substance use in conjunction with the use of condoms, and yet a number of others described that, for a variety of reasons, substance use compromised their ability to achieve sexual safety.

In many ways, our data fit the cognitive escape model proposed by McKirnan and his colleagues (1996). The relationship described between substances and sexual risk was complex and appeared to be affected by factors that were both personal and contextual. At the personal level, we observed that substance use had behavioral, cognitive, and emotional effects. Despite the power of personal characteristics (behavioral, cognitive, and emotional) in determining how substance use and sex came together for the men, contextual elements also clearly affected the situation. Setting is an important factor that is explored in depth in chapter 12 (this volume); the relevant point in this chapter is that in some situations, the sexual norms for a particular setting seemed to be important in determining sexual safety, but in other situations, substance use appeared to affect sexual risk within the context of the prevailing norms. Partner type and substance use by sexual partners also were important in affecting the relationship between substance use and sex.

A final contextual factor that bears more investigation is the reporting by some men in both cities that they thought high rates of HIV among minority gay and bisexual men may be due to the fact that substance use was more common in those communities. Researchers have not successfully explained the ethnic differences in HIV rates because there are only minimal racial differences for most risk domains. A recent study found that those who binged on methamphetamine use were more likely to be racial minority men than were those who did not binge (Semple, Patterson, & Grant, 2003). It may be that a model that accounts for the additive effects of multiple stressors may help to explain these differences (e.g., Díaz, Ayala, Bein, Henne, & Marin, 2001; Stall et al., 2003).

One important caution regarding the conclusions in this chapter is that these data cannot establish whether substance use causes sexual risk, despite the language used by many of the men and despite some of the interpretations of the data. Many studies have shown a link between drinking or drug use and sexual risk behavior among gay and bisexual men, but other studies have failed to find a link (Gillmore et al., 2002). Part of the reason for these different findings may be the way the studies were designed (Leigh & Stall, 1993). But even the quantitative studies cannot tell us that substance use causes risk; they can only tell that the two are associated.

The data from the narratives of the HIV-positive gay and bisexual men in our sample make it clear that these men have a complex relationship with alcohol and other drugs. Although many HIV-positive men use substances with few harmful effects on their lives or relationships, others reported problematic relations with substances. Although we did not specifically ask about substance abuse or try to diagnose the participants, it appears that some of the men, currently or previously, had a substance abuse disorder. Regardless of whether they chronically abused substances, many men reported that they used substances in sexual situations and that sometimes this use was related to an increased likelihood of sexual risk. It appears, however, that the equation for risky sex is much more complex than simply whether substances were used or not. A host of personal and contextual factors appear to work together to increase or decrease the likelihood that substance use and risk occur together. Thus, it is likely that an individualized approach to HIV prevention activities may be helpful for this population, because for each man, the factors that affect the interaction between sex and substance may be different. In addition, however, group interventions with substance using gay and bisexual men who have different but overlapping factors affecting them might be helpful to reduce both substance use and sexual risk (Batki & Nathan, 1999). Given this complexity, it is important to try to understand in a more refined manner how and why gay and bisexual men use substances and what effects substances have on their sexual behavior. By increasing our understanding of this complex phenomenon, we can then determine how important substance use is for HIV transmission and how we might best work with HIV-positive gay and bisexual men and their partners.

REFERENCES

Batki, S. L., & Nathan, K. I. (1999). HIV/AIDS and substance use disorders. In M. Galanter & H. D. Kleber (Eds.), *Textbook of substance abuse treatment* (2nd ed., pp. 503–510). Washington, DC: American Psychiatric Association.

Díaz, R. M., Ayala, G., Bein, E., Henne, J., & Marin, B. V. (2001). The impact of homophobia, poverty, and racism on the mental health of gay and bisexual Latino men: Findings from 3 US cities. *American Journal of Public Health, 91*, 927–932.

Freese, T. E., Miotto, K., & Reback, C. J. (2002). The effects and consequences of selected club drugs. *Journal of Substance Abuse Treatment, 23,* 151–156.

Gillmore, M. R., Morrison, D. M., Leigh, B. C., Hoppe, M. J., Gaylord, J., & Rainey, D. T. (2002). Does "high = high risk"? An event-based analysis of the relationship between substance use and unprotected anal sex among gay and bisexual men. *AIDS and Behavior, 6,* 361–370.

Harrington, R. D., Woodward, J. A., Hooton, T. M., & Horn, J. P (1999). Life-threatening interactions between HIV-1 protease inhibitors and illicit MDMA and gamma-hydroxybutyrate. *Archives of Internal Medicine, 159,* 221.

Klitzman, R. L., Pope, H. G., & Hudson, J. I. (2000). MDMA ("Ecstasy") abuse and high-risk sexual behaviors among 169 gay and bisexual men. *American Journal of Psychiatry, 157,* 1162–1164.

Leigh, B. C., & Stall, R. (1993). Substance use and risky sexual behavior for exposure to HIV. *American Psychologist, 48,* 1035–1045.

Lewis, M., & Ross, M. (1995). *A select body: The gay dance party subculture and the HIV/AIDS pandemic.* New York: Cassell.

Mansergh, G., Colfax, G. N., Marks, G., Rader, M., Guzman, R., & Buchbinder, S. (2001). The circuit party men's health survey: Findings and implications for gay and bisexual men. *American Journal of Public Health, 91,* 953–958.

McKirnan, D. J., Ostrow, D. G., & Hope, B. (1996). Sex, drugs and escape: A psychological model of HIV-risk sexual behaviors. *AIDS Care, 8,* 655–669.

McNall, M., & Remafedi, G. (1999). Relationship of amphetamine and other substance use to unprotected intercourse among young men who have sex with men. *Archives of Pediatric and Adolescent Medicine, 153,* 1130–1135.

Molitor, F., Truax, S., Ruiz, J. D., & Sun, R. K. (1998). Association of methamphetamine use during sex with sexual behaviors and HIV infection among non-injection drug users in California. *Western Journal of Medicine, 168,* 93–97.

Purcell, D. W., Campos. P. E., & Perilla, J. L. (1996). Therapy with lesbians and gay men: A cognitive behavioral perspective. *Cognitive and Behavioral Practice, 3,* 391–415.

Purcell, D. W., Parsons, J. T., Halkitis, P. N., Mizuno, Y., & Woods, W. J. (2001). Substance use and sexual transmission risk behavior of HIV-positive men who have sex with men. *Journal of Substance Abuse, 13,* 1–16.

Rawson, R. A., Washton, A., Domier, C. P., & Reiber, C. (2002). Drugs and sexual effects: Role of drug type and gender. *Journal of Substance Abuse Treatment, 22,* 103–108.

Semple, S. J., Patterson, T. L., & Grant, I. (2003). Binge use of methamphetamine among HIV-positive men who have sex with men: Pilot data and HIV prevention implications. *AIDS Education and Prevention, 15,* 133–147.

Stall, R., Mills, T. C., Williamson, J., Hart, T., Greenwood, G., Paul, J., et al. (2003). Association of co-occurring psychosocial health problems and increased vulnerability to HIV/AIDS among urban men who have sex with men (MSM). *American Journal of Public Health, 93,* 939–942.

Stall, R., & Purcell, D. W. (2000). Intertwining epidemics: A review of research on substance use among men who have sex with men and its connection to the AIDS epidemic. *AIDS and Behavior, 4,* 181–192.

Stall, R., & Wiley, J. (1988). A comparison of alcohol and drug use patterns of homosexual and heterosexual men: The San Francisco Men's Health Study. *Drug and Alcohol Dependence, 22,* 63–73.

Sullivan, P. S., Nakashima A. K., Purcell D. W., Ward, J.W., & the Supplement to the HIV/AIDS Surveillance Study Group. (1998). Geographic differences in noninjection and injection substance use among HIV-seropositive men who have sex with men: Western United States versus other regions. *Journal of Acquired Immune Deficiency Syndromes and Human Retrovirology, 19,* 266–273.

Westermeyer, J. (1999). Cross cultural aspects of substance abuse. In M. Galanter & H. D. Kleber (Eds.), *Textbook of substance abuse treatment* (2nd ed., pp. 75–85). Washington, DC: American Psychiatric Association.

Woody, G. E., Donnell, D., Seage, G. R., Metzger, D., Marmor, M., Koblin, B., et al. (1999). Non-injection substance use correlates with risky sex among men having sex with men. *Drug and Alcohol Dependence, 53,* 197–205.

Woody, G. E., VanEtten-Lee, M. L., McKirnan, D., Donnell, D., Metzger, D., Seage, G., III, et al. (2001). Substance use among men who have sex with men: Comparison with a national household survey. *Journal of Acquired Immune Deficiency Syndromes, 27,* 86–90.

12

BRIEF ENCOUNTERS: THE ROLES OF PUBLIC AND COMMERCIAL SEX ENVIRONMENTS IN THE SEXUAL LIVES OF HIV-POSITIVE GAY AND BISEXUAL MEN

JEFFREY T. PARSONS AND KALIL VICIOSO

The particular venues at which HIV-positive gay and bisexual men seek sex partners may play a critical role in their ability to engage in safer sex behaviors. Two such venues that are commonly described by such men are commercial sex environments (CSEs), such as bathhouses and sex clubs, and public sex environments (PSEs), such as parks, alleys, or other outdoor areas.

CSEs are commercial venues at which sexual activity between men takes place. Some facilities provide private rooms in which men can have sex, some have large open areas for sexual activity, and others have both. Men usually cruise one another for sex while either nude or wearing only a towel. CSEs have been associated with unprotected sex and substance use

The authors thank Mark Flores, Eric Martin, Diane Tider, and Jason van Ora for their assistance in preparing this chapter.

for many years, and many were closed or strictly regulated as a result of the HIV epidemic (Berube, 1996). Some argue that such venues provide the opportunity for socialization among gay and bisexual men, as well as the opportunity to provide HIV prevention messages (Binson et al., 2001; Woods, Binson, Mayne, Gore, & Rebchook, 2000). A recent study in Los Angeles found that young gay and bisexual men who frequented CSEs were more likely than other men to be HIV-positive, have a history of STDs, report more sexual partners, engage in more risky sexual behaviors, and have used drugs or alcohol during their last sexual experience (Brown, Reidy, Johnson, & Bingham, 2000).

PSEs are other venues in which men can meet other men to have sex. Unlike CSEs, which usually require payment of an admission fee and are commercial establishments, PSEs are typically outdoor, public areas where men can cruise for sex partners. Studies have shown that many men who have sex with men frequent such venues (de Wit, de Vroome, Sandfort, & van Griensven, 1997; Flowers, Hart, & Marriott, 1999), including men who do not identify as gay or bisexual (Earl, 1990). Two evaluations of HIV prevention interventions delivered in PSEs have been recently published (French, Power, & Mitchell, 2000; Hospers, Debets, Ross, & Kok, 1999). Two studies of Latino gay and bisexual men identified anonymous sex in PSEs as a significant predictor of unprotected anal sex (Díaz, Stall, Hoff, Daigle, & Coates, 1996; Díaz, Morales, Bein, Dilan, & Rodriguez, 1999). PSEs do not have the financial costs associated with CSEs and thus may be more popular for men who have sex with men with less disposable income.

In this chapter, men from the Seropositive Urban Mens Study (SUMS; see chap. 1, this volume) tell their stories of sexual experiences in PSEs and CSEs. Our primary goals are to describe the unique characteristics of the two different types of venues according to the men who frequent them, present the reasons that HIV-positive gay and bisexual men use such venues, and illustrate the impact that these venues have on serostatus disclosure and sexual practices. From a total of 250 qualitative interviews from SUMS, the data for this chapter were derived from sexual narratives of the 64 men who reported sexual activity in either a PSE or a CSE.

CHARACTERISTICS OF PUBLIC SEX ENVIRONMENTS

Participants reported sexual encounters in a variety of PSEs: parks, alleys, streets, and beaches. In many of these venues, the PSE described had a reputation as a location where men cruised for sex. Several specific characteristics of PSEs were cited by participants: (a) the spontaneity of sex in PSEs; (b) group sex experiences and voyeuristic aspects; (c) the presence of non-gay-identified men; and (d) a thrill factor associated with sex in a public venue.

Locations for "Unexpected" Sex

Men frequently described their sexual encounters in PSEs as being spontaneous or unexpected. Many reported not necessarily looking for sex but that the sexual situation "just happened." The layered structure of PSEs makes this explanation possible because the men can meet at the periphery or even the perimeter of the venue. One participant described having sex in a park on his way to his SUMS project interview:

> I got there [a park] earlier today trying to kill some time. . . . Until finally it was just like maybe an hour before I had to be here [at the interview]. . . . And I was feeling frustrated by this time because all I wanted to do was just like get off all day and I couldn't. . . . And I kind of steered the conversation towards sex because he was only 19 years old. And I pulled my dick out and it was semi-hard. And then I let him play with it. (Black male, age 30, New York)

Other participants who reported having sex in cruising parks further illustrate this trend by describing their brief encounters in PSEs as happening as a result of being in the "right place at the right time":

> I was just—I got some bad news from my doctor yesterday, and it overtook me. I said I needed time for myself to take a little walk. And I end up walking, and I got up and hot and horny seeing all these men passing through [the park]. (Black male, age 27, New York)

> Oh, oh, okay. I was walking my dog in Forest Park. And I just met some guy who was very attractive. Never—didn't even know his name. I was just walking my dog in the park, and he just grabbed his leg. And I saw like this enormous dick. And I was like, oh my god. (laughter) And I mean, I just—I gave the guy a blow job. (Latino male, age 31, New York)

Some interviews included contradictory statements, in which participants reported seemingly unexpected sexual encounters in PSEs but when questioned further, did report some indication that they were, in fact, expecting to have sex. When asked by the interviewer what he was doing at the park, one participant stated

> Just walking. Walking, sometimes I—the area where I go it's like a path and it's surrounded by water where there's ducks in the water, a pond, so I bring bread sometimes and I feed, you know, as I'm walking around I'm feeding the little ducks or the birds or whatever. . . . I like going to that place, it's just very serene and present, you know, it looks nice, it's just private, you know. (White male, age 40, New York)

But when asked if he had been expecting to have sex, he answered "Yeah." Another participant described a similar experience where he was not expecting to have sex in a park.

> When you go to the park, you cruise at night. When you're in the park you got the trails, you got the woods, you got, you know, other surroundings what make, what makes it more appealing for guys to come together. . . . So I went to the park that evening and I met up with a guy. . . . So at the time, I didn't have any condoms, I didn't really expect to get into anything sexually. (Black male, age 28, New York)

Group Sex and Voyeurism

Many participants reported sexual experiences in PSEs that involved multiple partners through group sex situations. Some men described this as an attractive feature of PSEs in terms of enhancing the erotic aspect of the brief encounters:

> So he was trying to do me, and it got so that a lot of people came around. We began to have a crowd. . . . He had his pants down to his ankles and a couple of guys were standing there with their dicks in my face. And it was a total—it was my—it was basically my fantasy. I had, like, three guys upon me. . . . And it was, like, I was just circled with all these guys, like three or four guys, and we—everybody was getting off, and then we all came and then that was it. And then everybody separated. Nobody said nothing to nobody. (Black male, age 35, New York)

> I enjoy group sex. And in a park, if I walk up on a couple of guys who are having sex, and then they notice me, and then they stop having sex but I haven't left the area where they're from, and, in fact, I move closer toward them and provoke some kind of response to my presence from them, to either join them or—or "Back off, you're in my space and don't come any closer." (Latino male, age 34, San Francisco)

Some participants, however, described the voyeuristic aspect of sex in PSEs as distracting and unpleasant. These participants would often describe going to specific areas of PSEs with less foot traffic to maintain greater privacy. One participant specifically contrasted this aspect of sex in a PSE with sex in a CSE:

> Is anybody watching us? That's the question about that place: is anybody watching us? Some people like that, I don't, you know. I'm going to be going back to the club [bathhouse] pretty soon; it's going to be getting cold out anyway. It's nice to have the [cruising park] in the summer, though, you know, that's why I go there more often, once the weather changes, I go to the club. (Black male, age 29, New York)

Sex With "Straight" Men

Some men described the presence of non-gay-identified or "straight" men at PSEs as an attractive feature of the venue. It is likely that these straight-identified men seek out these venues because of the unplanned "it just happened" aspect of sex in PSEs, which may help diffuse any questions regarding their sexual orientation:

> And he was married, because he had a wedding band on. (laughter). And that was actually what turned me on, you know. That, oh my God, this guy is married. I always liked that. I always thought that was a turn on. (Latino male, age 31, New York)

> Mostly the more straight-acting men or men who are bisexual or so-called "straight" men, most of them, they come to the park, and that's a lot of what comes to the park these days. They don't want to use condoms. (Black male, age 44, San Francisco)

Thrill Factor

Some men discussed a thrill aspect connected with having sex in public venues. Often, this was focused around the excitement and exhilaration related to the possibility of getting caught or the potential for danger associated with sex in outdoor areas:

> How was I feeling? I felt frightened. My adrenaline was up. I felt like I might be getting into trouble, and I realized that that's probably part of the reason that people go there [to the park], because of the fear aspect, fear of getting caught or wanting to get caught. But my adrenaline was up, and I was very nervous. But it didn't stop me from doing what I did. (White male, age 55, San Francisco)

> It was about 3 a.m. . . . . Well, in the back of my mind I was thinking I was gonna get caught. But at the time I didn't really care. . . . [I was just thinking about] the pleasure of it, I guess—and the danger. (mixed race/ethnicity male, age 34, San Francisco)

Other men talked about the thrill of sex in PSEs in terms of the pleasure and the process of obtaining a sex partner. This was frequently characterized as a way to enhance sexual excitement and was often tied to the process of finding a partner and "scoring" (having sex with him): "It just makes me feel wanted, you know. I just like the joy, you know. I just enjoy the thrill of it" (Black male, age 45, New York).

> Sometimes the most fun about it is the chase, you know. Once it's over, it's like, you know, "Good-bye, get away from me." It's just how I am. I don't mean to be that way, but it's how I am. (Black male, age 29, New York)

CHARACTERISTICS OF COMMERCIAL
SEX ENVIRONMENTS

Participants reported engaging in sex activities in a number of CSEs, including peep shows and adult movie theaters, although most reported activities in bathhouses or sex clubs:

> A bathhouse is a place of social gathering when one wants to get clean. Ha, ha, ha. It's a place; a bathhouse is a place. They have like a lot of little rooms that you go in. You pay like $20 and you have your room for like 8 hours. It's got a little twin bed and a little place to put your cigarettes and your booze on. And they also sell booze and drugs in there. You know, I'm sure they'd be out of business if they stuck to the law. And it actually has showers and has a sauna and it has a steam room and it has all that stuff. And it has a work out room and an exercise room and a lounge and a movie room and stuff. So you can walk around there and do what you want. But most people go there for sex. And let me tell you some of the boys in that place on Friday night, oh my God. I mean, you would chew your right arm off to look like half of them. (White male, age 34, New York)

As described, CSEs, unlike PSEs, are places where men go explicitly to have sex. When they go to CSEs, men are focused on the sexual experience that they will have and not on other sources of stimulation such as the thrill of the risk of getting caught or the possibility of having sex with men who identify themselves as straight. Several themes emerged from participant narratives involving CSEs: (a) drug and alcohol use; (b) attractiveness of clients and the ability to see many potential sex partners in states of undress; (c) absence of verbal communication; and (d) the power differential between those with and without rooms.

Drug and Alcohol Use

Drug and alcohol use seems to play a particularly important role in CSEs and was frequently described as part of a larger theme of escaping thoughts of HIV. (For more discussion of the role of substance use, see chap. 11, this volume.) In response to what he was getting high on, one respondent answered:

> I don't know, whatever anybody had. (laughter) Crystal, coke. . . . I was not as high as I've ever been or not as high as I wanted to be. When I go out for myself, I want to lose touch with reality. And that's my whole, sole purpose, to just get away, because it relieves every bit of—if you have an outlet, whether it's playing golf or whether it's going to the movies by yourself or it's gardening, whatever it is that totally you can get away from. . . . When I go out and I party and stuff, I don't

have a care in the world. And I'm really like relaxing myself. I'm really happy about life. And I really don't have to think about AIDS and dying and all this other shit. . . . Well that day I got high and then I got horny. So then I went to the bathhouse. (White male, age 34, New York)

If the participant was not under the influence of alcohol or drugs while in the CSE, his partner often was. Some participants attributed certain sex practices to particular drugs, especially the relationship between playing the passive (receptive) role in anal sex acts and use of crystal methamphetamine. One participant described how he attributed certain sexual activities to his partner being tweaked (a common term for being under the influence of methamphetamine):

> I also questioned whether he was on drugs, whether he was tweaked, because of, one, how fast his legs went up in the air. Which is interesting that I relate the two together. . . . But, it also has a lot to do with the stereotype of the bath house. You know? I used to go there a lot when I was tweaked. And I guess I'm very much alert of that going on, and I'm pretty much suspicious of everyone. For some reason, the fact that he threw his legs up in the air so fast really plays a big part. Because I know that when I used to be tweaked, I used to really like to get fucked because that was the only way I could get off. (White male, age 32, San Francisco)

Many participants reported the use of poppers (nitrate inhalants) in conjunction with their activities in CSEs, typically inhaled just before anal sex. Often, it was presented as a requirement to being in a CSE, and these participants were clear that poppers were essential to a satisfying CSE experience. "I'm not even going to go [to the bathhouse] if I don't have any poppers, you know what I mean?" (Black male, 37, New York).

> I had my poppers with me, of course. Because I like taking a sniff or two of that. . . . I only do them right before penetration, because it like opens, you know, if you are sniffing poppers you can get a fist up there. (White male, age 28, New York)

Attractiveness

Men described CSEs as places to find many attractive men wearing little or no clothing. For men who desire the opportunity to view many naked men, CSEs are a better option than PSEs, where most men will be clothed. The men often focused their discussions on the physically beautiful men with whom one can have sex in CSEs. One participant described his experience as follows:

> It is amazing. It is the kind of night where it has gotten known, like around, that that's the night when all the really beautiful hot looking

beautiful butt men all go there, and there is a hundred beautiful guys walking around in towels and the animalism in me comes out and I am looking and I am going "yummmm" and you just want to like attack them, and just like just eat them all up and you don't know which one to choose from because there is so many of them. . . . It is like being a young kid and walking into Disney World. You are just like, okay, I am ripping off my clothes and trying to get into my towel because I am just like, you know, waiting to get on that first ride so to speak. (White male, age 28, New York)

Absence of Verbal Communication

Consistent with other studies (Somlai, Kalichman, & Bagnall, 2001), men described CSEs as places in which verbal communication was not practiced. Some felt that talking was an unnecessary factor in obtaining sex at CSEs, and others sought out such venues specifically because of their desires to avoid verbal communication. "Well, because, I mean, when it comes to sex, you know, you go to a sex club, you don't need to speak English" (Asian or Pacific Islander male, age 32, San Francisco).

Well I don't talk [in bathhouses]. I'm the type of person, maybe I say one word. But I'm not like a talking person. . . . If he says something, I don't even remember, okay. (Latino male, age 41, New York)

Some participants explained how nonverbal communication in CSEs can be quite communicative and how it is used to indicate desired sexual activities to potential sex partners at these venues:

And I grabbed his ass and he didn't move so I knew that it was all right, that he wanted me to fuck, so I reached for the condom, and I was putting the condom on he was moving his asshole up. And so we got on the bed and I started fucking him for about a good 10 minutes. (White male, age 34, New York)

Although the previous participant reported engaging in unprotected sex as a result of nonverbal communication, other participants, as illustrated by the following quote, reported the use of nonverbal techniques resulting in protected sex:

This guy was sitting on the bed. And he was, you know, face up as opposed to face down. And we made eye contact and he beckoned me into the room. . . . And I took off my towel and he started to suck my dick. . . . I, you know, turned him over and stuck my tongue up his ass and then played with the area and came to the conclusion that he wanted me to fuck him. And he handed me a condom, you know, which is the international symbol for "I want you to use a condom." (White male, age 34, New York)

The Power of the Rooms

Some participants talked specifically about their need to have a private room in bathhouses to have potential sex partners come to them, rather than the other way around. Often, this was discussed in the context of the power that is associated with having a private cubicle in a CSE:

> When I go to the baths, I tend to—I always take a room, and I always pretty much have people come into my room rather than my walking the halls. It's a sense of power I guess, you know, and it's also a sense of protection with people. I'm not being rejected; people have to come to me. (White male, age 44, New York)

Further illustrating the need of some men to have a room in CSEs, one participant was willing to wait over an hour in line to get a room rather than just a locker:

> But when you get that [a locker], then you are like—you don't have the option; you are there in their corner, like you have to like go in their rooms, you know, that kind of thing. You don't have the power and the control. (White male, age 28, New York)

NEEDS MET (AND NOT MET) BY BRIEF ENCOUNTERS

Men described a number of needs that they felt were met through frequenting PSEs and CSEs. Specifically, participants talked about the ways in which these venues satisfied sexual, physical, and emotional needs. Some men, however, explained that going to such venues failed to meet certain other needs.

Sexual Release and Physical Needs

Most men were clear in articulating how PSEs and CSEs met their physical and sexual needs:

> The most recent experience was just 2 days ago when I was at a bathhouse. . . . I was there for three reasons, and out of the three reasons, two of the things happened. I was there to have—to have anal sex, to get fucked, and I was there to fuck someone, and then to get sucked off and then suck someone else off, so I guess that's four. And so, only two of those happened, or maybe three. (mixed race/ethnicity male, age 43, San Francisco)

Although many participants engaged in sexual behaviors at these venues with individuals that they perceived to be attractive, for other men the attractiveness of the partner was clearly secondary to the physical need to have sex. One participant described his unsatisfying sexual experience in a park:

> I wasn't attracted to the person but all I wanted was to just go ahead and cum and that was it. So I really didn't want to get to know that person, so I just wanted to get my shit off and that was it. . . . But he didn't arouse me the way I like to be aroused so it really didn't turn me on that much; it was like something I wanted to hurry up and get over with. (Latino male, age 32, New York)

Some men specifically differentiated using PSEs and CSEs to meet sexual needs from finding partners in other venues to meet more emotional needs:

> Well if I meet somebody that I would like to take seriously, I try to put off sex; but otherwise, when I meet somebody and it's on that level that we're getting together, then it's just a matter of release it seems. . . . But if it's somebody that I've met and we make an actual date of it, then we try to have fun with it. (Latino male, age 33, New York)

Not all participants reported feeling comfortable with their use of PSEs and CSEs for sexual gratification. Some participants described feeling conflicted over the use of such venues to meet their sexual needs:

> I go—I go to that [bathhouse] periodically. . . . And I go there to basically, to get off. And you know, it's this stupid place, and it's a stupid way of spending a morning or an afternoon or an evening or whatever, but you wander around, go around in circles, look at people; they look at you. You feel good about yourself; you feel bad about yourself. (White male, age 42, New York)

Emotional Needs

Some men reported having their emotional needs met as a result of sexual activities in PSEs and CSEs. Men reported frequenting such venues to deal with feelings of loneliness, depression, and a desire for intimacy:

> And being gay—it's really hard, it's just really hard. And it can be a pretty lonely life, you know, and having sex with even people I don't know somehow relieves the loneliness. Just someone touching you or whatever. Sometimes I go to the bath house, not specifically to have sex, but to have someone who will hug me, just touch me, and that's it. (Asian or Pacific Islander male, age 31, San Francisco)

> I was just depressed, and I didn't have any plans. I wasn't working, and it was like, I know how good the night on Sunday is there [at a bathhouse], so then I drove all the way into the city for a specific purpose, you know. (White male, age 28, New York)

Some men specifically cited an emotional need to escape thinking about their HIV status as a reason for frequenting PSEs and CSEs:

> And of course always HIV, it's like a helicopter hovering around me. And, that doesn't stop me. I just go and do it, you know. I just finish what I went there for because that was the purpose of my visit to the place [the bathhouse]. Find a person that I liked. And I did. And what happens sexually? I don't really care. (Latino male, age 41, New York)

Other men talked about these venues as places they could go to feel more attractive on the basis of the attention they received from potential sex partners:

> The need to know that people like you—we all like to look good. It's all about looking good, you know, and it feels good when people like me, you know. When you're having a good time with that, you know what I mean, you're treated for that. (Latino male, age 32, New York)

Unmet Needs

Some participants specifically spoke about the lack of fulfillment of emotional and relationship-oriented needs from brief sexual encounters in PSEs and CSEs. Feelings of guilt, depression, loneliness, and a general sense of dissatisfaction were reported by some men in response to these encounters. Some spoke about the guilt and shame they felt cheating on their boyfriends by having sex with anonymous partners at these venues:

> I go to the bathhouse and just, for 8 hours straight, you know, and then a lot of times I end up going in the room and just sleeping most of it. Just go there and someone gets it—gets off real quick, and I'm sitting there laying and think, "Man, why'd I go spend my money to come in here, you know?" And, that's how I always—I always—every time I go there, I go there, one or two encounters, and then I go lay down and I go to sleep, and it's time to go, and then I—you know, to me, I wasted my money. (Latino male, age 34, San Francisco)

> But then I did get a bit guilty, you know, a guilty streak that went "Oh my God, I am getting my ass plowed by some guy who is really hot and beautiful, and my boyfriend is in Kentucky." (White male, age 28, New York)

Other participants talked about how although they had frequented PSEs and CSEs regularly in the past, their needs had shifted and thus went to these venues less often:

> I would go out to [a cruising park] late at night for sex. No matter how tired I was, my dick would drag me out the door even though my body wanted to go to bed, you know. And that still happens sometimes, but

not nearly as much. . . . I'm much more interested in connecting with someone. (White male, age 34, San Francisco)

I went to [this sex club] maybe a year ago and just didn't feel right while I was there. I used to go to [this sex club] a lot. It was real strange to go to a familiar place and feel like, "This doesn't feel good." I did stay, and I did go to a glory hole where somebody sucked my dick, and unusually—and the situation was very unsatisfying. It's part of what lead to things changing; I felt like, "This is too anonymous." It just was too anonymous. (White male, age 50, San Francisco)

IMPACT ON WHAT HAPPENS SEXUALLY

Frequenting PSEs and CSEs were related to two critical aspects of the sexual lives of HIV-positive gay and bisexual men. First, attendance at these venues played a role in making assumptions about the HIV serostatus of sexual partners as well as serostatus disclosure. Second, men expressed the ways in which being in such sexually charged venues either did or did not result in sexual-risk practices.

Assumptions About Serostatus and Disclosure

Just being in PSE and CSE venues resulted in some participants making assumptions about the serostatus of their anonymous partners. (For a more detailed discussion of assumptions about partner serostatus, see chap. 8, this volume.) In most cases, participants made the assumption that their partner was also HIV-positive:

In these sex clubs and stuff, I assume that most of them are positive. And I assume that maybe most of them are there for the same reason I'm there for, and that's to have sex. And that's to get off. (Native American male, age 41, San Francisco)

In addition to making assumptions about the serostatus of their partners, some men used these assumptions and the nature of the sexual venue as justification for not disclosing their HIV-positive status to their sexual partners. (For a more detailed discussion of disclosure issues, see chap. 7, this volume.) When asked if HIV status was a factor, this man replied:

Not in the baths. Oh I—I think I always think of the person as if they have HIV and they're just not telling me. . . . But as far as in the baths, I don't tell people what my HIV status is. (White male, age 66, New York)

Other men failed to disclose their HIV status because they felt that such communication was either awkward or indicated that they would disclose their status if anyone actually asked:

I just—it's—you know, in a place like that [a bathhouse], it's kind of hard when you've just met somebody to say "Oh, by the way, I'm HIV positive." Although I have a few times. But it's basically that I don't want somebody to; you know, it's complicated, I don't like that. (White male, age 42, New York)

People don't ask you. If they come up front and ask me "Are you HIV-positive or no?", I'm going to say, "Yes." Because they're asking me. But nobody asks. (Latino male, age 41, New York)

Some participants explained how, although not inclined to disclose their status in a PSE or CSE, they typically disclose their HIV status when they meet potential sex partners outside of these venues:

And 99.9% of the time, if I meet someone somewhere, I let them know I am HIV. . . . When I don't want a relationship, I go to the bathhouse. . . . That's the only place I don't tell no one I'm HIV because I feel 99.9% of them are probably already HIV, because there's so much unsafe sex there, you know, and I know they don't tell you if they're HIV or not, you know, and I don't say nothing. That's why I say 99.9%, you know. (Latino male, age 34, San Francisco)

Sexual Risk Behaviors

Some participants explained how being in a PSE or CSE increased their likelihood of unprotected sex, frequently because of assumptions made about their partners at these venues or because they felt that each person should take responsibility for their own actions:

I don't insist on it [condom use] in the baths, for example, where I assume everybody is taking responsibility for themselves, their own risk, their own level of risk that they'll accept. (White male, age 46, New York)

Most of the boys [at the parks] don't want to use a condom; they just throw their dick in your throat. They don't give a fuck, some of them. . . . They ask you when it's all over, "I hope you don't have nothing." I've met a lot of boys like that. "I hope you don't have anything" after they fuck you. . . . You should have thought about that before we got into this shit. (Black male, age 45, New York)

One participant assumed that a partner he had met in a cruising park who had said that he was HIV-negative was not telling the truth and ended up having unsafe sex with him because he believed that his partner was lying:

I said, "You have rubbers?" He said, "No." I said, "Oh well." He said, "No, I don't care." I said, "Oh, really? But you don't even know if I'm sick or not." He said, "I know." So, I had to ask if he was positive. He said, "No." But he never asked me. So I didn't tell him. . . . I assumed he was positive when he told me he didn't care. . . . And to this day I really do think he was positive. And he just lied and told me, "No." That's why we had unprotected sex, 'cause I didn't believe him. . . . If I had really, really thought he was negative, I wouldn't have had sex with him. I might have—I might have—we might have had oral sex, but there definitely would have been no penetration. (Black male, age 32, New York)

Other participants voiced distress about their unprotected sex at these venues. Sometimes this was expressed as concern about possible HIV transmission, but other times it reflected fear about the participants becoming infected with an STD:

Actually, I didn't really think about much. Afterwards, I felt really bad. I did. I felt like, "Oh my god." And the first thing I thought of was like, "Oh my god, what if I get something in my throat, and I bring this home?" (Latino male, age 31, New York)

Other participants were just as likely to report safer sex behaviors in PSEs and CSEs as in other venues:

I was at [a cruising park] and I was walking through the park on the side where they cruise and everything. And, I met this cute little young blond boy and he came up to me and he said, "Oh, black daddy, I want you to fuck me," and I said, "Okay, sure, why not?" So, I asked him if he had any condoms and he said, "No." I said, "Well, we can't do it without condoms," and he wanted to do it without a condom. Fortunately, I had one in my wallet. (Black male, age 32, San Francisco)

Basically, I try not to have oral sex because it just gets so complicated, and I don't need it. I don't know, I have reached the point where I'm almost just happy enough to just jerk off with somebody and that satisfies; it satisfies him. I know it's safe. I know it's perfectly safe. So, I was in this cubicle [at the bathhouse] with this guy, and I jerked off by him and he jerked off by me. (White male, age 42, New York)

One participant even specified that he felt that the nature of CSEs made it easier to maintain the commitment to practicing safer sex:

For me, sex clubs and bathhouses are actually safer places for people like me because if I had been in a situation where someone wanted to penetrate me without a condom, which is what happened when I got infected, I could have said more easily, "No"; but because I was at the person's house, I felt like more obligated in a way. It was hard for me to set up those boundaries. (White male, age 41, San Francisco)

DISCUSSION

PSEs and CSEs clearly meet the sexual needs of some HIV-positive gay and bisexual men and provide a reliable source of sexual and physical release. Although quantitative studies have suggested that frequenting these venues is associated with unprotected sexual activity (Brown et al., 2000; Díaz et al., 1996, 1999; Parsons & Halkitis, 2002), these findings were not necessarily supported qualitatively. We heard stories from men who were perfectly capable of and committed to safer sex practices at these venues. We did, however, also hear stories from men who suggested that the spontaneity, anonymity, and lack of verbal communication associated with sex in PSEs and CSEs may facilitate having unprotected sex.

Interviews revealed that sex can "just happen" in PSEs when walking one's dog, riding one's bike, or trying to clear one's head. This is mainly a result of the layered structure of the venues. The aspect of PSEs that makes it seem like sex "just happened" makes them particularly appealing for men who identify as straight as well as the men who seek them out, most likely because men can justify to themselves that they were not seeking out sex with another man. The need to disown a sexual event may be important for men who are conflicted about seeking out these experiences because of struggles with their own sexual orientation, internalized homophobia, involvement in a monogamous relationship, or HIV-positive serostatus.

PSEs were often characterized as places to have group sex (or at least an audience) with the added bonus of the thrill and danger associated with the potential of being caught or arrested for having sex in a public place. These added dimensions made sex in PSEs much more desirable to some of the participants. Additional research should explore why this danger is such a salient characteristic of PSEs and whether it is a function of sexual sensation seeking or sexual compulsivity.

CSEs were somewhat more overt sexual venues. They provide men with a place to go specifically to seek out sex with other men. People do not just happen on CSEs. Men often described CSEs as a sexual playground or candy store where they could go to escape and indulge in a myriad of hot, beautiful, naked men, all there with one thing on their minds: sex. Limited verbal communication was often cited by men as a reason for frequenting CSEs. Instead of speaking, men communicate their desire and availability for sex through nonverbal strategies. Which sex acts are of interest to a particular person are indicated through gestures, such as pointing or turning on their stomach and lifting the buttocks in the air. Nonverbal communication is also used in CSEs to indicate the desire for protected sex.

Drugs facilitated the escape function that CSEs serve for many men. Recreational drugs, particularly crystal methamphetamine, poppers, and other club or party drugs, were used to intensify sexual sensations and make certain types of sex possible and enjoyable. The drug use, availability of many men all looking for sex, and the lack of verbal communication inherent in bathhouses and sex clubs may interact in such a way that HIV-positive gay and bisexual men use CSEs to facilitate a sense of cognitive escapism (McKirnan, Ostrow, & Hope, 1996). The venues permit men to escape thoughts about their HIV status, and, in some instances, escape perceptions of responsibility for safer sex practices or serostatus disclosure.

It is important to recognize that although certain needs are met by frequenting PSEs and CSEs, other needs are not. Men often described negative feelings resulting from the use of these venues for brief sexual encounters. Guilt, depression, loneliness, isolation—these were all feelings that some men attributed to sex environments. Although these places provide an opportunity for physical release, men are complex creatures, with a multitude of needs and desires, not all of which can be addressed by frequenting sex venues.

Intervention efforts need to address the impact of the structural aspects of both PSEs and CSEs. Although these venues may set men up for similar HIV risk behaviors, the specific motivations for frequenting them clearly differ. Moreover, the different conditions (public versus commercial, covertly sexual versus overtly sexual) of PSEs versus CSEs indicate distinct avenues of arriving at similar risk behaviors. Interventions aimed at CSEs might be built on their overtly sexual natures, and it would make the most sense to implement educational campaigns and programs directly in these venues to intervene with men in the heat of the moment. For example, some cities now offer HIV and STD testing inside bathhouses and sex clubs. Conversely, interventions aimed at PSEs must take into account the logistics of using condoms in public settings not typically used for sexual activity, as well as the fact that sexual acts often occur in the dark, when the participants are contending with the risk of being observed. Men may benefit from learning how to use condoms more effectively in these settings, as well as how to quickly negotiate safer sex behaviors. The presence of HIV outreach workers in PSEs may be useful in creating a cultural climate in which safer sex becomes the norm. However, it is likely that the men who frequent PSEs because of the anonymity afforded by them will be reluctant to engage with an outreach worker. Such efforts would need to be consistent and prolonged to become acceptable to men in PSEs (French et al., 2000).

Motivational interviewing has shown promise in one study of PSEs and CSEs (Harding, Dockrell, Dockrell, & Corrigan, 2001). This brief counseling approach uses a style that is client-centered and nonjudgmental. The goal is to create discrepancy between the goal and the actual behavior, or what the client is doing versus what the client wants to be doing. Thus, contrasting the feelings that HIV-positive gay and bisexual men have about not wanting to infect others with feelings of wanting to obtain quick, sexual release and escaping thoughts of HIV may be helpful in motivating the use of condoms (Parsons, 2004). Targeting men for motivational interviewing-based interventions while they are physically in the PSE or CSE seems particularly appropriate, because this may be an ideal time to explore discrepancy and issues of ambivalence regarding safer sex practices and HIV transmission and risk behaviors.

REFERENCES

Berube, A. (1996). The history of gay bathhouses. In F. C. Coller, W. Hoffman, F. Pendleton, A. Redick, & D. Serlin (Eds.), *Policing public sex* (pp. 187–220). Boston: South End Press.

Binson, D., Woods, W., Pollack, L., Paul, J., Stall, R., & Catania, J. (2001). Differential HIV risk in bathhouses and public cruising areas. *American Journal of Public Health, 91,* 1482–1486.

Brown, A. D., Reidy, W. J., Johnson, D. F., & Bingham, T. A. (2000, November). *Young men who have sex with men in commercial sex venues in Los Angeles: Comparing risks/assessing needs.* Paper presented at the American Public Health Association Annual Meeting, Boston.

de Wit, J. B., de Vroome, E. M., Sandfort, T. G., & van Griensven, G. J. (1997). Homosexual encounters in different venues. *International Journal of STD and AIDS, 8,* 130–134.

Díaz, R. M., Morales, E. S., Bein, E., Dilan, E., & Rodriguez, R. A. (1999). Predictors of sexual risk in Latino gay/bisexual men: The role of demographic, developmental, social cognitive, and behavioral variables. *Hispanic Journal of Behavioral Sciences, 21,* 480–501.

Díaz, R. M., Stall, R. D., Hoff, C., Daigle, D., & Coates, T. J. (1996). HIV risk among Latino gay men in the Southwestern United States. *AIDS Education and Prevention, 8,* 415–429.

Earl, W. L. (1990). Married men and same sex activity: A field study on HIV risk among men who do not identify as gay or bisexual. *Journal of Sex and Marital Therapy, 16,* 251–257.

Flowers, P., Hart, G., & Marriott, C. (1999). Constructing sexual health: Gay men and "risk" in the context of a public sex environment. *Journal of Health Psychology, 4,* 483–495.

French, R., Power, R., & Mitchell, S. (2000). An evaluation of peer-led STD/HIV prevention work in a public sex environment. *AIDS Care, 12,* 225–234.

Harding, R., Dockrell, M. J., Dockrell, J., & Corrigan, N. (2001). Motivational interviewing for HIV risk reduction among gay men in commercial and public sex settings. *AIDS Care, 13,* 493–501.

Hospers, H. J., Debets, W., Ross, M. W., & Kok, G. (1999). Evaluation of an HIV prevention intervention for men who have sex with men at cruising areas in the Netherlands. *AIDS and Behavior, 3,* 359–366.

McKirnan, D., Ostrow, D., & Hope, B. (1996). Sex, drugs, and escape: A psychological model of HIV risk sexual behaviors. *AIDS Care, 8,* 655–669.

Parsons, J. T. (2004). HIV-positive gay and bisexual men. In S. C. Kalichman (Ed.), *Positive prevention: Reducing HIV transmission among people living with HIV/AIDS* (pp. 99–133). New York: Kluwer Academic.

Parsons, J. T., & Halkitis, P. N. (2002). Sexual and drug-using practices of HIV-positive men who frequent public and commercial sex environments. *AIDS Care, 14,* 815–826.

Somlai, A. M., Kalichman, S. C., & Bagnall, A. (2001). HIV risk behaviour among men who have sex with men in public sex environments: An ecological evaluation. *AIDS Care, 13,* 503–514.

Woods, W. J., Binson, D. K., Mayne, T. J., Gore, L. R., & Rebchook, G. M. (2000). HIV/sexually transmitted disease education and prevention in US bathhouse and sex club environments. *AIDS, 14,* 625–626.

13

WISHFUL THINKING? HIV TREATMENT OPTIMISM AND SEXUAL BEHAVIOR AMONG HIV-POSITIVE GAY AND BISEXUAL MEN

ROBERT H. REMIEN AND THOMAS M. BORKOWSKI

Highly active antiretroviral therapy (HAART) has introduced a new dynamic into the epidemiology of HIV transmission and the field of HIV prevention. Renewed health and interest in romantic relationships and an active sex life among HIV-positive people may contribute to continued transmission of HIV, including the transmission of multiple drug resistant strains of HIV. This is a grave concern that affects the individual and the public health. There are also concerns that HIV-infected people and their uninfected partners may have a false sense of security because they believe in reduced infectivity as a result of undetectable viral load in plasma and because they may have diminished concern about the negative consequences of HIV infection. These beliefs and attitudes may contribute to increased complacency with regard to safer sex practices.

There is evidence that reduced viral load in those receiving HAART therapy may lead to a reduction in level of infectiousness. Some reports provide evidence that reduced viral load in the plasma may be paralleled by a similar reduction in genital secretions (Gupta et al., 1997; Vernazza et al., 1997); other reports show a lack of association between the ability to culture virus in semen and viral RNA level in blood (Coombs et al., 1998; Liuzzi et al., 1996; Zhang et al., 1998). Thus, although there may be a correlation between the amount of virus in blood and in genital secretions, this correlation is not 1:1. Nevertheless, it has been reported that plasma viral load was the strongest predictor of HIV transmission within heterosexual HIV serodiscordant couples in Africa (Quinn et al., 2000). There is concern that such population-based findings will be interpreted by some as permission to engage in unprotected sex if the viral load of the infected partner is low or undetectable (Remien & Smith, 2000).

Although findings are mixed, some evidence indicates that changing attitudes toward HIV, because of new treatments, are leading to increases in transmission-risk behaviors (Dilley, Woods, & McFarland, 1997; Elford, Bolding, Maguire, & Sherr, 2001; Halkitis & Wilton, 1999; Kalichman, Nachimson, Cherry, & Williams, 1998; Kelly, Hoffman, Rompa, & Gray, 1998; Ostrow et al., 2002; Remien, Wagner, Carballo-Dieguez, & Dolezal, 1998; Rietmeijer, Patnaik, Judson, & Douglas, 2003; Wolitski, Valdiserri, Denning, & Levine, 2001). According to surveys of gay men, those who report episodes of unprotected anal sex are more likely to believe that it is safe to have unprotected anal sex with an HIV-positive man who has an undetectable viral load or is on combination antiretroviral therapy (Ekstrand, Stall, Paul, Osmond, & Coates, 1999; Kalichman et al., 1998), believe that combination antiretroviral therapy is effective in reducing serious illness, and report being less worried about HIV infection now than in the past (Van de Ven, Kippax, Knox, Prestage, & Crawford, 1999). Some HIV-positive men say they have practiced safer sex less often since new AIDS treatments became available (Kelly et al., 1998). A study of HIV serodiscordant male couples showed that the HIV-negative partners associated these attitudes with their sexual risk behavior within the couple, whereas the HIV-positive partners did not (Remien et al., 1998); however, a study among both HIV-positive and HIV-negative gay men in London found associations between treatment optimism and unprotected anal sex with men of opposite HIV status (Elford et al., 2001).

This chapter examines the evidence for changes in sexual risk behavior as a consequence of HIV treatment advances and level of optimism regarding disease management. The phenomenon is analyzed by exploring various meanings of sex for gay and bisexual men in different relationship and social contexts. The chapter is based on a qualitative study with a total of 250 participants from the New York and San Francisco metropolitan areas. Most participants in this qualitative study did not describe what they believed to be a significant change in sexual risk behavior; neither in their own lives nor among gay and bisexual in general, as a result of medical treatment advances. Most men said that despite important treatment advances contributing to improved health and longevity for many people, they believed that it is still important to practice safer sex and that risks remained for self and others regarding transmission of HIV and sexually transmitted diseases (STDs). Nevertheless, enough participants discussed what they believed to be significant changes in sexual behavior and sexual risk behavior for themselves and for the broader community of gay and bisexual men that speak to these associations. This chapter focuses on the beliefs that the participants had about significant changes in sexual behavior and sexual risk behavior and discusses implications for the development of effective interventions to help prevent future HIV and STDs among gay and bisexual men.

THE QUALITATIVE STUDY

Using qualitative data from the Seropositive Urban Men's Study (SUMS; see chap. 1, this volume, for methods), we examined participant responses to open-ended questions about the potential effect of successful medical treatments for HIV (i.e., HAART) on sexual behavior in general and on sexual risk behavior in particular. Although 58% of the participants reported taking a treatment regimen that included one or more protease inhibitors, all participants were asked to discuss their personal feelings, experiences, and behaviors related to treatment options. All participants were also asked about their perception of what others in the gay community thought about this issue. The objective was to determine whether changes in sex and sexual risk behavior have occurred in association with HIV treatment advances and, where changes were acknowledged, to elucidate the specific beliefs, attitudes, and emotions associated with those changes. The goal of this study was not to generalize findings from this convenience sample of HIV-positive gay and bisexual men living in New York City and San Francisco to all gay and bisexual men living with HIV in these cities, nor in other geographic locations. Rather, this study was undertaken to identify how they view the phenomenon of HIV treatment advances, associated optimism, and its potential effect on sexual behavior in their own lives and in the larger community.

Analysis of quantitative data from the SUMS cohort found that HIV-positive men receiving antiretroviral therapy rated their perception of risk (for either HIV transmission to uninfected partners or a worsening of health for infected partners) higher than did men not receiving antiretroviral therapy. We also found that among the men on antiretroviral therapy there was an association between perception of risk for transmission of HIV and actual sexual behavior with partners of HIV-negative or unknown status and between perceptions of risk for reinfection or negative health effects with actual sexual behavior with other HIV-positive men. That is to say that men who engaged in unprotected anal sex with partners of HIV-negative or unknown status were more likely to rate their perception of risk for transmission of HIV as lower than were men who did not engage in this risk behavior. Similarly, men who engaged in unprotected anal sex with HIV-positive partners were more likely to rate their perception of risk for negative health outcomes (e.g., infection with resistant virus or worsening of health) as lower than were men who did not engage in this risk behavior (Remien, Halkitis, O'Leary, Wolitski, & Gómez, in press). Clearly, causality cannot be determined from this and other cross-sectional studies, and indeed the association between these beliefs and sexual risk behavior may in fact be post hoc rationalizations rather than premeditated decisions (Remien & Smith, 2000). However, it is possible that this subset of men takes sexual risks for a variety of reasons, as has been shown in extensive behavioral research of the past two decades, but now, in the context of HAART, has an added rationale for the behavior. It is hoped that our qualitative data analysis will lend clarity to these issues while providing useful information to assist with the development of effective interventions to help reduce HIV and sexually transmitted disease (STD) transmission among gay and bisexual men.

IMPACT OF HIGHLY ACTIVE ANTIRETROVIRAL THERAPY

Rarely were direct and specific cause-and-effect relationships clearly described between attitudes and beliefs regarding risk perception and sexual risk behavior; nor were associations described consistently in the same direction. Rather, it seems that a dynamic relationship exists among these factors that can change with time, is at times contradictory regarding causal direction, and is often context specific (i.e., dependent on sex partners and environment). In general, discussions fell into the following themes: (a) greater sexual interest and frequency of sex because of treatment advances, (b) treatment optimism (or pessimism) and its role in sexual behavior, and (c) specific beliefs about viral control and sexual risk taking. Personal experiences and perception of community norms, as articulated by the men in the study, will be presented within these three themes.

General Changes in Sexual Interest and Frequency of Sex as a Result of Treatment Advances

As is often found in studies of people living with HIV, men in the sample described a general loss of interest in sex since becoming HIV-positive. This loss has been described as being attributable to one or more of the following: psychological consequences of knowing that one is infected with a life-threatening illness that can be transmitted via sex, the direct physical consequences of the virus in the body, the effects of associated illnesses, and the side effects from antiretroviral medication. This participant identified his treatment regimen as the cause of a diminished sex drive and impotence; as a result of this personal observation, he discontinued his medication:

> A lot of times it makes me impotent—taking the medication. Nothing happens. Like, nothing. I mean sexually, I'm completely turned off. It takes—it overpowers my sexual drive at times when I'm on the medication. So I take myself off to be more sexually active. (Latino male, age 35, New York)

In contrast, many men described how their desire for sex reemerged after they began HAART, similar to the way it was before becoming infected with HIV: "I couldn't have sex, and I remembered the desire was two times a month, and now I'm very sexually active. Yeah, I think I come back to the place I was without HIV" (Latino male, age 38, San Francisco). This was articulated by another participant who altered his identity from a person living with AIDS to being HIV-positive: "Well, I think I've been more sexual, you know, once I'm feeling better. I mean, I've been diagnosed with AIDS, and now I don't tell people I have AIDS; I tell them that I'm positive" (Asian or Pacific Islander male, age 47, San Francisco).

For many men in the sample the effectiveness of the medications used to treat HIV gave them a positive outlook on their sex lives, which includes the interest and frequency of sex as well as an expansion of their sexual behavioral repertoire, "You know, I'm a typical gay, HIV-positive man with four libidos, not one. I think the medications that I'm taking right now have caused even more of a sex drive" (mixed race/ethnicity male, age 37, New York) and "Now I have energy, sexual energy, I can be top or bottom or both. My fantasy's both at the same time [laughter]" (Latino male, age 38, San Francisco). Although the men did not make the direct link to increased sexual risk behavior, they made some indirect references to likely increases in risk-taking behavior associated with renewed sexuality and an expansion of behaviors:

> When I was taking Crixivan and stuff, it did [have an effect on sexual behavior]. I just because I felt awful, and I looked horrible, and I didn't want to, I didn't feel attractive or anything . . . [later] . . . and I guess I am getting kind of scared because it is making me feel like I can go out there and have sex now. And I can go out there and party and drink and do all the stuff I did before. (Latino male, age 23, San Francisco)

Men described sexual behavior change associated with improved health and physical appearance. Not too long before these interviews were conducted, wasting syndrome and Kaposi's sarcoma had devastating effects for HIV-positive men in a community that values physical appearance and image. For many men, a healthy appearance was tied to the men's sexual prowess, and lack of a healthy appearance was associated with fear of rejection. As this quotation demonstrates, HAART has had a positive effect on feelings of sexual attractiveness for some:

> Well, I mean, physically, yeah. I do more things. I look better. I attract more people. I don't feel like I look like death anymore . . . I'm having more sex. I'm not as afraid that someone is not going to like me. (Latino male, age 38, San Francisco)

It was also interesting that it was not necessary for an individual to have personally experienced physical benefits from treatments for him to feel a part of this wave of optimism:

> It's not benefiting me, but I'm still, um, benefiting from—from the high of the whole thing. And like—and people are thinking about sex more. And it's making me think about sex more and, ah, you know, I'm trying to be positive, ah, that something will happen. (White male, age 39, New York)

Treatment Optimism and Its Role in Sexual Risk Behavior

In addition to HAART's contribution to improved sexual interest and functioning, many men spoke about HAART's contribution to their improved general health, longevity, and hope for the future. At the same time, they also spoke about fears and concerns about long-term toxicities and pessimism about the lack of a cure for HIV disease.

> I'm involved in all of them [the medications] . . . 2 years ago if I had gone through what I had went through 6 months last year, I would not have made it. I wouldn't be here . . we got control of the virus somewhat in the body, and I've been able to bounce back . . . But, they're not a cure. They're not a cure. (Latino male, age 40, New York)

And although treatment optimism was generally high, many men spoke of the continued importance of continuing to be safe: "Not on my sexual behavior, no [in reference to changes since effective treatments became available]. I don't think this is a cure, by any means. No, I think we still need to be very careful" (White male, age 40, San Francisco). However, some men expressed concerns about how treatment optimism was contributing to a reduced concern among HIV-positive men about negative health consequences resulting from unprotected sex:

> I think their reasoning, which is a little different than mine, is that they're positive anyway, so—and they're taking really, really good care

of themselves—so they can withstand being reinfected. Many of them are on protease inhibitors; others are on alternative healing therapies. None of them are in denial. Every one of my HIV-positive friends is doing something proactive about his health, and he's feeling healthy, and he's feeling so healthy that he figures that even—and it's not like they're having unsafe sex all the time, but there are occasions when they have an unsafe encounter here and there, and they'll say, "Well, yes, but I doubt that I'm going to get reinfected." (Black male, age 45, New York)

According to men in this study, another way that treatment advances may be contributing to increased sexual risk behavior was via reduced concern about primary prevention in light of the many challenges of living long-term with HIV. As the following quotation suggests, concerns about transmission of HIV to others may be low on their list of priorities relative to many other concerns:

I know people who have sold their insurance, sold their homes, sold their businesses, and they going to find out they are going to be living another 10 years probably. That's our biggest problem now. That is really the biggest problem. Not whether you have a condom on or not, but whether you can deal with the next 2, 3, 4, 5 years, whatever you've got coming, because you are going to get more . . . and you are going to get— if you are on the road with AZT, 3TC, works for you, and then you get to the inhibitors, and they are working for you because those weren't getting, you know, your viral loads were starting to creep up and this and that and you go to the cocktails. . . . So, I think that's a much bigger issue. . . . They might have unprotected sex and get back into drugs and drinking alcohol and all that stuff because that's scary; the unknown is much more scary than getting caught by this thing again. (Black male, age 56, New York)

In contrast, some men described how optimism and hope contributed to a reduction in sexual risk behavior and an increased motivation to use protection:

When I first found out, which was 3 years ago—this is before protease inhibitors which is a big factor in everybody's life now—my sexual behavior didn't change, meaning it didn't lessen at all. I just had sex but I denied the HIV thing and I didn't deal with it as much as I could, so I still went out and I had sex and I did whatever, you know, but I was also more willing to have sex without a condom. After protease, when the protease came out and people started living longer and there was all this good hope about, you know, the whole thing and, you know, like all of a sudden it wasn't such a fatalist thing, there was some kind of future, you know, all those kinds of issues that come up. After protease, now being HIV-positive, I am more—I'm more protective of myself because I know that being HIV-positive, I'm more susceptible to a lot of, like, diseases out there that normally people who aren't HIV-positive can handle easily but I can't. . . . So, after the protease inhibitor, the introduction into the market, there was a totally different change, like I was more protective of me. Before, I didn't care about me. I only cared if I cared about someone, you know, like if I wanted to see them again or if I had a relationship with them or something like that; that's the only time I cared about them. Now I care about me more, so I'll try and have sex without a condom—I mean, with a condom. You know, I won't be as careless even though I have been careless a couple of times, but not on the receiving end, on the giving end. (White male, age 32, New York)

Note that this man's description of increased safety was about protecting himself, not necessarily about protecting others. This exemplifies the somewhat idiosyncratic manner in which some men may think about these issues.

Specific Beliefs About Viral Control and Sexual Risk Taking

Beyond a more general optimism about the benefits of HAART, the men in this study specifically discussed the belief that being on HAART and having an undetectable viral load means reduced or negligible risk for transmission of HIV:

There's a thing going on with the protease inhibitors. I haven't fooled myself in this sense, but I know that I've heard other people around me; where there's a positive and a negative partner and the negative partner's having unsafe sex with the positive partner, and the reason they think it's okay is because he's on protease inhibitors and his viral load is undetectable. This is a big deal right now because we don't know what that means . . . there are a lot of people that feel that if they're undetectable, there's a very strong chance they cannot transmit the virus. (White male, age 37, New York)

This same man went on to say, "I want stronger proof before I'm going to believe that," but he contradicted himself and then admitted, "It gives me a little more comfort to know that my viral load is so low that it is undetectable because I do believe the higher it is, the higher the chance you're going to transmit." Although some men said that medical advances have not affected their own risk behavior, they do see the association between medical advances and increased risk behavior as a phenomenon out in the community: "It doesn't for me, but I do realize it has [influenced] a lot more people. I'm really surprised that a lot more people are having more unprotected sex" (Asian or Pacific Islander male, age 32, San Francisco). Other men spoke about how it is their perception that others are thinking this way and admitted that it is part of their own thinking too:

> It starts making you feel that you're not carrying as much of the virus. I mean, you know you're still infected, but I think it's giving a lot of guys a sense of being a little safer, you know. I don't think anybody completely fools themselves and thinks that they're totally safe, but I think it does have an effect on people feeling that—well, it just feels like they're not going to. I think some guys are thinking that it's—it's—if it's not coming up in large numbers in your blood, that it's reducing the—the chance of you exposing somebody. You know? And I think that kind of gives people a—maybe a little bit of a sense of false security. But—but, you know, like I said, I can't speak for anybody else, but it sort of does that for me in a way. (mixed race/ethnicity male, age 46, New York)

Several men spoke in terms that demonstrated misinformation or inaccuracy in their understanding of the biology and basic science of the issue. For example, some equated undetectable with zero, some spoke of HIV no longer being in the sperm rather than understanding that it is carried in the seminal fluid, and some equated plasma viral load with the viral load of genital secretions. One participant said, "I believe that if I have zero viral load per cubic, my blood, whatever—I can't say it in English—the chances of the AIDS virus being in my sperm is maybe less than a few years ago (Latino male, age 33, New York); and another said, "Well, I have a zero viral load; I'm not going to pass anything on" (Black male, age 36, San Francisco). As another participant put it, "Taking those drugs doesn't mean you can go out and you're not contagious any more. People believe that. There is a lot of twisted concepts around all this that is going on out there" (Latino male, age 40, New York).

Some men said that they were looking for answers from the experts about these things but felt frustrated that the answers were not available:

> I asked—at some point I asked my therapist, I said, "You know, okay, I'm—my viral load is undetectable now. What does that mean? Does that mean it's only in the blood? Or does that mean it's in semen? Has there been any tests that have been done to show that if it's not detectable in the blood, then maybe it's not detectable in the semen, and does that mean that I'm not able to transmit it?" He didn't have an answer. There hasn't been research done. You know? (White male, age 37, New York)

The way that some men discussed the issue suggests that there is not a clear cause-and-effect relationship between beliefs about viral load and risk for transmission of HIV but rather that the likelihood of reduced infectiousness can be used as a post hoc rationalization. In other words, men may find themselves engaging in sexual risk behavior for a variety of reasons, but after the fact they may use their improved health status as an excuse that gives them some reassurance. For example, "It gives leeway to people who are in a form of denial that want anything that they can latch on to. I think this is another reason why some positive men are—why more positive men are starting to have unsafe sex" (White male, age 37, New York). Another man said that he gets some reassurance when risk behavior occurs simply from being on medication, even though he admits to having a high viral load:

> It makes me feel more healthier, meaning that if I do practice unsafe— which is not good—but if I do practice unsafe sex, there is a chance that the medication might correct my mistake or, you know, something like that. Like, I think I have more leverage to play with now. I feel like I could go a bit further, knowing that there is a certain drug that, okay, if you are taking drugs and you are feeling good, the risk thing starts, you start losing all those sides, some of the things go down and you start doing certain things that, hey, this can't be bad, though I have a very high viral load. (Black male, age 34, New York)

Another man whose partner was also HIV-positive expressed it this way:

> I think that probably contributed to slipping, particularly on my boy-friend's part although his viral load is still slightly elevated. And we talked about it, and he admits that—he says, yeah, with improvements in his blood work, it makes him feel like—although he knows intellectu-ally that it makes a difference, he feels kinda less—it feels less dangerous. (Asian or Pacific Islander male, age 36, San Francisco)

Some men specifically spoke about the issue of reinfection:

> I know I can get reinfected. And I know—but I also know that I go every 3 months to St. Vincent's in the city and every year for the past 4 years—well, actually, since I started the medication, T-cells are always high, but then my viral load was real high. Now it is undetectable. I feel safe. It's kind of like a permission to be promiscuous again, with all these new drugs that they have. It's a good thing and it's a bad thing. You think people would have learned. (White male, age 36, New York)

Other men articulated a concern about the development of viral resis-tance when HIV-positive men have unprotected sex with each other:

> If I don't use a rubber, it's going to feel a lot better. Well, with the drugs they have out now, it's under control. At least my viral load's under control. How about you? That type of—that type of mind-set. "Oh, yeah, well, I'm taking the same thing you are and it's—and my

viral load's undetectable, too, so we might as well do it to each other. Who cares?" Rather than saying, "Well, do you ever think about the fact that this virus may be under control but may be mutating and change somewhere down the road; it could be a supervirus, and that we have nothing, you know, that will fight it?" (Native American male, age 41, San Francisco)

This same respondent describes how concern about reinfection or the development of a resistant virus can be a reason for insisting on using condoms:

Barebacking is like going back to raw sex, without a rubber. Especially if you're on protease inhibitors and stuff. Since your viral load has already decreased to the point of undetectable, then a lot of them are getting to the point where they're saying, "Well, if I bareback, I have an undetectable level of virus, so you don't have to worry about"—but, see, that's what I don't like hearing. Because I tell them to use a rubber anyway . . . you know, the virus that he may have may be undetectable, but still he could change what I've got.

Thus, knowledge about possible negative health consequences associated with unprotected sex between two HIV-positive men can motivate some men to maintain protective behaviors.

DISCUSSION

Most men seemed to be realistic about the fact that HIV is still an extremely serious disease and that there is a continued need to practice safer sex. However, many men discussed changes in their own behavior and observed changes in the larger gay and bisexual communities that support the concern among experts in HIV and STD prevention about increased risk-taking behavior in this community. At the same time it has become clearer that simple and straightforward conclusions cannot be made about the association between attitudes and beliefs about effective treatments and their link to sexual risk behavior. Neither universal nor consistent patterns between treatment optimism and associated beliefs and risk behavior were found; rather, these patterns were contradictory and at times idiosyncratic. Directions of the associations also differed. For example, although some men spoke about how treatment optimism has contributed to increases in sexual risk behaviors, others spoke about ways in which it has contributed to increases in protective behaviors. Furthermore, associations vary according to whether the concern is about personal health (i.e., reinfection, the development of resistant virus, or the acquisition of coinfections) or the health of others (i.e., transmission of HIV to sex partners). Similarly, men made clear distinctions between their own behavior and what they observe in the community; at times there were some implicit contradictions regarding attribution of risk and behavior change.

The concern about the role of treatment optimism that may be associated with these changes is warranted in light of relatively recent reports on increases in sexual risk behavior, sexually transmitted infections and incidence of HIV among gay men in Europe, Australia, and North America (Dodds, Nardone, Mercey, & Johnson, 2000; Rietmeijer et al., 2003; Stolte, Dukers, de Wit, Fennema, & Coutinho, 2001; Van de Ven, Prestage, Crawford, Grulich, & Kippax, 2000; Wolitski et al., 2001) and cases of transmission of multiple drug resistant strains of HIV (Boden et al., 1999; Hecht et al., 1998; Little et al., 1999). Although clear and consistent cause-and-effect relationships were not found between treatment optimism and beliefs and sexual risk behavior, men more typically spoke of increased comfort with the risks they find themselves taking because of a general treatment optimism and the reduced likelihood of transmission of HIV while receiving HAART. Thus, even if these rationalizations for engaging in sexual risk behavior are post hoc, they may be worthy of addressing in prevention interventions for gay men. Men may need to be challenged on not being able to use these beliefs as excuses for engaging in behaviors that put themselves and others at risk.

These collective findings have specific implications for the development of prevention messages and intervention programs. Although it may be important to develop community-wide messages that speak to the continued seriousness of HIV disease and the need to protect oneself and others from HIV and other STDs, there is also a need for individual tailoring of prevention interventions. Tailored interventions are needed because many men have developed their own idiosyncratic interpretations of HIV transmission risk and risk for other negative health outcomes. These issues may be best addressed in a one-on-one setting. Healthcare providers and counselors should speak directly to patients about sexual risk behavior and reinforce prevention messages in each encounter. Although a counselor may have more time to go into detail discussing risk, psychosocial factors associated with risk, and the challenges of maintaining safer sex behaviors, medical providers need to reinforce specific messages to specific patients. They may start by assessing the patient's understanding of risk of transmitting HIV to others and risk of reinfection or becoming infected with STDs. The provider can then reinforce the message that HIV can be transmitted to others even when there is no detectable viral load in the blood, that reinfection with HIV is possible and could have negative health consequences, and that getting new STDs can further damage one's immune system and lead to increases in HIV viral load. It is also important to address these primary prevention issues in the broader context of addressing the multiple concerns and challenges faced by people living with HIV so that they feel they are being treated as whole individuals with a range of personal needs.

Prevention messages also need to address different motivations for behavior change and maintenance. In other words, concern about personal health and concern about the health of sex partners should be addressed separately. It also seems clear that the scientific and prevention community needs to develop clear, scientifically based messages regarding risk for transmission in the context of effective therapies and undetectable viral load and to be more clear about the basic biology of transmission.

REFERENCES

Boden, D., Hurley, A., Zhang, L., Cao, Y., Jones, E., Tsay, J., et al. (1999). HIV-1 drug resistance in newly infected individuals. *Journal of the American Medical Association, 282,* 1135–1141.

Coombs, R. W., Speck, C. E., Hughes, J. P., Lee, W., Sampoleo, R., Ross, S. O., et al. (1998). Association between culturable human immunodeficiency virus type 1 (HIV-1) in semen and HIV-1 RNA levels in semen and blood: Evidence for compartmentalization of HIV-1 between semen and blood. *Journal of Infectious Diseases, 177,* 320–330.

Dilley, J. W., Woods, W. J., & McFarland, W. (1997). Are advances in treatment changing views about high-risk sex? *New England Journal of Medicine, 337,* 501–502.

Dodds, J. P., Nardone, A., Mercey, D. E., & Johnson, A. M. (2000). Increase in high risk sexual behaviour among homosexual men, London, 1996–1998: Cross sectional, questionnaire study. *British Medical Journal, 320,* 1510–1511.

Ekstrand, M. L., Stall, R. D., Paul, J. P., Osmond, D. H., & Coates, T. J. (1999). Gay men report high rates of unprotected anal sex with partners of unknown or discordant HIV status. *AIDS, 13,* 1525–1533.

Elford, J., Bolding, G., Maguire, M., & Sherr, L. (2001). HIV positive and negative homosexual men have adopted different strategies for reducing the risk of HIV transmission. *Sexually Transmitted Infections, 77,* 224–225.

Gupta, P., Mellors, J., Kingsley, L., Riddler, S., Singh, M. K., Schreiber, S., et al. (1997). High viral load in semen of human immunodeficiency virus type 1-infected men at all stages of disease and its reduction by therapy with protease inhibitors and nonnucleoside reverse transcriptase inhibitors. *Journal of Virology, 71,* 271–275.

Halkitis, P. N., & Wilton, L. (1999). Optimism and HIV treatment advances: The impact on sexual risk-taking among gay men. *Health Psychologist, 21,* 10–12.

Hecht, F. M., Grant, R. M., Petropoulos, C. J., Dillon, B., Chesney, M. A., Tian, H., et al. (1998). Sexual transmission of an HIV-1 variant resistant to multiple reverse-transcriptase and protease inhibitors. *New England Journal of Medicine, 339,* 307–311.

Kalichman, S. C., Nachimson, D., Cherry, C., & Williams, E. (1998). AIDS treatment advances and behavioral prevention setbacks: Preliminary assessment of reduced perceived threat of HIV/AIDS. *Health Psychology, 17,* 546–550.

Kelly, J. A., Hoffman, R. G., Rompa, D., & Gray, M. (1998). Protease inhibitor combination therapies and perceptions of gay men regarding AIDS severity and the need to maintain safer sex. *AIDS, 12,* 91–95.

Little, S. J., Daar, E. S., D'Aquila, R. T., Keiser, P. H., Connick, E., Whitcomb, J. M., et al. (1999). Reduced antiretroviral drug susceptibility among patients with primary HIV infection. *Journal of the American Medical Association, 282,* 1177–1179.

Liuzzi, G., Chirianni, A., Clementi, M., Bagnarelli, P., Valenza, A., Cataldo, P. T., et al. (1996). Analysis of HIV-1 load in blood, semen and saliva: Evidence for different viral compartments in cross-sectional and longitudinal study. *AIDS, 10,* 51–56.

Ostrow, D. E., Fox, K. J., Chimel, J. S., Silvestre, A., Visscher, B. R., Vanable, P. A., et al. (2002). Attitudes towards highly active antiretroviral therapy are associated with sexual risk taking among HIV-infected and uninfected homosexual men. *AIDS, 16,* 775–780.

Quinn, T. C., Wawer, M. J., Sewankambo, N., Serwadda, D., Li, C., Wabwire-Mangen, F., et al. (2000). Viral load and heterosexual transmission of human immunodeficiency virus type 1. *New England Journal of Medicine, 342,* 921–929.

Remien, R. H., Halkitis, P. N., O'Leary, A., Wolitski, R. J., & Gómez, C. A. (in press). Risk perception and sexual risk behaviors among HIV-positive men on antiretroviral therapy. *AIDS and Behavior.*

Remien, R. H., & Smith, R. A. (2000). HIV prevention in the era of HAART: Implications for providers. *AIDS Reader, 10,* 247–251.

Remien, R. H., Wagner, G., Carballo-Dieguez, A., & Dolezal, C. (1998). Who may be engaging in high-risk sex due to medical treatment advances? *AIDS, 12,* 1560–1561.

Rietmeijer, C. A., Patnaik, J. L., Judson, F. N., & Douglas, J. M. (2003). Increases in gonorrhea and sexual risk behaviors among men who have sex with men. *Sexually Transmitted Diseases, 30,* 562–567.

Stolte, I. G., Dukers, N. H., de Wit, J. B., Fennema, J. S., & Coutinho, R. A. (2001). Increase in sexually transmitted infection among homosexual men in Amsterdam in relation to HAART. *Sexually Transmitted Infections, 77,* 184–186.

Van de Ven, P., Kippax, S., Knox, S., Prestage, G., & Crawford, J. (1999). HIV treatments optimism and sexual behaviour among gay men in Sydney and Melbourne. *Journal of Acquired Immune Deficiency Syndromes, 13,* 2289–2294.

Van de Ven, P., Prestage, G., Crawford, J., Grulich, A., & Kippax, S. (2000). Sexual risk behaviour increases and its association with HIV optimism among HIV-negative and HIV-positive gay men in Sydney over the 4-year period to February 2000. *AIDS, 14,* 2951–2953.

Vernazza, P. L., Gilliam, B. L., Flepp, M., Dyer, J. R., Frank, A. C., Fiscus, S. A., et al. (1997). Effect of antiviral treatment on the shedding of HIV-1 in semen. *AIDS, 11*, 1249–1254.

Wolitski, R. J., Valdiserri, R. O., Denning, P. H., & Levine, W. C. (2001). Are we headed for a resurgence of the HIV epidemic among men who have sex with men? *American Journal of Public Health, 91*, 883–888.

Zhang, H., Dornadula, G., Beumont, M., Livornese, L., Jr., Van Uitert, B., Henning, K., et al. (1998). Human immunodeficiency virus type-1 in the semen of men receiving highly active antiretroviral therapy. *New England Journal of Medicine, 339*, 1803–1809.

14

WITH A LITTLE HELP FROM MY FRIENDS: COMMUNITY AFFILIATION AND PERCEIVED SOCIAL SUPPORT AMONG HIV-POSITIVE GAY AND BISEXUAL MEN

KELLY R. KNIGHT

Insight into how HIV-positive gay and bisexual men define their communities and affiliate themselves into these communities can help us understand how HIV affects their self-identity with regard to family, cultural group, peer group, and larger society. This understanding can provide a basis for understanding how HIV-positive gay and bisexual men build social and sexual relationships and perceive their social support after receiving their diagnosis. It is well understood that many gay and bisexual men experience stigma, stress, and social isolation as a result of an HIV diagnosis (Crandall & Coleman, 1992; Herek, 1999; Thompson, Nanni, & Levine, 1996). These psychosocial pressures can influence the willingness of HIV-positive gay and bisexual men who may fear sexual and social rejection, discrimination, and hostility, to disclose HIV status (Chesney & Smith, 1999).

A potential implication of these pressures is the increased likelihood for HIV-positive gay and bisexual men to participate in unprotected sexual behavior that could transmit HIV to uninfected partners (Wenger, Kusseling, Beck, & Shapiro, 1994). Reluctance to disclose HIV status because of limitations on sexual partnering and a potential loss of intimacy can create conflicts in terms of relationships and sexual experiences (Hoff, McKusick, Hilliard, & Coates, 1992). The perceived responsibility to disclose is often weighed against the social and sexual costs of disclosure (Hays et al., 1993).

Sociostructural factors also play a significant role in the self-identity and behavior of gay and bisexual men. Poverty, homophobia, and racism have been found to be associated with sexual risk taking among gay and bisexual men (Díaz, 1998). Among young Latino men engaging in sex with other men (MSM), attachment to ethnic community has been associated with greater social support in sexual matters (O'Donnell et al., 2002). Among Black gay and bisexual men, an integrated self-identity as both Black and gay has been associated with higher levels of self-efficacy for HIV prevention and stronger social networks (Crawford, Allison, Zamboni, & Soto, 2002).

Ramirez-Valles (2002) has argued that community involvement can moderate the association between these sociostructural factors and sexual risk behaviors because it influences peer norms about safer sex, self-efficacy toward HIV risk reduction, and positive self-identity. The framework also contends that community involvement reduces feelings of alienation, particularly among gay and bisexual men of color, who are at increased risk for stigmatization and oppression (Ramirez-Valles, 2002). It is important to understand how HIV-positive gay and bisexual men define and create their communities, what their communities mean to them in terms of self-identity and social support, and how their community affiliation might influence their sexual relationships and behavior.

The research summarized in this chapter originates from the Seropositive Urban Men's Study (SUMS; see chap. 1, this volume for details). This chapter discusses what SUMS participants described as their communities and what they perceived their level of acceptance and support to be within these communities. It also explores the relationship between community affiliation and support and sexual risk taking. Men in the sample were asked a series of questions that included, "People often consider themselves part of communities such as a neighborhood, religious community, gay community, ethnic community, trade or professional community. Do you feel a part of any particular communities? If so, which?" and, "How supported or accepted do you feel as an HIV-positive gay/bisexual/MSM man in each of the communities you mentioned?" Answers were analyzed, coded, and organized according to emergent themes.

DEFINING COMMUNITY AND COMMUNITY AFFILIATION

The men described a variety of communities to which they felt they belonged; these communities were often overlapping and not mutually exclusive from each other.

> I'm a part of many different communities, but, um, I guess I would define it as a group of like-minded people with common values and common goals. And I move in and out of several different communities where I feel comfortable and welcome. (White male, age 40, New York)

Most men reported feeling they were members of the gay community, but there was great variability when they attempted to define what *gay community* meant to them. The degree of belonging to the gay community varied significantly and could mean being highly involved in political and service work or perceiving that one was a member by default, as a gay man, with little or no gay social involvement. Other communities varied broadly as well, from being based on race/ethnicity and cultural background to being created around living in a specific apartment complex or engaging in a specific sexual scene, such as the "leather community." Many men reported active membership in a church or spiritual community; many others reported membership in communities built around recovery from drug and alcohol use.

Identifying the multiple communities in which they live, work, socialize, and have sexual relationships was initially challenging for many of the men. This difficulty is not surprising given that each community has extensive and often overlapping histories for the men, most of which are complex to define and describe.

> [Laughter] Community. No, I don't think I have a community. I'm not really sure what you mean by community . . . most of the people I know, that I'm friendly with, are HIV-positive. You know. A couple of my family members know, but the majority of people that I, you know, associate with, you know, are HIV-positive. So you know, we're all going through the same thing, basically. (Black male, age 34, New York)

Some men felt very little community affiliation and balked at the question, feeling that the notion of community created segregation on the basis of sexual orientation or race/ethnicity or preferring to refer to themselves as "loners."

> Skip the question, not because I feel uncomfortable about answering, but because I don't believe there is a community. And I don't think

there's more of a gay community than there is of a, you know, just people in general. . . . Maybe some people would feel that they can answer that. But as far as I'm concerned, there is no gay community any more than there's a straight community. (White male, age 34, New York)

Type of community also varied tremendously, with many men reporting that their main community affiliation was to their family and friends, not a broader social group with whom they may share similar characteristics or backgrounds. Others reported strong identification to social groups that share a common heritage or set of behaviors. Some men felt a strong affiliation to the HIV/AIDS community, yet others were more likely to consider themselves as an HIV-positive person in another community than to perceive the HIV/AIDS community as distinct. Some men felt that HIV was so intertwined with gay identity that it provided the main definitional and political axis for the gay community.

> There's a level of admiration, trust, camaraderie, brotherhood among people that deal with this stuff [HIV]. . . . This is—the first gay community I think, is the HIV community. Where people have common goals and really work toward them. I mean, I'm not negating the political work that was done in pre-AIDS, but I'm saying that political power has definitely been a side effect of HIV/AIDS power. More powerful the community gets, more powerful the extended gay community gets by association, and I think that's true of people's respect of the gay community too, straight people, people out in the middle of the country. (White male, age 52, New York)

In addition to focusing on the political dimensions of HIV within the gay community, many men described their affiliation with other HIV-positive gay and bisexual men as a necessity for bolstering social support and engendering a sense of belonging. Seeking out other HIV-positive men in social or service settings became a way for the men to create community that provided both service networks and a social life of peers that served to reduce feelings of social isolation.

> I—so I decided to go after a new community. And that was the HIV community. . . . Of course, that HIV community was accepting of me. The fact I'm able to share what was going on, I enjoyed that. So I was accepted. I didn't feel isolated. (White male, age 51, New York)

> So it is nice. It's nice. I like it. And now I made some friends, maybe two or three friends. They are very supportive. They call me. We cry sometimes. We laugh. We walk, doing things like that, to—to the ballet or something like that. I know. I know, so really this institution is helping me a lot, a lot, to break the, um, the isolation. (Latino male, age 39, New York)

THE CHALLENGE OF HIV DISCLOSURE

The degree of community affiliation and comfort with HIV disclosure were reciprocally related. Although most men felt that they were members of the gay community, many were uncomfortable being visible as HIV-positive. The reluctance to disclose HIV status stemmed from negative personal experiences and from negative assumptions about the outcome of disclosure conversations. For some men, negative experiences with family and friends when they came out as gay men made them wary of revealing their serostatus. "The gay community has been very, very positive. The straight community and family have been absolutely horrible. In fact, I don't talk to any of my family anymore" (White male, age 42, San Francisco).

> My support system is basically a hospital, yes. I don't call [HIV service agency] or those kind of places very often, you know, I'm more or less still in the closet, you know. My parents are Jehovah's Witnesses, so I haven't seen them in a while because, you know, they know. . . . They know that I'm gay, and that's—you know, we haven't spoken in years. (White male, age 43, New York)

Stories of families' and friends' responses to the HIV-positive gay and bisexual men's coming out as gay came up frequently as the subtext for how men define community and how supported they feel within it. Gay men's experiences of coming out to family and peers are often poignant and traumatizing. Many gay men experienced rejection and social alienation from their families and cultures of origin on revealing their sexual orientation. Stories of familial and cultural rejection were so common that men who did not experience such rejection consistently pointed out how lucky they had been to have had this unusual experience, thereby underscoring the significant role that this initial rejection plays in HIV disclosure decision making.

> [A program for HIV-positive men] could be for people who don't have any friends, who don't have any supporting family also, you know. We need that out here 'cause a lot of people, a lot of families, a lot of friends are not supportive of things like that. I'm—I'm one of the lucky ones, the very few lucky ones. My family and my friends know about my situation and they love me regardless. Yes, that's [a program for HIV-positive men] a good idea. (Black male, age 23, New York)

Among men of color, lack of acceptance of homosexuality was a common theme and continually referenced as a reason for not disclosing either gay orientation or HIV or for being estranged from their cultural or ethnic community of origin.

> I don't think I really put it out there. Well, if I haven't put it out there, there must be a fear of nonacceptance. There's still a fear in the black

community, you know. . . . It hasn't came up, but I wouldn't advertise it in my community. If I was speaking at schools around the community, for younger people, I wouldn't have a fear of that, just to put it out, where I live, where I wake up, walk, and go to the store every day, nah. (Black male, age 24, San Francisco)

When another man was asked how supported and accepted he felt as an HIV-positive gay man in the Latino community, he replied:

Not very well. I—I don't have—I don't have much contact with other people. I don't have contact with my family 'cause they—they rejected me because I was homosexual first. And when I disclosed to them that I was HIV-positive, it's like, you know, they just couldn't—they don't want to be bothered; so that's cool, you know. (Latino male, age 41, New York)

Some men of color showed great resiliency in their ability to join communities of color within the gay community and gain support as HIV-positive gay men; others served as crusaders within their ethnic and cultural communities to combat HIV stigma and homophobia.

I feel that the Asian community is really, I mean, really kind of helps to try to bridge the gap from the regular gay community to bring them into the HIV programs and stuff. Because most of the Asians are very closeted and don't want to talk about it or deal with it. There are really a lot of issues, and I've been on the board of the agency and been working with the different programs and trying to bridge some gaps because I feel that I can bring something else to the table, rather than all the hang-ups. (Asian or Pacific Islander male, age 36, San Francisco)

I think there are still a lot of people, a lot of Latinos, that hide the fact that they're positive. I'm one of the ones that's trying to change that. I always say, "I am positive. I do have AIDS." I volunteer at the clinic. . . . I don't do the counseling, I'm the receptionist there, you know. . . . But people sit there in the lobby and start talking, and they say this and that. I say, "Hey, I'm here and I have AIDS," 'cause I have nothin' to hide. (Latino male, age 38, San Francisco)

The difficulty around the disclosure of both sexual orientation and HIV status led some men to feel that it was not necessary or desirable to disclose either.

But it is none of anyone in the community's business that I am positive. I am not going to be, you know, exchanging bodily fluids with these people I come in contact with, so I don't know—as far as community goes, I don't consider it an issue; just like my homosexuality, I don't go around saying that . . . I have no plans on being a camp counselor and being like I am a flaming homosexual. So, as far as community goes, as far as—I just don't make it an issue with that or with the homosexuality. (White male, age 28, New York)

Difficulty with self-acceptance as a gay man influenced some men's ability to seek support for their HIV, thereby increasing their social isolation.

> Well, you know, I—I tend not to get close to people as much as I used to. So, ah, I kind of protect myself, you know, now. I never used to feel like I had to protect myself or hide anything from anybody until this happened, you know, and I live with that every day, you know, where I—I know I'm hiding something, you know, again. It's like it took me years and years and years to finally come out of the closet and feel comfortable letting people know I'm gay. (mixed race/ethnicity male, age 46, New York)

Other men, although they felt no conflict about being out as gay, felt that their HIV status was not something to disclose in all settings.

> And I'm openly gay everywhere, but I'm not necessarily HIV-positive everywhere I go. When it comes up, I don't shy away from it, but I don't introduce it the way I introduce being openly gay. So there are environments that I am in sometimes where people know that I'm gay but they don't necessarily know that I'm positive. (Black male, age 45, New York)

Community-Level AIDS Fatigue and HIV Denial

The response of the gay community to HIV-positive men became an important factor for the men when evaluating their perceived acceptance and social support. Many men felt that there was a clear split in the community between men who are HIV-positive and men who are uninfected. This split stemmed from what some men referred to as "AIDS fatigue," a community-level response to the tremendous toll that decades of loss have taken on the community.

> Ah, in my community, ah, very-well supported among the people with HIV. Not so much with people who aren't. It's kind of changed through the years. It's a little bit less supportive and people are tired of it now. They don't want to—to know about it, even people with AIDS. . . . And it's kind of like, you know, people are tired of AIDS, and they don't want to know about or deal with it as much. Everyone is building their bodies up and it's like, especially AIDS is like not popular, you know. It used to be very popular to walk around, ah, with wasting [phonetic] your CMV retinitis on Eighth Avenue in Chelsea and feel comfortable. So it's not easy to be sick. (White male, age 39, New York)

Not only did AIDS fatigue affect how many men felt that they were perceived by the gay community at large but it reflected the reality of how the number of AIDS causalities had completely depleted the existing social networks of many men. These men felt that they were without support because their select group of HIV-positive peers had all died. "Well, I had no support from family. I have really no support from friends. Most of my good friends are dead, and a couple that are alive are not HIV-positive" (White male, age 36, New York).

Perceived discrimination and lack of support from within the gay community made many men reluctant to disclose their HIV status for fear of lack of acceptance. Men expressed anger at the fact that many other HIV-positive men in the community are participating in the silence around HIV by not disclosing themselves. This left HIV-positive men experiencing isolation within the gay community, while they were in fact surrounded by other HIV-positive men who were equally fearful of disclosure.

> What I find is that there are a lot of people who have it but are not accepting it. And there are people who have it right within your community who won't admit to the fact of having it, and you know they won't admit it to the community as well. And it's like if they know that you have it, then it's like they'll also look down on you, like knowing that they have it as well but won't admit to it. (Black male, age 32, New York)

This community-level silencing around HIV left few places for some men to access support with regard to their HIV.

> [I]n general, gay men are very, very uptight about it [HIV]. I feel, you know, they—it's still something that people, you know, the only place that gay men ever open up about it is maybe a—a support group, a gay, you know, HIV support group. In those environments you can open up, you know, but even those people that attend those groups, I'll bet you, you know, 90% of them probably don't tell the people they're around day to day. (mixed race/ethnicity male, age 46, New York)

> People are really rough; people are really rough and rude to you, and no, I don't feel accepted at all by the community. I think it has more to do with—I think it's more of a self-reflective quality because I think that they're not accepting it about themselves, so, therefore, if they see it, they don't want to accept it either. (Latino male, age 33, New York)

HIV Visibility and Social Support

Among the men who did feel a high level of social support, the key elements of that support were self-acceptance of their HIV and the degree to which they disclosed their HIV status. The characteristics that these men shared were a supportive—or at least a not entirely negative—response to their sexual orientation disclosure among family and friends and an ability to overcome their fear of rejection because of their HIV status. These characteristics were linked for some men. A supportive coming-out process paved the way to seek more support and increased self-acceptance. Many men also felt that they created the acceptance and support because they were so public about their HIV status. In other words, by acting self-accepting and demonstrating pride in themselves as HIV-positive individuals, they found social support reflected back to them.

> But I feel supported in the sex community, I feel supported in the political community, I feel supported by my relatives. Even though they don't really understand what it is that I'm going through, they still support me in it because I'm so adamant and so strong and so out about it. (Black male, age 45, New York)

> Exceptional [support], absolutely exceptional. I'm very open and very honest about my lifestyle and about where I am in my health situation, not that I look at it as an impediment, but it brings out the best in people, brings out communication, brings out tolerance, brings out education. And being very active in the gay community in [home state], there's not many people that don't know, and I haven't lost any friends; I've only gained. (White male, age 32, New York)

Other men felt they that they had truly earned the support that they had for HIV. After experiencing severe family rejection and loss of peers to AIDS, some men were able to remark on their own perseverance and bravery and gained strength from that to continue to seek out social support for their HIV.

> But I'm not lost on the fact that I survived, where a lot of people I know didn't; so it's almost like this grieving period, where I go into schools and tell my story, and students actually hear what I'm saying. And I'm like, "Oh my god, that's so unreal." Like I remember telling the story of my mom disowning me, maybe a month or so ago, and hearing that and actually responding to it, with the pain of it hitting me after all these years, and that I actually lived through that. But what I've learned is that if you try hard enough, you can get through it, you can move past all the heartbreak, the devastation and loss, whatever it was that we've gotten through, and you can move on with your life. (Asian or Pacific Islander male, age 36, San Francisco)

In a similar vein, a subgroup of men felt a great deal of social support from their recovery communities. These men expressed a general sense that the struggle to remain free of alcohol and drug use created a strong bond of acceptance of each other as addicts or alcoholics. Many of these men also remarked that others in their recovery support groups and programs were also HIV-positive, providing a community that shared even greater commonality.

Ah, I think that, number one, it is because a lot of the other members of my recovering addict groups are HIV-positive and are gay. So we have—we all have that, all that in common together. You know we are recovering from drugs; plus, we are battling this virus, you know. And I, ah, a lot of them are Spanish or Black, and we're minorities, and I think in those three senses, you know, for me, Hispanic, drug addict, homosexual, HIV—I think that's four. So, I am like a four-time minority, I feel. (Latino male, age 31, New York)

Another subgroup of men gained social support from their church or spiritual community. Many men described religious and cultural upbringings that were oppressive and discriminatory against homosexuality. This oppression and discrimination also permeated many men's early or current experiences with HIV/AIDS. Recalling the history of rejection from a religious community was an important component of explaining their current community affiliation and social support.

It's a little better now; then it was terrible. . . . They [the church] find out that the member is infected, or has AIDS, or whatever, and they completely disassociated themselves with that member. Okay? That member has a mother and a father and whatever, and so they also disassociate themselves with that whole family. And so that would force that person that was infected to go out of the church entirely. . . . But it went on like that for quite a while, long enough for enough people to die, you see, that should not have died alone, with nobody. It was just a little too much . . . sometimes when I think about the ones that did go on without even a prayer, you know, from their home congregations, it saddens me even now. (Black male, age 50, San Francisco)

In response to their HIV diagnoses, many men were able to reconnect with their spiritual roots by finding fellowships and congregations that were accepting of them as HIV-positive gay men; this provided a central new community and source of social support

Church. You know. Five out of seven days [laughter]. I'm in church a lot. You know? And they have welcomed me there. They know who I am. They know what I am. They know about my past. They know I'm HIV-positive. And they don't care. You know, they've accepted me with open arms, and I feel like that's my home, or my second home. You know? I just found a lot of love and respect. You know. And friends. New friends. (Latino male, age 31, New York)

Those who expressed greater social support were more likely to be open about their HIV status in a variety of social settings, to express self-acceptance of their HIV, and to project a sense of resiliency and pride toward the struggles they had been through as HIV-positive gay men.

I have no problem with it whatsoever when people—people ask me. I say, "Yes, ma'am, I can talk about this." You know, people ask, "How can you be proud of being HIV?" I say, "Because I've been alive for so long." I'm very proud of it. You know, there's not very many people who can say they're still around and stopped using drugs and stopped drinking, stopped having unsafe sex. You know? It's changed my life for the better. (Black male, age 32, San Francisco)

ACCEPTANCE, SOCIAL SUPPORT, AND SEXUAL RISK

The men in the sample drew connections between their community acceptance, social support, and sexual risk taking, both for them and for other HIV-positive gay and bisexual men. Several issues arose when these links were drawn. Worry about sexual rejection, limits in sexual partnering, lack of disclosure, social isolation, and depression were all expressed as contributing factors to unsafe sex.

The only issue I have is when I meet somebody and I start dating them, and then I tell them I'm HIV-positive, and sometimes I get dropped like a hot potato; so that's where I don't find I'm accepted. (White male, age 44, New York)

Limited on sexual partnering was a frequent theme when men discussed the effects of community acceptance on their lives as HIV-positive men. Some men felt the degree of social separation on the basis of serostatus more acutely than others, but most agreed that disclosing HIV status led to rejection in many dating and sexual situations. To many men this rejection in the relationship realm paralleled a general social rejection they experienced in the gay community.

Because I mean there are some people that if they know, even as a gay, if they know you're positive, they don't want to be bothered with you. . . . Even though they're gay! . . . You think people will be all together; they're not! They only want other negative people. . . . I have other friends, on the other hand, where being positive doesn't matter to them; but when it comes to sex, if they know you're positive, their approach to you is completely different. (Black male, age 43, New York)

This sexual rejection has led many men to seek social and sexual relationships exclusively with other HIV-positive men to avoid rejection and mediate a negative response to themselves as HIV-positive men. The alternative was to remain closeted in social and dating situations.

Well, in the gay community there is a lot of negative feelings about HIV-positive people. I mean, like I read these [personal] ads. . . . They are not interested in HIV-positive people. I do feel that gay community in and of itself is very supportive of this. But in terms of socializing or relating sexually with people, they will run if you tell them this, most of them. . . . Now, what I have been doing is I have been going to HIV dances, and I haven't joined an HIV support group for gay men. But I am thinking about doing that—and of gay men of color—but for the most part it hasn't really affected me that much in my social life because I don't tell people that. (Black male, age 48, New York)

This fear of rejection and general lack of acceptance as HIV-positive men led to difficulty with disclosure in sexual situations. Some men chose to not disclose their HIV status because of concerns over rejection, and others were struggling with the issues of disclosure with their potential sex partners.

Um, and I normally don't discuss any of this with anyone. Um, and again, I've only just begun to talk to three guys that I was, quote, dating, um, nothing—nothing sexual, just dating. But I said it up front to all three. . . . Ah, and I had also told three of my best friends, and I've got one more to tell, and I haven't gotten around to him yet. And that's as far as I've gone with it. I will not discuss it with anyone else. (Latino male, age 38, New York)

An HIV diagnosis led some men to reevaluate their place in the gay sexual culture. The conflicts that arise over social acceptance and sexual partnering among the men made many sites for socializing in gay culture seem out of reach. Bars and sex clubs, which had defined participation in the gay community for some men, became problematic places to navigate disclosure and sexual negotiations. "Yeah, it was only like bath houses occasionally and gay bars. I stopped the bars and the baths once I found out I was positive. I felt I didn't belong there" (White male, age 39, New York).

Some men described a community norm of unsafe sex within the gay culture, particularly in bars and sex clubs. This community-level indictment arose out of a conversation about how supported they felt as HIV-positive men and reflected a way in which the community was not taking care of them.

I guess I've just seen a lot and heard a lot, and, I mean, I'm not exactly pleased, I mean, with the way the gay community is handling this epidemic, so to speak. But I mean, I've just seen—seen and heard so much unsafe sex that, I mean, it's just incredible. I mean, right there in front of you at every bar people are having sex. I mean in all the bathrooms, and you can't get away from it. There are—there is no protection used. (White male, age 28, New York)

The sense of social isolation and separation from the gay community and other communities contributed to unsafe sexual behaviors. Men who had not disclosed their HIV status in social situations and within their communities found it even more difficult to disclose or insist on condom use during sexual encounters. When asked why he felt other HIV-positive men have unprotected sex, one man responded as follows:

> [For] the same reasons I have . . . I am telling this to you because I know. I have conversations with different men, and they are telling me the same thing. They need escape. . . . They need—they need to feel loved, to feel important to someone else, at least if it's only for 5 minutes, but you feel that you are liked. . . . Ah, the rejection is a fact in our life, someone is rejecting us 24 hours per day. It's the society, the community, the policemen, the government in the same organization, that someone is rejecting of. If you feel that this guy is coming to you, and he's trusting that moment of—of fun, that's—that's—that's nice. So they don't behave differently than I behave. It's my idea, my conclusion. (Latino male, age 39, New York)

DISCUSSION

For HIV-positive gay and bisexual men, community is a rich but problematic topic. This is in part because the HIV-positive gay community has an incredibly diverse membership, the commonality of which is sexual orientation, behaviors, and disease status, which are socially stigmatized. Research on stigma suggests that although the experience of stigma is powerful and commonplace among HIV-positive individuals, it is experienced to a varying degree from individual to individual (Crandall & Coleman, 1992; Lee, Kochman, & Sikkema, 2002). Among the HIV-positive gay and bisexual men in this study, community definitions, community affiliation, and perceived social support were all influenced by the degree of stigma that men had experienced coming out as gay men to their families, friends, cultures of origin, and social groups. The influence of support or rejection by family members was particularly poignant in our sample, as has been shown with other samples of gay men and HIV-positive gay men (Turner, Hays, & Coates, 1993; Fisher, Goldschmidt, Hays, & Catania, 1993; Kimberly & Serovich, 1999).

Three broad groups of HIV-positive men emerged in relation to community affiliation and perceived social support. First, men with intact familial and social support for their identity as gay men tended to reflect greater integration into the gay community and other social arenas as HIV-positive men. Another group felt community affiliation as gay men but experienced discrimination and rejection as HIV-positive men from within the gay community itself and from other social groups, such as their religious communities and cultures of origin. A third group felt little community affiliation or support because they resisted categorization as a gay or HIV-positive person or because they were in complete isolation as closeted gay and HIV-positive individuals.

In terms of sexual relationships and behavior, the men in the sample reflected on limitations in their ability to build sexual relationships and choose sex partners for fear of rejection and discrimination because of their HIV-positive status. The fears that were raised about HIV disclosure in the social areas of family, neighborhood, and church easily transferred to sexual situations. Some men expressed disappointment in the gay community for not supporting safer sex norms. Men also described searching for emotional connection through unsafe sex to ameliorate the pain of past oppression and rejection, which has been noted in other studies of gay men (Díaz, 1998).

A perceived split within the gay community with regard to serostatus caused many HIV-positive men to feel conflict about their community affiliation; they expressed both a feeling of belonging and of anger toward the gay community. HIV-positive gay and bisexual men have experienced multiple levels of rejection that have alienated them from their traditional sources of social support, first from family, cultural of origin, and religious community, then in some cases from the gay community itself. Davison, Pennebaker, and Dickerson (2000) suggested that these multiple experiences of alienation can put a premium on social support that is geared toward HIV-positive individuals. This may help to explain the resiliency and pride many of the men expressed at their ability to not only physically survive HIV disease but to survive its social consequences. These HIV-positive gay and bisexual men created their communities and earned the social support that they experienced by overcoming tremendous psychosocial and socio-structural barriers.

Prevention programs serving HIV-positive gay and bisexual men should explore the multiple community contexts in which the men may be operating and the relationship between community affiliation, social support, and sexual risk behavior. Such an exploration could identify points of social vulnerability and personal resiliency that significantly affect HIV disclosure practices, sexual risk taking behavior, and psychological well-being.

REFERENCES

Chesney, M. A., & Smith, A. W. (1999). Critical delays in HIV testing and care: The potential role of stigma. *American Behavioral Scientist, 42,* 1162–1174.

Crandall, C. S., & Coleman, R. (1992). AIDS-related stigmatization and the disruption of social relationships. *Journal of Social and Personal Relationships, 9,* 163–177.

Crawford, I., Allison, K. W., Zamboni, B. D., & Soto, T. (2002). The influence of dual-identity development on the psychosocial functioning of African-American gay and bisexual men. *Journal of Sex Research, 39,* 179–189.

Davison, K. P., Pennebaker, J. W., & Dickerson, S. S. (2000). Who talks? The social psychology of illness support groups. *American Psychologist, 55,* 205–217.

Díaz, R. M. (1998). *Latino gay men and HIV: Culture, sexuality, and risk behavior.* New York: Routledge.

Fisher, L., Goldschmidt, R. H., Hays, R. B., & Catania, J. (1993). Families of homosexual men: Their knowledge and support regarding sexual orientation and HIV disease. *Journal of the American Board of Family Practice, 6,* 25–32.

Hays, R. B., McKusick, L., Pollack, L., Hilliard, R., Hoff, C., & Coates, T. J. (1993). Disclosing HIV seropositivity to significant others. *AIDS, 7,* 425–431.

Herek, G. M. (1999). AIDS and stigma. *American Behavioral Scientist, 42,* 1106–1116.

Hoff, C., McKusick, L., Hilliard, R., & Coates, T. J. (1992). The impact of HIV antibody status on gay men's partner preferences: A community perspective. *AIDS Education and Prevention, 4,* 197–204.

Kimberly, J. A., & Serovich, J. M. (1999). The role of family and friend social support in reducing risk behaviors among HIV-positive gay men. *AIDS Education and Prevention, 11,* 465–475.

Lee, R. S., Kochman, A., & Sikkema, K. J. (2002) Internalized stigma among people living with HIV-AIDS. *AIDS and Behavior, 6,* 309–319.

O'Donnell, L., Agronick, G., San Doval, A., Duran, R., Myint, U. A., & Stueve, A. (2002). Ethnic and gay community attachments and sexual risk behaviors among urban Latino young men who have sex with men. *AIDS Education and Prevention, 14,* 457–471.

Ramirez-Valles, J. (2002). The protective effects of community involvement for HIV risk behavior: A conceptual framework. *Health Education Research, 17,* 389–403.

Thompson, S. C., Nanni, C., & Levine, A. (1996). The stressors and stress of being HIV-positive. *AIDS Care, 8,* 5–14.

Turner, H. A., Hays, R. B., & Coates, T. J. (1993). Determinants of social support among gay men: The context of AIDS. *Journal of Health and Social Behavior, 34,* 37–53.

Wenger, N. S., Kusseling, F. S., Beck, K., & Shapiro, M. F. (1994). Sexual behavior of individuals infected with the human immunodeficiency virus. *Archives of Internal Medicine, 154,* 1849–1854.

15

LISTENING TO GAY AND BISEXUAL MEN LIVING WITH HIV: IMPLICATIONS OF THE SEROPOSITIVE URBAN MEN'S STUDY FOR PSYCHOLOGY AND PUBLIC HEALTH

RICHARD J. WOLITSKI

The narratives of the 250 men who participated in the Seropositive Urban Men's Study (SUMS) are a powerful testament to the resilience of individuals living with HIV and to the diversity and complexity of their experiences. These men provided important insights into the very human experiences that HIV-positive gay and bisexual men struggle with as they seek to establish and maintain sexual relationships that satisfy their emotional and physical needs.

The data and analyses from SUMS provide a new perspective on the sexual lives of HIV-positive gay and bisexual men. The study goes beyond

This chapter was authored by an employee of the United States government as part of official duty and is considered to be in the public domain. Any views expressed herein do not necessarily represent the views of the United States government, and the author's participation in the work is not meant to serve as an official endorsement.

most existing work in this area, which has, with few exceptions, focused primarily on the risk that individuals living with HIV pose to their uninfected partners. The literature has generally failed to acknowledge the importance of a healthy sex life for HIV-positive individuals and has largely ignored the potential psychological, social, legal, and physical risks that unprotected sex poses for them.

ROMANTIC AND SEXUAL RELATIONSHIPS

Earlier studies have described the prevalence and correlates of risky sexual practices, but they have not adequately documented the fact that many men are able to sustain emotionally and physically satisfying relationships with little or no risk for HIV transmission. These romantic and sexual relationships take many forms and present a range of inherent challenges and potential rewards. Although some men with main partners considered their primary relationships to be mutually monogamous, many did not (see chap. 3, this volume). Open relationships that involved agreements about sex with other partners were fairly common. Professionals who work with HIV-seropositive gay and bisexual men should not assume that these relationships conform to any particular standard. Men who are in a primary relationship may or may not have other sex partners, and sex outside of the main-partner relationship may or may not be a source of distress. The range and variety of relationship types observed in SUMS are not unique to HIV-seropositive gay and bisexual men (see Greenan & Tunnell, 2003), but HIV can introduce additional issues and problems into these relationships.

Men in open relationships often differentiated emotional intimacy with their main partner from the needs that were met by casual sexual encounters with other partners. A desire to have sex outside the relationship may reflect a need to satisfy unmet sexual needs and may not be indicative of other problems in the relationship. However, seeking sex outside of a main partner relationship (particularly when partners do not have an explicit agreement about sexual encounters with others) also can be a symptom of broader dissatisfaction in the relationship or HIV-related fears on the part of one or both partners. Gay and bisexual men living with HIV may fear a loss of physical attractiveness and want validation that they are sexually desirable to others. They also may feel shame about their HIV status or dissatisfaction with safer sex practices and seek anonymous or HIV-seropositive partners with whom serostatus or sexual safety may be perceived to be less important. The accounts of the HIV-positive men suggest that fears about HIV-related illness, disability, and death may cause some men or their partners to withdraw emotionally or sexually. In these situations, seeking sex outside of the relationship may represent a conscious or unconscious strategy to ward off the emotional pain associated with these anticipated losses.

Feelings about a main partner, greater intimacy, and personal history as a couple sometimes were related to different patterns of sexual behavior with main and nonmain partners (see chap. 3, this volume). It was common for men with main and nonmain partners to express a greater desire to protect their main partner's health and exhibit less concern for nonmain partners, especially those who were anonymous. That is not to say that unprotected sex did not occur in main-partner relationships. Greater trust and intimacy in main partner relationships, a desire to please one's partner, and communication about preferred sexual activities contributed to risky sexual practices in these primary relationships. Patterns of sexual behavior with main and nonmain partners, satisfaction with these activities, and the perceived risk of these activities are important issues to explore with HIV-seropositive clients.

CONCERNS ABOUT HIV TRANSMISSION

Most HIV-positive gay and bisexual men are sexually active and are concerned about the possibility that they might transmit the virus to someone else (see chaps. 3, 4, and 10, this volume). Most SUMS participants saw themselves as having a special responsibility to protect their partners from HIV infection and had taken action to do so (see chap. 10, this volume). Concern about the possibility of infecting a sex partner affected the quality and nature of men's sexual relationships, their decision to be sexually active, and the sexual practices they were willing to engage in with or without condoms. For some, the fear of infecting a partner was so great that it led them to sacrifice relationships with partners for whom they cared deeply. Some men directly addressed their reasons for ending the relationship, others talked about fabricating excuses, and a few described how they had provoked their partner to break up with them.

Some respondents dealt with their fear of transmitting HIV to others by avoiding relationships with HIV-negative partners. Although choosing to have sex only with other HIV-positive men is a valid choice, deciding to end relationships with seronegative partners may reflect misperceptions or a sense of shame about being HIV positive. For example, a small number of men were worried that deep kissing might transmit HIV, even though this behavior is associated with a near-zero-risk for HIV transmission. Saliva that is not contaminated with blood is not a viable source of infection, and only one potential case of HIV transmission associated with kissing has been identified since AIDS was first recognized in 1981 (Centers for Disease Control and Prevention, 1997).

Clinicians and interventionists who work with HIV-positive men should know the risks of specific sexual practices (see Appendix 15.1 for a list of information sources) and should explore their clients' understanding of these risks. Men who fear transmitting HIV through extremely low-risk activities may simply not understand how HIV is transmitted or may feel shame, guilt, or other unresolved emotions about their HIV status, intimacy, or their relationship with their partners. HIV-positive gay and bisexual men should be encouraged to adopt risk-reduction strategies that include low-risk sexual practices that they can enjoy without having to be concerned about the adverse effects that their behavior may have on their partners' health (see Appendix 15.1 for information sources).

OTHER CONCERNS

SUMS participants' concerns about the risks associated with sexual activity were not limited to transmitting HIV. Some expressed strong concerns about the risk that unprotected sex presented to their own health (see chap. 4, this volume). These concerns included fear of reinfection or superinfection with another strain of HIV and exposure to other sexually transmitted pathogens. Definitive data about the real risk for superinfection and its effect on disease progression are not currently available, but until the magnitude of this risk is better understood, experts recommend that HIV-positive men avoid unprotected sex with HIV-positive partners (Blackard, Cohen, & Mayer, 2002).

Clear evidence does exist, however, about the risks associated with other sexually transmitted infections (STIs) that may adversely affect the health of HIV-positive men (Nkengasong et al., 2001; O'Brien et al., 1999; Wiley et al., 2000) and increase their ability to transmit HIV to others (Fleming & Wasserheit, 1999). As described in this volume and elsewhere, some HIV-positive gay and bisexual men may be unaware of these consequences of STIs or may consider STIs to be easily treated or inconsequential compared with already having HIV (Wolitski, in press). Interventions for HIV-positive gay and bisexual men should address bacterial and viral STIs: their consequences and how they can be prevented. Condom use provides good protection from most STIs (National Institute of Allergy and Infectious Diseases, 2001). However, some STIs can be transmitted by activities for which most gay and bisexual men typically do not use condoms or other barrier methods (such as oral sex and oral–anal contact) because of the relatively low risk for HIV transmission associated with these sexual practices

(Belcher, Sternberg, Wolitski, Halkitis, & Hoff, 2003; Doll & Ostrow, 1999; Halkitis & Parsons, 2000; Kalichman et al., 1997; Wolitski & Branson, 2002). Because individual STIs and HIV are transmitted differently, understanding this complex information is difficult and may cause some individuals to believe that they have few acceptable options for protecting themselves if they wish to remain sexually active. Given this reality, it may be best to tailor STI information to the specific risk-reduction needs, preferences, and concerns of individuals living with HIV. In doing so, the greatest attention should be paid to known risks and viral STIs, which may have life-long consequences.

RISK-REDUCTION STRATEGIES

In general, HIV-positive gay and bisexual men are well aware of the potential health risks associated with sexual activity and have adopted a number of risk-reduction strategies (see chap. 4, this volume). These strategies are often based on the men's understanding of the relative risks of specific sexual practices and the known or assumed serostatus of their partners. The strategies go well beyond using condoms during anal intercourse and include avoiding situations that led to unprotected sex in the past; selecting partners on the basis of serostatus or perceived risk characteristics; abstaining from penetrative sex and other specific sexual practices; avoiding exposure to body fluids (including withdrawing before ejaculation); and inspecting partners' genitals for discharges, sores, or other signs of STIs.

Some men described how they adopted different sexual roles, depending on the serostatus of their partner, in an effort to reduce the risk for HIV transmission. This strategic positioning is not limited to this sample of men and is used by both HIV-negative and HIV-positive gay and bisexual men (Van de Ven et al., 2002). Strategic positioning is a practice in which HIV-positive gay and bisexual men are more likely to adopt the receptive role during unprotected anal intercourse with HIV-negative partners than with HIV-positive partners. On the other hand, HIV-negative men are more likely to adopt the insertive role with partners they know to be HIV-positive than with seroconcordant partners. These same patterns are not observed, however, for condom-protected sex.

The effectiveness of strategic positioning as a real-world risk-reduction strategy is not known at this time, but it is consistent with epidemiological data indicating that receptive anal intercourse places uninfected partners at greatest risk for HIV (Vittinghoff et al., 1999; Wolitski & Branson, 2002). Although strategic positioning may reduce the risk for HIV transmission, it does not provide full protection, even for men who adopt the insertive role during anal sex. Until there is evidence that strategic positioning significantly reduces risk for HIV, prevention messages for HIV-positive gay and bisexual men and their partners should continue to encourage condom use for anal sex, regardless of the specific role that each partner adopts. When condoms are not available, lower risk behaviors (such as oral sex or nonpenetrative sexual activities) would probably be preferable to strategic positioning. Future research needs to examine the effectiveness of the multiple strategies that gay and bisexual men are using. Although the risk-reducing effects of some of these strategies are well documented (i.e., abstinence, not having penetrative sex, using condoms), a need remains for additional research that can clarify the effects of strategic positioning, withdrawal, and other risk-management strategies on HIV transmission. Given the possibility that some risk-management strategies have the potential to increase risk (as was found with the spermicide nonoxynol-9, which many HIV-positive gay and bisexual men believed provided protection against HIV), the need for this research is particularly urgent (Mansergh, Marks, Rader, Colfax, & Buchbinder, 2003; Wolitski, Halkitis, Parsons, & Gómez, 2001).

PSYCHOLOGICAL AND INTERPERSONAL DYNAMICS

Although risk perceptions appeared to play an important role in the sexual decision making of SUMS participants, these beliefs may not be the most important determinants of unsafe sexual practices among HIV-positive gay and bisexual men. Different respondents attached different meanings to their sexual relationships and used sex to meet a wide range of physical and emotional needs (see chap. 2, this volume). Establishing a connection with another human being, experiencing intimacy, expressing and receiving love, and feeling attractive and desirable to others were basic needs that were met through sexual relationships. The same needs were described by some respondents as leading to risky sexual encounters. For some men, having unprotected sex and the exchange of body fluids were symbols of intimacy and trust that differentiated highly valued sexual relationships from less valued relationships (see chaps. 2 and 3, this volume). It is important for clinicians and other providers to help HIV-positive men recognize the value that they place on specific sexual practices and to weigh the value of these activities against the potential risks. As shown by the experiences of other SUMS participants, these needs can be satisfied within healthy sexual relationships that can take many different forms but share a common characteristic of respect and responsibility for one's self and one's partners.

Mental health issues are inextricably intertwined with risk-taking behavior, and a considerable number of SUMS participants talked about having sex, drinking alcohol, or using drugs to cope with the stress of being an HIV-positive gay or bisexual man (see chap. 11, this volume). Some men described engaging in these behaviors to deal with depression, loneliness, anger, or shame about their HIV status. Worrying about the possibility of infecting a partner, conforming to safer sex norms, and violating personal or normative standards for sexual behavior added to the stress that some respondents experienced. The physical release, validation, and emotional connections associated with sexual encounters seemed to help some men cope with these mental health issues but left others feeling empty or feeling conflicted about their sexual practices or substance use (see chaps. 2, 11, and 12, this volume). This seemed to be true especially when substance use or other factors led to encounters that caused men to be concerned about their health, the health of a partner, or other aspects of their lives. Achieving sustained reductions in risky sexual practices may require either short-term or extended psychotherapeutic interventions tailored to the specific needs of a given individual. Prevention programs working with HIV-positive gay and bisexual men should develop active linkages to local mental health service programs for individuals living with HIV.

Mental health service providers should assess the sexual practices and substance use behavior of their HIV-positive clients to ascertain whether these behaviors are placing the client or others at risk and explore issues that the client may have that contribute to risk taking behavior. In some instances, it may be beneficial for clinicians to work with clients to identify patterns in their behavior, explore their feelings about these behaviors, and examine the underlying needs that they are trying to satisfy. For clients who engage in risky sexual practices, it may be beneficial to identify situations or triggers that are associated with risk taking and to foster the development of strategies for managing these triggers. The nature of some therapeutic relationships and the complexity of some clients' information needs may make it difficult to adequately address these issues with each client. Therefore, mental health service providers should identify programs that provide primary and secondary prevention services in their community so that they can facilitate referrals to these agencies as necessary. Unfortunately these programs may not be available in rural areas and some urban communities. Providers in these communities may need to access information and refer clients to services available via the Internet or telephone. A partial listing of nationally available resources for professionals and people living with HIV is provided in Appendix 15.1.

Other HIV-related mental health issues seemed to cause some men to withdraw emotionally from sex partners or seemed to affect the types of relationships they had. The effects of HIV-related stigma and losses brought about by the AIDS epidemic, in particular the death of a partner, caused some men to avoid intimate sexual relationships or to seek sexual experiences with anonymous partners in settings such as bathhouses, sex clubs, and other public sex environments (see chaps. 2 and 12, this volume). HIV status was less likely to be disclosed to anonymous sex partners than to main or regular partners. Sex with anonymous partners sometimes shifted responsibility for safer sex to the partner because of the casual nature of the relationship or the perception that men seeking sex in public sex environments are aware of the potential risks involved.

Attributions about one's own HIV infection also affected perceived responsibility and the willingness of a minority of men to engage in sexual practices that pose a high risk for HIV transmission to uninfected partners (see chap. 9, this volume). It may be beneficial for clinicians to explore HIV-positive clients' beliefs about how they contracted HIV and whether they attribute responsibility to themselves or others. Men who attribute responsibility to someone other than themselves may be at greater risk for transmitting HIV to others. Clinicians should work with these men to develop a sympathetic or empathetic orientation (see chap. 9, this volume) that seeks to resolve personal issues about the circumstances surrounding their infection and supports the development of a strong sense of personal responsibility for protecting the health of others.

DISCLOSURE OF HIV STATUS

Another issue for clinicians to examine with HIV-positive clients is serostatus disclosure. Whether or not to disclose; with whom this personal information should be shared; and when, where, and how to reveal their serostatus were all issues that caused some men considerable distress (see chap. 7, this volume). Public health recommendations encourage HIV-positive individuals to disclose their HIV status to potential sex partners (Centers for Disease Control and Prevention, 2003a). The philosophical foundation for these recommendations is the belief that uninfected individuals should know if their partners have HIV so that HIV-negative men can make informed decisions about the potential risks that they are willing to accept during a sexual encounter. These recommendations are also based on the expectation that disclosure will reduce the probability that unprotected sex will occur between HIV-positive and HIV-negative individuals.

The experiences of many participants in SUMS and studies published elsewhere (Marks & Crepaz, 2001; Wolitski, Rietmeijer, Goldbaum, & Wilson, 1998) raise important cautions about the relationship between disclosure and risk-taking behavior. Some men believed that they had "done their part" when they disclosed their HIV status and were more willing to have unprotected sex if their partner did not bring up safer sex or expressed a willingness to have risky sex. Disclosure may also foster greater intimacy in relationships, which some SUMS participants described as a factor that contributed to risk taking. Disclosure of HIV status should be encouraged to promote informed decision making on the part of uninfected individuals; however, it cannot be automatically assumed that disclosure will reduce the risk for HIV transmission. Clinicians and prevention program staff should help HIV-positive men develop communication skills that promote early disclosure of HIV status. It is unreasonable to assume that all men will always disclose. Disclosure will not be possible in every situation because of the constraints of some environmental settings and potential for a violent reaction. It is important to encourage men to think about and build skills for handling disclosure in different settings and with different types of partners.

When and how to disclose HIV status was a particularly difficult issue for many of the SUMS participants because of the stigma associated with HIV and fear of being rejected (see chaps. 7 and 14, this volume). For many, negative experiences reinforced their reluctance to disclose their serostatus. These experiences included partners' refusal to have sex, loss of valued relationships, and, for a few, verbal or physical assault. As a result, some men opted to use nonverbal strategies that provided clues about their HIV status rather than raise the issue directly. It is possible that some of the nonverbal cues described by SUMS participants (e.g., talking about being involved in AIDS-related causes, discussing upcoming physician appointments, keeping medication bottles visible) may have been missed or misinterpreted by uninfected partners with little exposure to HIV-related issues. The value of nonverbal strategies may be in raising the issue of HIV status in a less threatening manner, but HIV-positive men should be encouraged to talk directly and frankly about their serostatus to avoid misunderstandings. Men who waited to disclose their HIV status until intimacy and trust had been established experienced the most distress when disclosure was met by negative reactions from partners who felt deceived. For some men, a strategy of disclosing their serostatus early in a relationship (before the first sexual encounter) seemed to work best. Although these men reported sometimes being rejected by their partners, this rejection occurred before strong emotional attachments had developed; therefore, they avoided potential negative reactions from partners who felt betrayed because this information had been withheld.

When serostatus was not discussed, some men made assumptions about the serostatus of their partners that affected the level of risk they took (see chap. 8, this volume). Most of these assumptions served to justify unprotected sex in the heat of the moment or rationalize it after the fact. Although some assumptions were influenced by knowledge of how HIV and HAART affect the bodies of HIV-positive men, others were influenced by indicators that only have a weak association or no association at all with serostatus. These nonspecific indictors included the setting in which partners were met and the partner's age, neighborhood of residence, or willingness to have unprotected sex. Clinicians and prevention programs should raise awareness of the fallibility of these assumptions and should encourage serostatus disclosure to reduce reliance on potentially faulty assumptions. Because serostatus disclosure is usually a mutual process, the contribution of assumptions to risk behavior is yet another reason for prevention programs to encourage HIV-negative gay and bisexual men to disclose their HIV status and ask partners about their status. It should not be assumed, however, that disclosure will reduce the risk of HIV transmission to uninfected partners. HIV-positive gay and bisexual men should be encouraged to adopt safer sex practices regardless of whether information about HIV status has been shared.

IMPLICATIONS FOR PREVENTION EFFORTS

Despite the efforts of many HIV-seropositive gay and bisexual men to limit the risk of HIV transmission, some regularly engage in high-risk sexual practices and others experience occasional lapses in safer sex behavior. It is important to acknowledge this risk and take steps to intervene on this behavior and confront the very serious consequences that unprotected sex can have. Understanding the complexity of men's motivations and of the risks of unprotected sex is an important place to start, but just understanding the reasons behind these behaviors is not sufficient. There is a need for additional effort on the part of public health agencies, community-based organizations, and individual practitioners to address influences that affect HIV-seropositive gay and bisexual men's ability to maintain safer sex practices and disclose their HIV status to potential sex partners. These efforts should include improving access and adherence to antiretroviral therapy as well as behavioral and psychotherapeutic interventions that promote behavior change (Janssen et al., 2001; Wolitski, Janssen, Onorato, Purcell, & Crepaz, in press).

Public health officials have acknowledged the potential role of effective HIV treatment and viral suppression in limiting the spread of HIV in the United States (Janssen et al., 2001). For SUMS participants, the effects of highly active antiretroviral treatment (HAART) on sexual behavior varied (see chap. 13, this volume). The availability of HAART reduced some respondents' concern about the possibility of transmitting HIV; this may be particularly true for men with undetectable plasma viral load. This belief, however, was by no means universal. HAART was associated with decreased sexual activity among some respondents and greater sexual desire and activity among others.

Beliefs about HAART may have contributed to increased risk taking by at least a minority of HIV-positive gay and bisexual men in the study (see chap. 13, this volume). The fact that these beliefs are based on scientific evidence that demonstrates a positive association between viral load and perinatal and heterosexual transmission of HIV raises complicated public health issues (Quinn et al., 2000; Sperling et al., 1996; Tovanabutra et al., 2002). Identifying individuals with undiagnosed HIV and improving access and adherence to medical care may benefit communities by reducing HIV incidence and may benefit HIV-positive individuals by dramatically slowing disease progression. At the same time, decreases in the transmissibility of HIV can be offset by an increased willingness of at-risk individuals to engage in unprotected sex (Blower, Gershengorn, & Grant, 2000; Katz et al., 2002). Thus, the HIV epidemic could expand even if HIV treatments lead to community-level reductions in viral load and decrease the ease with which HIV can be transmitted. This possibility, coupled with the fact that plasma viral load may not always correspond with seminal viral load (Kalichman et al., 2001), continue to make it important for HIV-positive individuals to maintain safer sex practices. Messages encouraging all HIV-positive gay and bisexual men to maintain safer sex practices (even if they are receiving HIV treatment or have an undetectable viral load) should be a part of all prevention programs for this population. Similar messages should be directed also to the HIV-negative partners of HIV-positive men and to gay and bisexual men in general.

Given the complexity of these issues, a particularly important setting for the delivery of messages for HIV-positive gay and bisexual men may be the clinics where they receive medical care. Health care providers are trusted sources of medical information, and brief interactions with providers can lead to significant health behavior change (Neumann, Marks, & Purcell, 2003). Unfortunately, however, many health care providers fail to engage their HIV-positive patients in discussions about safer sex (Margolis, Wolitski, Parsons, & Gómez, 2001; Marks et al., 2002). In recognition of this problem, recommendations on how to incorporate HIV prevention into the medical care of individuals living with HIV have recently been issued and provide useful information for physicians and other providers involved in the care of HIV-positive individuals (Centers for Disease Control and Prevention, 2003a; Neumann et al., 2003).

Other types of interventions will also be needed. Structured behavioral interventions delivered in a range of clinical and community-based settings have been found to reduce HIV risk behavior. Two early interventions that were designed to reduce depression and increase the ability of HIV-seropositive individuals to cope with HIV-related stress demonstrated that behavioral interventions can reduce risk behavior among people living with HIV (Coates, McKusick, Kuno & Stites, 1989; Kelly et al., 1993). Since that time, a number of other studies have been initiated, but only a small number of published intervention trials have provided compelling data showing significant reductions in transmission risk behavior among HIV-seropositive individuals (Kalichman et al., 2001; Margolin, Avants,

Warburton, Hawkins, & Shi, 2003; Rotheram-Borus et al., 2001). These three studies evaluated group-level interventions for HIV-positive youth, adult men and women, and methadone maintenance clients. They found that respondents receiving these interventions reported a greater reduction in risk behavior relative to those who were assigned to a comparison group. A summary of these interventions and prevention case management, a one-on-one intervention that may be of particular interest to mental health providers, has been developed by the Centers for Disease Control (CDC; 2004).

The narratives of the SUMS participants illustrate the many common experiences that people living with HIV share. Relatively few differences associated with city of interview, race/ethnicity, or other demographic characteristics emerged from the data. That is not to say that these characteristics are unimportant. For example, respondents' responses to direct questions about the effects of race and ethnicity provided insights into the additional challenges faced by HIV-positive gay and bisexual men of color (see chap. 6, this volume). Broad challenges included the stresses of coping with racism in addition to homophobia and HIV-related stigma, which sometimes affected the interactions of men of color with other HIV-positive gay and bisexual men. Race and ethnicity played a role in the partner preferences of men from varied racial and ethnic backgrounds. Race and ethnicity shaped sexual interactions because of perceptions that respondents and their partners brought to sexual encounters between men of the same or different races or ethnicities. These interactions sometimes reflected racial or ethnic stereotypes that some respondents had of men from their own or other racial and ethnic groups. These stereotypes were sometimes translated into discriminatory behavior that negatively affected the self-image of some men of color. The narratives of some SUMS respondents hint at the complexities of interracial and intraracial sexual relationships that are compounded by HIV serostatus (see chap. 6, this volume). SUMS only scratched the surface of these issues. Much remains to be learned about the ways in which culture affects sexual practices, disclosure of HIV status, access to care, and adherence to care. This information is essential for the further development of culturally competent interventions that effectively reduce the disproportionate burden of HIV infection and AIDS among Black and Latino individuals in the United States.

Although HIV-positive gay and bisexual men bear a special responsibility to protect others from becoming infected, the influence of partner preferences and the responsibility of HIV-negative individuals to protect themselves cannot be ignored. Numerous men described direct and indirect requests for unprotected sex that were made by partners who were HIV-negative or with whom serostatus had not been discussed. Differences in the perceived risk of some sexual activities, willingness to accept risk, and preferences for specific sexual behaviors were a considerable source of stress and tension for some respondents who were in relationships with uninfected partners. Most of these partners did not appear to be "bug chasers" (individuals who seek unprotected sex with infected partners so that they can contract HIV). SUMS provides little insight into the motivations and risk factors of HIV-seronegative gay and bisexual men. Correlates of high-risk sexual practices among HIV-negative gay and bisexual men have been the subject of extensive research and deserve continued study (for reviews see Hospers & Kok, 1995; Stall, Hays, Waldo, Ekstrand, & McFarland, 2000).

As greater emphasis is placed on the prevention needs of HIV-positive gay and bisexual men, there is a potential danger that insufficient resources will be devoted to the needs of those who are uninfected and that their responsibility to protect themselves from HIV infection will be minimized. The need to reach uninfected individuals who are at greatest risk of contracting HIV is underscored by an analysis suggesting that most new cases of HIV infection are transmitted by individuals who are unaware of their serostatus (Marks, Crepaz, Senterfitt, & Janssen, 2003). Proven behavioral interventions exist for gay and bisexual men that reduce risky sexual practices that put uninfected men at risk for contracting HIV (Johnson et al., 2002). It is critical that these interventions, HIV testing, and STI treatment continue to be readily available to HIV-negative gay and bisexual men. Interventions should be directed toward subgroups of gay and bisexual men who are at greatest risk of contracting HIV, such as Black and Latino men, young men under the age of 30, men who use methamphetamines or other substances associated with high-risk behavior, men who meet sex partners on the Internet, barebackers (men who intentionally seek out unprotected anal sex), and men who are seeking treatment for or have a diagnosis of an STI (Gross, 2003; Halkitis & Parsons, 2003; Stall et al., 2000; Wolitski, Validiserri, Denning, & Levine, 2001; Wolitski, in press).

SUMS represents the largest and most comprehensive qualitative study of HIV-positive gay and bisexual men conducted to date, but the time that the data were collected (1996–1997), the way in which they were collected, and the focus of the research raise potential limitations. Since the late 1990s, HIV treatments have continued to improve; some men have become less concerned about HIV; and rates of risk behavior, STIs, and HIV diagnoses have risen (for reviews, see Ciesielski, 2003; Jaffe, 2003; Wolitski, in press; Wolitski et al., 2001). Awareness of barebacking, which had just become an identifiable phenomenon at the time of this study, has become widespread. By the early 2000s, 27% of HIV-positive gay and bisexual men recruited for an intervention study in New York City and San Francisco identified themselves as barebackers (Halkitis et al., in press). The ability of the Internet to facilitate sexual encounters, increased methamphetamine use, prevention fatigue, and other changes in the gay community have profound implications for public health and strongly indicate a need to reevaluate, reinvent, and reinvigorate HIV prevention efforts for gay and bisexual men (Wolitski, in press).

Because SUMS was conducted to provide information for a behavioral intervention for HIV-positive gay and bisexual men, some important issues that affect the sexual lives of the respondents may have been missed or underemphasized. For example, we collected little information about sexual dysfunction, a problem that can significantly affect the sex lives of HIV-positive men (Catalan & Meadows, 2000; Collazos, Martinez, Mayo, & Ibarra, 2002; Colson et al., 2002). And although the large number of interviews allowed for the representation of many different segments from the population of HIV-positive gay and bisexual men, the volume of data was overwhelming and presented considerable challenges to data management, analysis, and reporting of findings. Identifying and analyzing subgroup differences was particularly challenging, and some differences may have been missed. Even with an entire book dedicated to this single study, we could not present information on all relevant aspects of HIV-positive gay and bisexual men's experiences or communicate the complexity and variety of these experiences. We hope to address some of these other issues in future qualitative and quantitative reports.

Key findings from SUMS provide an important foundation for the development of prevention programs for HIV-positive gay and bisexual men. They demonstrate that most gay and bisexual men who are living with HIV are actively concerned about the ways in which their sexual behavior can affect the physical and emotional health of their partners and their own well-being (e.g., superinfection, exposure to other STIs, legal consequences of HIV transmission). These narratives complement the quantitative data collected from SUMS participants (for a review, see Wolitski, Parsons, & Gómez, 2004) by promoting a deeper understanding of the multiple barriers that HIV-positive gay and bisexual men face as they try to maintain safer sex practices across a wide range of interpersonal, social, and environmental contexts. They help explain the varied approaches that these men adopt in an effort to balance the risks of sexual relationships against the inherent pleasures. To address barriers to safer sex, prevention programs for HIV-positive gay and bisexual men may often need to go beyond informational, cognitive, and skills-building activities that are the mainstay of HIV behavioral interventions. Successfully changing risk practices may require mental health and other intervention services that address underlying psychological and substance abuse issues that are long-standing and undermine individuals' efforts to make conscious and responsible choices about their sexual behavior.

Prevention programs for gay, bisexual, and other individuals living with HIV are an important and necessary component of a comprehensive HIV prevention strategy. Such a strategy should include readily accessible HIV testing to reach individuals with undiagnosed HIV infection, HIV treatment and other medical and supportive services for individuals who receive positive HIV test results, and prevention programs for uninfected individuals (CDC, 2003b; Janssen et al., 2001). Despite a compelling public health rationale for placing greater emphasis on prevention for HIV-positive individuals, this emphasis has the potential to indirectly blame individuals with HIV for the continued spread of the virus in the United States and to further a rift in the gay community that is defined by HIV serostatus. Signs of such a rift are already evident and have been associated with adverse effects on the mental health of HIV-positive gay and bisexual men (Díaz, in press, 2003; Wolitski, Dey, Parsons, Gómez, & the SUMS Research Group, 2002). A balanced approach to prevention that addresses risks to the health of HIV-positive individuals and their partners should help avoid victim blaming. Such an approach must work to reduce and buffer the effects of HIV-related stigma on the health and well-being of individuals living with HIV (see chap. 14, this volume). Buffering the negative effects of stigma may involve individual interventions that teach people how to cope with the stresses of being HIV positive, promote a positive self-image and acceptance of their HIV status as one aspect of their lives, and foster the development of supportive relationships.

As the qualitative interviews from SUMS show, the experiences and perspectives of people living with HIV can teach a great deal to those who are concerned about stopping the spread of HIV. People living with HIV are invaluable partners in public health and community efforts to stop the further spread of HIV and AIDS. We need to ensure that they are actively involved in these efforts and that an open and honest dialogue about the difficulties and responsibilities of living with HIV is established. Maintaining this dialogue will require that we listen to people living with HIV and learn from their experiences. No one else is in a better position to articulate how HIV infection affects one's life and how challenges to protecting the health of people living with HIV and their partners can be overcome.

APPENDIX 15.1:
SELECTED INTERNET RESOURCES FOR PROFESSIONALS
AND PEOPLE LIVING WITH HIV OR AIDS

- AIDS Educational Global Information System (AEGIS)
  The AEGIS Web site (http://www.aegis.org) provides access to information, fact sheets, newsletters, and research findings from around the world. The site has extensive links to other Internet resources.

- American Psychological Association (APA)
  The APA Public Interest Directorate Web site has a wealth of information for clinicians and other professionals. The Web site (www.apa.org/pi/aids/resource.html) includes technical information about HIV/AIDS, information about working with clients with HIV/AIDS, curriculum resources, and information about training programs for professionals and students.

- Centers for Disease Control and Prevention (CDC)
  The Divisions of HIV/AIDS Prevention Web site (www.cdc.gov/hiv/dhap.htm) contains updated statistics, general information about HIV and AIDS, medical treatment guidelines, prevention tools, and research information. The site also contains information about the Advancing HIV Prevention initiative, which is focused specifically on the prevention needs of people living with HIV.

- HIV Insite
  This site (http://www.hivinsite.ucsf.edu/) is a comprehensive treatment and prevention resource that is administered by the University of California, San Francisco. Extensive information is provided in three domains: (a) HIV treatment and care, (b) prevention, and (c) policy. Easy-to-read fact sheets that summarize prevention-related research and issues are available in English and Spanish (www.caps.ucsf.edu/FSindex.html).

- Human Resources Services Administration (HRSA)
  HRSA is responsible for funds provided by the Ryan White CARE Act, which is the primary source of funding for HIV and AIDS-related medical and mental health services in the United States. The site (http://hab.hrsa.gov) provides information about HRSA activities and has links to other resources for mental health and medical professionals.

- National Prevention Information Network (NPIN)
  NPIN operates a national hotline (800-458-5231) and online resource directory that helps professionals locate information about HIV, STIs, and tuberculosis. The Web site (http://www.cdcnpin.org) provides access to a daily summary of HIV-related news and scientific reports, a searchable prevention resource database, information about funding for programs and research, and a directory of local conferences.

- National Association of People Living With AIDS (NAPWA)
  NAPWA is a national organization that advocates for the rights and needs of people living with HIV. The Web site (http://www.napwa.org) describes NAPWA's programs and provides access to the *Positive Voice* newsletter.

- National Institutes of Health (NIH)
  The NIH is the primary source of funding for HIV and AIDS-related research. This research is coordinated by the Office of AIDS Research (OAR). The OAR Web site (http://www.nih.gov/od/oar/index.htm) provides updated information about research funding OAR initiatives.

- National Minority AIDS Council (NMAC)
  NMAC is a national organization that is "dedicated to developing leadership within communities of color to address the challenges of HIV/AIDS." The Web site (http://www.nmac.org) has many features, including the ability to search for local community-based organizations and hotlines that provide HIV-related information and services.

- Project Inform
  The Project Inform Web site (http://www.projectinform.org) provides detailed information about approved and experimental treatments for HIV infection. Special sections provide information for people who are newly diagnosed with HIV, women, and Spanish-speaking users.

- The Body
  The Body Web site (http://www.thebody.com) is a comprehensive and easy-to-understand resource for people living with HIV. The site provides medical information and "Ask the Experts" sections for people who are newly diagnosed with HIV as well as those with advanced HIV disease. A special section is tailored to the needs of women living with HIV, and the site includes information in Spanish.

REFERENCES

Belcher, L., Sternberg, M., Wolitski, R., Halkitis, P., & Hoff, C. (2003, August). *Perceived HIV transmission risk and condom use among HIV-positive men who have sex with men.* Paper presented at the annual meeting of the American Psychological Association, Toronto, Canada.

Blackard, J. T., Cohen, D. E., & Mayer, K. H. (2002). Human immunodeficiency virus superinfection and recombination: Current state of knowledge and potential clinical consequences. *Clinical Infectious Diseases, 34,* 1108–1114.

Blower, S. M., Gershengorn, H. B., & Grant, R. M. (2000). A tale of two futures: HIV and antiretroviral therapy in San Francisco. *Science, 287,* 650–654.

Catalan, J., & Meadows, J. (2000). Sexual dysfunction in gay and bisexual men with HIV infection: Evaluation, treatment, and implications. *AIDS Care, 12,* 279–286.

Centers for Disease Control and Prevention. (1997). Transmission of HIV possibly associated with exposure of mucous membrane to contaminated blood. *Morbidity and Mortality Weekly Report, 46,* 620–623.

Centers for Disease Control and Prevention. (2003a). Incorporating HIV prevention into the medical care of persons living with HIV: Recommendations of CDC, the Health Resources and Services Administration, the National Institutes of Health, and the HIV Medicine Association of the Infectious Diseases Society of America. *Morbidity and Mortality Weekly Report, 52(RR-12),* 1–32.

Centers for Disease Control and Prevention. (2003b). Advancing HIV prevention: New strategies for a changing epidemic—United States, 2003. *Morbidity and Mortality Weekly Report, 52,* 329–332.

Centers for Disease Control and Prevention. (2004). *Advancing HIV prevention: Interim Technical Guidance for Selected Interventions.* Retrieved April 22, 2004, from http://www.cdc.gov/hiv/partners/Interim-Guidance.htm

Ciesielski, C. A. (2003). Sexually transmitted disease in men who have sex with men: An epidemiological review. *Current Infectious Disease Reports, 5,* 145–152.

Coates, T. J., McKusick, L., Kuno, R., & Stites, D. P. (1989). Stress reduction training changed number of sexual partners but not immune function in men with HIV. *American Journal of Public Health, 79,* 885–887.

Collazos, J., Martinez, E., Mayo, J., & Ibarra, S. (2002). Sexual dysfunction in HIV-infected patients treated with highly active antiretroviral therapy. *Journal of Acquired Immune Deficiency Syndromes, 31,* 322–326.

Colson, A. E., Keller, M. J., Sax, P. E., Pettus, P. T., Platt, R., & Choo, P. W. (2002). Male sexual dysfunction associated with antiretroviral therapy. *Journal of Acquired Immune Deficiency Syndromes, 30,* 27–32.

Díaz, R. M. (in press). In our own backyard: HIV/AIDS stigmatization in the Latino Gay community. In N. F. Teunis (Ed.), *Sexual inequalities: Essays from the field.* New York: Routledge.

Díaz, R. M. (2003, June). *HIV stigmatization and mental health outcomes in Latino gay men*. Paper presented at the Society for Community Research and Action Biennial, Las Vegas, NV.

Doll, L. S., & Ostrow, D. G. (1999). Homosexual and bisexual behavior. In K. K. Holmes, P. F. Sparling, P. A. Mardh, S. M. Lemon, W. E. Stamm, P. Piot, et al. (Eds.), *Sexually transmitted diseases* (3rd ed., pp. 151–162). New York: McGraw-Hill.

Fleming, D. T., & Wasserheit, J. N. (1999). From epidemiological synergy to public health policy and practice: The contribution of other sexually transmitted diseases to sexual transmission of HIV infection. *Sexually Transmitted Infections, 75*, 3–17.

Greenan, D. E., & Tunnell, G. (2003). *Couple therapy with gay men*. New York: Guilford Press.

Gross, M. (2003). The second wave will drown us. *American Public Health, 93*, 872–881.

Halkitis, P. N., & Parsons, J. T. (2000). Oral sex and HIV risk reduction: Perceived risk, behaviors, and strategies among young HIV negative gay men. *Journal of Psychology and Human Sexuality, 11*, 1–24.

Halkitis, P. N., & Parsons, J. T. (2003). Intentional unsafe sex (barebacking) among men who meet sexual partners on the Internet. *AIDS Care, 15*, 367–378.

Halkitis, P. N., Wolitski, R. J., Wilton, L., Parsons, J. T., Bimbi, D., & Hoff, C. (in press). Barebacking identity among gay and bisexual men: Psychological, behavioral and contextual correlates. *AIDS*.

Hospers, H. J., & Kok, G. (1995). Determinants of safe and risk-taking sexual behavior among gay men: A review. *AIDS Education and Prevention, 7*, 74–94.

Jaffe, H. W. (2003, July). *HIV/AIDS in America today*. Paper presented at the 2003 National HIV Prevention Conference, Atlanta, GA.

Janssen, R. S., Holtgrave, D. R., Valdiserri, R. O., Shepherd, M., Gayle, H. D., & DeCock, K. M. (2001). The serostatus approach to fighting the HIV epidemic: Prevention strategies for infected individuals. *American Journal of Public Health, 91*, 1019–1024.

Johnson, W. D., Hedges, L. V., Ramirez, G., Semaan, S., Norman, L. R., Sogolow, E., et al. (2002). HIV prevention research for men who have sex with men: A systematic review and meta-analysis. *Journal of Acquired Immune Deficiency Syndromes, 30*(Suppl. 1), S118–S129.

Kalichman, S. C., Cage, M., Barnett, T., Tharnish, P., Rompa, D., Austin, J., et al. (2001). Human immunodeficiency virus in semen and plasma: Investigation of sexual transmission risk and correlates. *AIDS Research and Human Retroviruses, 17*, 1695–1703.

Kalichman, S. C., Cherry, C., Williams, E., Abush-Kirsh, T., Nachimson, D., Schaper, P., et al. (1997). Oral sex anxiety, oral sexual behavior, and human immunodeficiency (HIV) risk perceptions among gay and bisexual men. *Journal of Gay and Lesbian Medical Association, 1*, 161–168.

Kalichman, S. C., Rompa, D., Cage, M., DiFonzo, K., Simpson, D., Austin, J., et al. (2001). Effectiveness of an intervention to reduce HIV transmission risks in HIV-positive people. *American Journal of Preventive Medicine, 21,* 84–92.

Katz, M. H., Schwarcz, S. K., Kellogg, T. A., Klausner, J. D., Dilley, J. W., Gibson, S., et al. (2002). Impact of highly active retroviral treatment on HIV seroincidence among men who have sex with men: San Francisco. *American Journal of Public Health, 92,* 388–394.

Kelly, J. A., Murphy, D. A., Bahr, G. R., Kalichman, S. C., Morgan, M. G., Stevenson, Y., et al. (1993). Outcome of cognitive–behavioral and support group brief therapies for depressed, HIV-infected persons. *American Journal of Psychiatry, 150,* 1679–1686.

Mansergh, G., Marks, G., Rader, M., Colfax, G. N., & Buchbinder, S. (2003). Rectal use of nonoxynol-9 among men who have sex with men. *AIDS, 17,* 905–909.

Margolin, A., Avants, S. K., Warburton, L. A., Hawkins, K. A., & Shi, J. (2003). A randomized clinical trial for a manual-guided risk reduction intervention for HIV-positive injection drug users. *Health Psychology, 22,* 223–228.

Margolis, A. D., Wolitski, R. J., Parsons, J. T., & Gómez, C. A. (2001). Are health-care providers talking to HIV-seropositive patients about safer sex? *AIDS, 15,* 2335–2337.

Marks, G., & Crepaz, N. (2001). HIV-positive men's sexual practices in the context of self-disclosure of HIV status. *Journal of Acquired Immune Deficiency Syndromes, 27,* 79–85.

Marks, G., Crepaz, N., Senterfitt, J. W., & Janssen, R. S. (2003). *Meta-analysis of high-risk sexual behavior in persons aware and unaware they are infected with HIV: Implications for HIV prevention.* Unpublished manuscript.

Marks, G., Richardson, J. L., Crepaz, N., Stoyanoff, S., Milam, J., Kemper, C., et al. (2002). Are HIV care providers talking with patients about safer sex and disclosure? A multi-clinic assessment. *AIDS, 16,* 1953–1957.

National Institute of Allergy and Infectious Diseases. (2001). *Workshop summary: Scientific evidence on condom effectiveness for sexually transmitted disease (STD) prevention.* Washington, DC: Author.

Neumann, M. S., Marks, G., & Purcell, D. W. (2003). Delivering human immunodeficiency virus (HIV) transmission prevention services to HIV-seropositive persons in clinical care. In J. Erwin, D. K. Smith, & B. S. Peters (Eds.), *Ethnicity and HIV: Prevention and care in Europe and the USA* (pp. 141–164). London: International Medical Press.

Nkengasong, J. N., Kestens, L., Ghys, P. D., Koblavi-Dème, S., Bilé, C., Kalou, M., et al. (2001). Human immunodeficiency virus type 1 (HIV-1) plasma virus load and markers of immune activation among HIV-infected female sex workers with sexually transmitted diseases in Abidjan, Côte d'Ivoire. *Journal of Infectious Diseases, 183,* 1405–1408.

O'Brien, T. R., Kedes, D., Ganem, D., Macrae, D. R., Rosenberg, P. S., Molden, J., et al. (1999). Evidence of concurrent epidemics of human herpes virus 8 and human immunodeficiency virus type-1 in US homosexual men: Rates, risk factors, and relationship to Kaposi's Sarcoma. *Journal of Infectious Disease, 180*, 1010–1017.

Quinn, T. C., Wawer, M. J., Sewankambo, N., Serwadda, D., Li, C., Wabwire-Mangen, F., et al. (2000). Viral load and heterosexual transmission of human immunodeficiency virus type 1. *New England Journal of Medicine, 342*, 921–929.

Rotheram-Borus, M. J., Lee, M. B., Murphy, D. A., Futterman, D., Duan, N., Birnbaum, J. M., et al. (2001). Efficacy of a preventive intervention for youths living with HIV. *American Journal of Public Health, 91*, 400–405.

Sperling, R. S., Shapiro, D. E., Coombs, R. W., Todd, J. A., Herman, S. A., McSherry, G. D., et al. (1996). Maternal viral load, zidovudine treatment and the risk of transmission of human immunodeficiency virus type 1 from mother to infant. Pediatric AIDS Clinical Trials Group Protocol 076 Study Group. *New England Journal of Medicine, 335*, 1621–1629.

Stall, R. D., Hays, R. B., Waldo, C. R., Ekstrand, M., & McFarland, W. (2000). The Gay '90s: A review of research in the 1990's on sexual behavior and HIV risk among men who have sex with men. *AIDS, 4*(Suppl. 3), S101–S114

Tovanabutra, S., Robison, V., Wongtrakul, J., Sennum, S., Suriyanon, V., Kingkeow, D., et al. (2002). Male viral load and heterosexual transmission of HIV-1 subtype E in northern Thailand. *Journal of Acquired Immune Deficiency Syndromes, 29*, 275–283.

Van de Ven, P., Kippax, S., Crawford, J., Rawstorne, P., Prestage, G., Grulich, A., et al. (2002). In a minority of gay men, sexual risk practice indicates strategic positioning for perceived risk reduction rather than unbridled sex. *AIDS Care, 14*, 471–480.

Vittinghoff, E., Douglas, J., Judson, F., McKirnan, D., MacQueen, K., & Buchbinder, S. P. (1999). Per-contact risk of human immunodeficiency virus transmission between male sexual partners. *American Journal of Epidemiology, 150*, 306–311.

Wiley, D. J., Visscher, B. R., Grosser, S., Hoover, D. R., Day, R., Gange, S., et al. (2000). Evidence that anoreceptive intercourse with ejaculate exposure is associated with rapid CD4 loss. *AIDS, 14*, 707–715.

Wolitski, R. J. (in press). The emergence of barebacking among gay men in the United States: A public health perspective. *Journal of Gay and Lesbian Psychotherapy*.

Wolitski, R. J., & Branson, B. M. (2002). "Gray area behaviors" and partner selection strategies: Working toward a comprehensive approach to reducing the sexual transmission of HIV. In A. O'Leary (Ed.), *Beyond condoms: Alternative approaches to HIV prevention* (pp. 173–198). New York: Kluwer Academic.

Wolitski, R. J., Dey, A., Parsons, J., Gómez, C., & the SUMS Research Group. (2002, November). *Is there a rift between HIV-seropositive and HIV-seronegative men in the gay community?* Paper presented at the annual meeting of the American Public Health Association, Philadelphia.

Wolitski, R. J., Halkitis, P. N., Parsons, J. T., & Gómez, C. A. (2001). Awareness and use of untested barrier methods by HIV-seropositive gay and bisexual men. *AIDS Education and Prevention, 13,* 291–301.

Wolitski, R. J., Janssen, R. S., Onorato, I. M., Purcell, D. W., & Crepaz, N. (in press). A comprehensive approach to prevention with people living with HIV. In S. C. Kalichman (Ed.), *Positive prevention: Reducing HIV transmission among people living with HIV-AIDS.* New York: Kluwer Academic.

Wolitski, R. J., Parsons, J. T., & Gómez, C. A. (2004). Prevention with HIV-seropositive gay and bisexual men: Lessons learned from the Seropositive Urban Men's Study (SUMS) and the Seropositive Urban Men's Intervention Trial (SUMIT). *Journal of Acquired Immunodeficiency Syndromes, 37*(Suppl. 2), S101–S109.

Wolitski, R. J., Rietmeijer, C. A., Goldbaum, G. M., & Wilson, R. M. (1998). HIV serostatus disclosure among gay and bisexual men in four American cities: General patterns and relation to sexual practices. *AIDS Care, 10,* 599–610.

Wolitski, R. J., Valdiserri, R. O., Denning, P. H., & Levine, W. C. (2001). Are we headed for a resurgence in the HIV epidemic among men who have sex with men? *American Journal of Public Health, 91,* 883–888.

AUTHOR INDEX

Numbers in italics refer to listings in reference sections.

Courtenay-Quirk, C., 10, *16*
Coutinho, R. A., *18*
Crandall, C. S., 217, 229, *230*
Crawford, I., 88, 99, 218, *230*
Crawford, J. M., 4, *18*, 41, *52*, 74, 84, *253*
Crepaz, N., 4, 6, *16*, 102, *119*, 236, 240, 245, *252, 254*
Cunningham, W. E., *119*
Curtin, L., 134, *145*
Cusick, L., 40, *52*

Daigle, D., 184, *199*
Dang, Q., 88, 99
Davidovich, U., 41, *52*
Davison, K. P., 229, *231*
Dawson, J. M., 102, *118*, 121, *131*
Day, R., *18, 253*
Debets, W., 184, *199*
DeCock, K. M., *251*
DeJong, G. M., *52*
de Luise, C., 5, *16*
Denning, P. H., 4, *19*, 245, *254*
Derlega, V. J., 40, *52*
De Rosa, C. J., 102, *118*
de Vroome, E. M., *71*, 184, *199*
de Wit, J. B. F., 41, *52*, *71*, 184, *199*
Dey, A., 247, *253*
Díaz, R. M., 73, *84*, 87, 88, 99, 178, *179*, 184, *199*, 218, 230, *231*, 247, *250, 251*
Dickerson, S. S., 229, *231*
DiFonzo, K., 56, *71, 252*
Dilan, E., 73, *84*, 184, *199*
Dilley, J. W., 122, *131, 252*
Dillon, B., *16*
Dockrell, J., 198, *199*
Dockrell, M. J., 198, *199*
Dolcini, M., 73, *84*
Dolezal, C., 39, 41, *52, 53*
Doll, L. S., 237, *251*
Domier, C. P., 164, *180*
Donnell, D., *181*
Dorrucci, M., *18*
Dorst, D., 102, *119*
Douglas, J., *253*
Duan, N., *253*
Dukers, N., *18*
Duran, R., *231*

Earl, W. L., 184, *199*
Ehrhardt, A., 74, *85*
Ekstrand, M. L., 4, *18*, 56, *72*, 102, *118*, 245, *253*
Elwood, W. N., 6, *18*
Epstein, J. A., 98, *100*

Facer, M., 74, *85*
Fisher, J. D., 22, *35*
Fisher, L., 229, *231*
Fisher, W. A., 22, *35*
Fiske, S. T., 134, *145*
Fitzpatrick, R., 57, *71*, 118, *131*
Fleming, D. T., 236, *251*
Flowers, P., 184, *199*
Folkman, S., 57, *72*
Freedberg, K. A., *119*
Freese, T. E., 164, *180*
French, R., 184, 198, *199*
Futterman, D., *253*

Galavotti, C., *16*
Gallo, R. C., 22, *36*
Ganem, D., *17, 252*
Gange, S., *18, 253*
Gant, L. M., 98, 99
Gardos, P. S., 74, *85*
Gayle, H. D., *251*
Gaylord, J., *180*
Gershengorn, H. B., 243, *250*
Ghys, P. D., *252*
Gibson, P., 7, *16*
Gibson, S., *252*
Gillis, J. R., 40, *52*
Gillmore, M. R., 179, *180*
Glunt, E. K., 40, *52, 53*, 118, *118*
Gold, R. S., 55, 57, 58, *71*, 74, *84*, 122, 129, 130, *131, 132*
Goldbaum, G. M., 102, *119*, 240, *254*
Golden, E., 73, *84*
Goldschmidt, R. H., 229, *231*
Gomez, C. A., 5, 10, *17, 18*, 22, *36*, 122, *132*, 238, 243, 246, 247, *252, 253, 254*
Gore, L. R., 184, *200*
Grant, I., 83, *85*, 178, *180*
Grant, P. J., 55, *71*
Grant, R. M., *16*, 243, *250*
Greenan, D. E., 234, *251*

SUBJECT INDEX

Communications strategies, *continued*
  directive behavior, 78–79
  environmental cues, 79–80
  negotiated safety, 74
  nonverbal communication, 78, 83, 84, 190, 197, 241
  normative communication, 81
  normative cues, 80–81
  sexual negotiation, 74
  verbal communication, 75–78, 82, 84
Community. *See also* Support, social
  affiliation, 219–220, 229
  defining, 219–220, 229
Condom use, 69
  and anal sex, 59–61, 237
  and attributions about becoming HIV-positive, 134
  avoiding, 122
  and communication, 73
  environmental cues, 79–80
  and fear of infecting a partner, 43–44
  and intimacy, 41, 122
  and oral sex, 67–68
  in public sex venues, 198
Coping
  and sex, 24, 34–35
Culture. *See also* Race and ethnicity
  effects on sexuality, 91

Dating, 44–48
  and discussion of HIV, 46–48
  effect of HIV seropositivity on, 44–45
  effect of improved HIV treatments, 46–47, 50
  with someone of similar status, 45
Denial, and substance use, 170–171
Depression
  influence on responsibility, 154
  interventions to reduce, 243–244
  and public and commercial sex venues, 192–192, 198
  and self-punishment, 137–138
  and sex, 24
  and sexual risk behaviors, 239
  and substance use, 174
Directive behavior, 78–79

Disclosure of HIV status, 14, 103–118, 240–242. *See also* Communications strategies; Seropositive Urban Men's Study; Support, social
  and avoiding intimacy, 113–114
  before sexual activity, 108–109
  catalysts for, 105–106
  challenge of, 107–108, 221–227
  fear of prejudice and rejection, 103–104, 109, 117–118, 152, 230
  indirect, 114–115, 117
  and intimacy, 240–241
  main vs. casual sex partners, 102, 105, 109, 110
  moral mandates, 106, 109, 110
  nondisclosure, 140, 141
  nonverbal communication of, 106, 114
  norms and sexual scripts, 104–105
  obfuscation practices, 115
  partners of similar status, 112, 117
  at public and commercial sex venues, 194–195
  responsibility for, 157
  and risk behaviors, 116–117
  and safe practices, 110, 117
  strategies for, 108–116, 118
Drug use. *See also* Substance use
  before sexual activity, 164, 166
  and minorities, 177, 178, 245

Ecstacy, 165. *See also* Substance use
Emotions
  effects of substance use, 172–175
  and public and commercial sex venues, 192–192
  and responsibility for HIV disclosure, 157–158
  and sex, 24–27
  and sexual negotiation, 74
  and sexual risk behaviors, 230
Empathetic orientation, 143
Ethnicity. *See* Race and ethnicity
EZ-Text Qualitative Analysis Software, 10

Family. *See also* Support, social
  rejection by, 221, 225, 230
  support of, 224, 229

Fantasy
and substance use, 170–171
Fears. *See also* Emotions; Rejection
of infecting a partner, 43–44, 47–48,
50, 150, 235
of losing a partner to AIDS, 47
of rejection, 44–45, 152, 221–222,
224–225, 228–229, 241

Gay Men's Health Crisis
Positive Testimonials campaign, 7
Group sex, and public sex environments,
186, 197
Guilt. *See also* Emotions
and nondisclosure of HIV status,
106
and public and commercial sex
venues, 198
taking responsibility to avoid, 151

Heterosexuality
and assumption of HIV status, 127,
129
Highly active antiretroviral therapy
(HAART), 14, 201–213, 242–
243. *See also* Seropositive Urban
Men's Study
and beliefs about being less
infectious, 56, 208–211, 212–
213, 242–243
and changes in sexual interest, 204–
206
and diminished sex drive, 205
improved health and appearance,
205–206
and increase in sexual risk
behaviors, 4–5, 22, 201, 202,
207, 208–210, 211
and interest in protecting self, 206–
208, 211
and misinformation, 209
and optimism, 4, 50, 206–208, 211–
212
reduction in viral load, 56, 201–
202
Human Immunodeficiency Virus (HIV).
See also Assumptions of HIV
status; Attributions about becoming HIV-positive; Disclosure of

HIV status; Seropositive Urban
Men's Study
and calculations of risk, 70, 244–245
concerns about transmission, 235–
236
experimental treatments for, 249
increase in rate of infections, 4

Inhalants (poppers), 164, 166. *See also*
Substance use
behavioral effects and, 167–168
and commercial sex environments,
189
Internet
to facilitate encounters, 245
resources, 248–249
Interventions. *See also* Seropositive
Urban Men's Study
implications for prevention efforts,
242–247
prevention programs, 230, 246–247
psychotherapeutic, 239–240
at public and commercial sex
venues, 198–199
recommendations for disclosure,
240–242
and sexually transmitted infections,
236
for sexual risk behaviors, 212
and substance use, 178
Intimacy, 26–27, 51. *See also* Relationships, sexual
avoidance of, 49–50, 51, 113–114
and disclosure, 240–241
and public and commercial sex
venues, 192–192
and sexual risk behaviors, 238

Judgment, impaired
and substance use, 169–170

Kissing
and HIV transmission, 235

Laws
against HIV transmission, 148
Lipodystrophy, 131

Loneliness, 35
    influence on responsibility, 154
    and public and commercial sex
        venues, 192–192, 198
    and sex, 24
    and sexual risk behaviors, 239

Marijuana, 164, 166. *See also* Substance use
    behavioral effects and, 169
Meanings of sex, 14, 21–35. *See also*
    Relationships, sexual; Sero-
    positive Urban Men's Study
    affirmation of self, 31–34
    and body image, 31–32
    coping with stress, 25–26, 34–35
    and emotional roles, 23–27
    drawbacks of successful treatments,
        22–23
    and intimacy, 26–27, 51
    and physical roles, 28–31
    roles of sex, 23–31
    and sexual identity, 21–22, 33–34
Mental health issues, 239–240
Methamphetamines, 164, 166, 189. *See*
    also Substance use
    behavioral effects and, 168
Minorities. *See* Race and ethnicity
Models of helping and coping, 142–143,
    144. *See also* Attributions about
    becoming HIV-positive; Sero-
    positive Urban Men's Study
    antipathetic orientation, 143
    apathetic orientation, 143
    empathetic orientation, 143
    sympathetic orientation, 142–143
Moral mandates
    and disclosure of HIV status, 106,
        109, 110
    and personal responsibility, 150–151

Negotiated safety, 74
Nonverbal communication, 78, 83, 84

Oral sex, 67–68. *See also* Sexual practices

Physical appearances
    and HIV assumptions, 123–124
    and feeling desirable, 234

Poppers. *See* Inhalants
Positive prevention, 4
Prevention programs, 246–247. *See also*
    Interventions
    community, 230
Public and commercial sex venues, 14,
    183–199. *See also* Commercial
    sex environments; Public sex
    environments; Seropositive
    Urban Men's Study; Sexual risk
    behaviors
    assumptions of HIV status, 126,
        194–195
    conflicts over use, 192
    and emotional needs, 192–193
    and interventions, 198–199
    meeting needs, 191–194, 196–197
    and responsibility assumptions, 157–
        158, 159
    sexual risk behaviors, 195–196, 197
    social norms against, 228–229
    unmet needs, 193–194, 198
Public sex environments. *See also* Public
    and commercial sex venues;
    Sexual risk behaviors
    characteristics of, 184–187
    described, 184
    and group sex, 186, 197
    thrill factor, 187, 197
    and "unexpected" sex, 185–186,
        187, 197
    and voyeurism, 186

Race and ethnicity, 14, 87–99, 222, 244.
    See also Seropositive Urban
    Men's Study
    in coping with HIV status, 88–91
    influence on partnerships, 91–94
    influence on sexual behaviors,
        94–95
    influence on sexuality, 91
    and perceived risk for HIV, 96–98
    rejection because of sexual
        orientation, 89, 221
    religious beliefs and, 90
    and sense of isolation, 88
    and shame, 89
    as source of disapproval, 89
    and stereotyping, 95–96, 98, 244
    and substance use, 177, 178, 245

ABOUT THE EDITORS

Perry N. Halkitis, PhD, is a health and educational psychologist and research methodologist, as well as an associate professor and chair of applied psychology at New York University and codirector of the Center for HIV/AIDS Educational Studies and Training. His research has focused on prevention for HIV-positive individuals, HIV treatment and adherence issues, and methamphetamine and other club-drug use in the gay community, among other issues. He was the recipient of the 1999 American Psychological Foundation Placek Award, the New York University 1999 Daniel E. Griffith's Research Award, the 2002 American Psychological Association (APA) Emerging Leader award, and the 2002 APA Award for Distinguished Contribution to Research in the lesbian gay bisexual transgender community. He received his doctorate in educational psychology from the City University of New York.

Cynthia A. Gómez, PhD, is an associate professor in the Department of Medicine and codirector of the Center for AIDS Prevention Studies at the University of California, San Francisco. Her scientific work has focused on the development of HIV prevention interventions for diverse populations as well as on the influence of social factors such as race, ethnicity, gender, and class on sexual behaviors. She has served on several national committees, including the Centers for Disease Control and Prevention's HIV and STD Advisory Council and the American Psychological Association's Committee on Psychology and AIDS. She served on the Presidential Advisory Council on HIV/AIDS under the Clinton and latter Bush administrations. She received her doctorate in clinical psychology from Boston University.

Richard J. Wolitski, PhD, serves as chief of the Community Intervention Research Section, Prevention Research Branch, Division of HIV and AIDS

Prevention, National Center for HIV, STD, and TB Prevention, at the Centers for Disease Control and Prevention. His research is devoted to furthering an ecological understanding of HIV risk in vulnerable populations and applying this knowledge to developing effective and sustainable interventions that limit the further spread of HIV. Following his own diagnosis with HIV in 1994, his work began to focus on psychological and interpersonal factors that affect HIV-positive individuals' risk of acquiring or transmitting sexually transmitted infections. This experience motivated him to author the program announcement under which the Seropositive Urban Men's Study was funded in 1996. He received his doctorate in community psychology from Georgia State University.